REVISION WORKBOOK

English Legal System

Third Edition

DR VICKNESWAREN KRISHNAN
LLB (Hons), LLM, MA, Barrister, ACI Arb, AIPFM, AFSALS, ACII, PhD

OLD BAILEY PRESS

OLD BAILEY PRESS
at Holborn College, Woolwich Road,
Charlton, London, SE7 8LN

First published 1997
Third edition 2003

© Holborn College Ltd 2004

All Old Bailey Press publications enjoy copyright protection and the copyright belongs to Holborn College Ltd.

All rights reserved. No part of this publication may be reproduced or transmitted in any form or by any means, electronic, mechanical, photocopying, recording or otherwise, or stored in any retrieval system of any nature without either the written permission of the copyright holder, application for which should be made to the Old Bailey Press, or a licence permitting restricted copying in the United Kingdom issued by the Copyright Licensing Agency.

Any person who infringes the above in relation to this publication may be liable to criminal prosecution and civil claims for damages.

ISBN 1 85836 549 X

British Library Cataloguing-in-Publication.

A CIP Catalogue record for this book is available from the British Library.

Printed and bound in Great Britain.

Contents

Acknowledgements		v
Introduction		vii
Studying English Legal System		ix
Revision and Examination Technique		xi
Table of Cases		xvii
Table of Statutes and Other Materials		xxi
1	Sources of Law	1
2	Statutory Interpretation	14
3	Law Reform and Agencies	34
4	The Doctrine of Precedent	40
5	The Judiciary and Magistrates	58
6	The Jury System	79
7	The Legal Profession	103
8	Tribunals and Alternative Dispute Resolution	110
9	Legal Services and Funding	116
10	Civil Justice System	128
11	Civil and Criminal Appeals	140
12	Arrest, Search and Seizure; Interrogations and Confessions	157
13	Prosecution and Bail	183
14	Classification of Offences and Committal Proceedings	197
15	Summary Trial	200
16	Trial on Indictment and Plea Bargaining	202

Acknowledgements

Some questions used are taken or adapted from past University of London LLB (External) and University of Wolverhampton LLB (Honours) by Distance Learning Degree examination papers and our thanks are extended to the Universities of London and Wolverhampton for their kind permission to use and publish the questions.

Caveat

The answers given are not approved or sanctioned by the University of London or the University of Wolverhampton and are entirely our responsibility.

They are not intended as 'Model Answers', but rather as Suggested Solutions.

The answers have two fundamental purposes, namely:

a) to provide a detailed example of a suggested solution to an examination question; and

b) to assist students with their research into the subject and to further their understanding and appreciation of the subject.

Introduction

This Revision WorkBook has been designed specifically for those studying English legal system to undergraduate level. Its coverage is not confined to any one syllabus, but embraces all the major English legal system topics to be found in university examinations.

Each chapter contains a brief introduction explaining the scope and overall content of the topic covered in that chapter. There follows, in each case, a list of key points which will assist the student in studying and memorising essential material with which the student should be familiar in order to fully understand the topic.

Additionally in each chapter there is a key cases and statutes section which lists the most relevant cases and statutory provisions applicable to the topic in question. These are intended as an aid to revision, providing the student with a concise list of materials from which to begin revision.

Each chapter usually ends with several typical examination questions, together with general comments, skeleton solutions and suggested solutions. Wherever possible, the questions are drawn from the University of London external English legal system papers, with recent questions being included where possible. However, it is inevitable that, in compiling a list of questions by topic order rather than chronologically, not only do the same questions crop up over and over again in different guises, but there are gaps where questions have never been set at all.

Undoubtedly, the main feature of this Revision WorkBook is the inclusion of as many past examination questions as possible. While the use of past questions as a revision aid is certainly not new, it is hoped that the combination of actual past questions from the University of London LLB external course and specially written questions, where there are gaps in examination coverage, will be of assistance to students in achieving a thorough and systematic revision of the subject.

Careful use of the Revision WorkBook should enhance the student's understanding of English legal system and, hopefully, enable you to deal with as wide a range of subject matter as anyone might find in a English legal system examination, while at the same time allowing you to practise examination techniques while working through the book.

Studying English Legal System

The study of English legal system is fundamental in assisting a student to understand the mechanics of the system, without which aspects of other subjects will remain puzzling. As the student will discover, English legal system has been described by many as the mother of all laws and, indeed, a thorough understanding of this subject is essential in the practice of law.

Firstly, the subject consists of a variety of topics, not all connected. Therefore, the volume of information the student must deal with is vast.

However, not all the areas can be easily compartmentalised and many examination questions will require the knowledge of perhaps three or more areas. For example, most questions on criminal procedure will require a knowledge of legal funding, bail and perhaps appeals. Recently there have been many changes affecting the civil and criminal justice systems. Major developments (amongst others) include Auld LJ's review of the criminal courts, the 2002 White Paper *Justice for All*, the Criminal Justice Act 2003 and the Courts Act 2003. The legal profession has also been the focus in terms of the competition and regulation in the legal services market. Of fundamental importance was the announcement by the Prime Minister on 12 June 2003 that the office of the Lord Chancellor was to be abolished and that the Lord Chancellor's Department (LCD) was to become the Department for Constitutional Affairs (DCA). Whilst the DCA is already functioning, the office of the Lord Chancellor is still in existence, although legislation is being drafted to completely abolish it. In the meantime, however, Lord Falconer of Thornton QC is holding the two offices of Lord Chancellor and Secretary of State for Constitutional Affairs.

Another problem that presents itself is the fact that the rules in many areas are, or have been, under review. This compounds the volume of research required by individuals. Questions on the English legal system often require an analysis of proposals for reform, the effectiveness of reform and occasionally criticisms of reforms that, although instituted, have perhaps not gone far enough. The only way a student can hope to keep abreast of such developments is by frequent reference to a journal, for example the *New Law Journal*, and by reading a quality newspaper every day.

Relatively speaking, there are perhaps fewer cases to deal with in studying English legal system than in most other areas of law. However, these cases are used differently. Rather than always referring to a case for its ratio alone, case law is used to illustrate a rule, for example cases that illustrate the approach of the court to statutory interpretation or cases that show how the doctrine of precedent may be avoided. Of course, in order to discover these features, students must read the case itself or parts of it, where time permits. This is a useful exercise and will aid understanding of the area.

Revision and Examination Technique

Revision Technique

Planning a revision timetable

In planning your revision timetable make sure you do not finish the syllabus too early. You should avoid leaving revision so late that you have to 'cram' – but constant revision of the same topic leads to stagnation.

Plan ahead, however, and try to make your plans increasingly detailed as you approach the examination date.

Allocate enough time for each topic to be studied. But note that it is better to devise a realistic timetable, to which you have a reasonable chance of keeping, rather than a wildly optimistic schedule which you will probably abandon at the first opportunity!

The syllabus and its topics

One of your first tasks when you began your course was to ensure that you thoroughly understood your syllabus. Check now to see if you can write down the topics it comprises from memory. You will see that the chapters of this WorkBook are each devoted to a syllabus topic. This will help you decide which are the key chapters relative to your revision programme, though you should allow some time for glancing through the other chapters.

The topic and its key points

Again working from memory, analyse what you consider to be the key points of any topic that you have selected for particular revision. Seeing what you can recall, unaided, will help you to understand and firmly memorise the concepts involved.

Using the WorkBook

Relevant questions are provided for each topic in this book. Naturally, as typical examples of examination questions, they do not normally relate to one topic only. But the questions in each chapter will relate to the subject matter of the chapter to a degree. You can choose your method of consulting the questions and solutions, but here are some suggestions (strategies 1–3). Each of them pre-supposes that you have read through the author's notes on key points and key cases and statutes, and any other preliminary matter, at the beginning of the chapter. Once again, you now need to practise working from memory, for that is the challenge you are preparing yourself for. As a rule of procedure constantly test yourself once revision starts, both orally and in writing.

Revision and Examination Technique

Strategy 1

Strategy 1 is planned for the purpose of quick revision. First read your chosen question carefully and then jot down in abbreviated notes what you consider to be the main points at issue. Similarly, note the cases and statutes that occur to you as being relevant for citation purposes. Allow yourself sufficient time to cover what you feel to be relevant. Then study the author's skeleton solution and skim-read the suggested solution to see how they compare with your notes. When comparing consider carefully what the author has included (and concluded) and see whether that agrees with what you have written. Consider the points of variation also. Have you recognised the key issues? How relevant have you been? It is possible, of course, that you have referred to a recent case that is relevant, but which had not been reported when the WorkBook was prepared.

Strategy 2

Strategy 2 requires a nucleus of three hours in which to practise writing a set of examination answers in a limited time-span.

Select a number of questions (as many as are normally set in your subject in the examination you are studying for), each from a different chapter in the WorkBook, without consulting the solutions. Find a place to write where you will not be disturbed and try to arrange not to be interrupted for three hours. Write your solutions in the time allowed, noting any time needed to make up if you are interrupted.

After a rest, compare your answers with the suggested solutions in the WorkBook. There will be considerable variation in style, of course, but the bare facts should not be too dissimilar. Evaluate your answer critically. Be 'searching', but develop a positive approach to deciding how you would tackle each question on another occasion.

Strategy 3

You are unlikely to be able to do more than one three hour examination, but occasionally set yourself a single question. Vary the 'time allowed' by imagining it to be one of the questions that you must answer in three hours and allow yourself a limited preparation and writing time. Try one question that you feel to be difficult and an easier question on another occasion, for example.

Misuse of suggested solutions

Don't try to learn by rote. In particular, don't try to reproduce the suggested solutions by heart. Learn to express the basic concepts in your own words.

Keeping up-to-date

Keep up-to-date. While examiners do not require familiarity with changes in the law during the three months prior to the examination, it obviously creates a good impression if you can show you are acquainted with any recent changes. Make a habit of looking through one of the leading journals – *Modern Law Review*, *Law Quarterly Review* or the *New Law Journal*, for example – and cumulative indices to law reports, such as the *All England Law Reports* or *Weekly Law Reports*, or indeed the daily law reports in *The Times*. The *Law Society's Gazette* and the *Legal Executive Journal* are helpful sources, plus any specialist journal(s) for the subject you are studying.

Examination Skills

Examiners are human too!

The process of answering an examination question involves a communication between you and the person who set it. If you were speaking face to face with the person, you would choose your verbal points and arguments carefully in your reply. When writing, it is all too easy to forget the human being who is awaiting the reply and simply write out what one knows in the area of the subject! Bear in mind it is a person whose question you are responding to, throughout your essay. This will help you to avoid being irrelevant or long-winded.

The essay question

Candidates are sometimes tempted to choose to answer essay questions because they 'seem' easier. But the examiner is looking for thoughtful work and will not give good marks for superficial answers.

The essay-type of question may be either purely factual, in asking you to explain the meaning of a certain doctrine or principle, or it may ask you to discuss a certain proposition, usually derived from a quotation. In either case, the approach to the answer is the same. A clear programme must be devised to give the examiner the meaning or significance of the doctrine, principle or proposition and its origin in common law, equity or statute, and cases which illustrate its application to the branch of law concerned. Essay questions offer a good way to obtain marks if you have thought carefully about a topic, since it is up to you to impose the structure (unlike the problem questions where the problem imposes its own structure). You are then free to speculate and show imagination.

The problem question

The problem-type question requires a different approach. You may well be asked to advise a client or merely discuss the problems raised in the question. In either case, the most important factor is to take great care in reading the question. By its nature, the question will be longer than the essay-type question and you will have a number of facts to digest. Time spent in analysing the question may well save time later, when you are endeavouring to impress on the examiner the considerable extent of your basic legal knowledge. The quantity of knowledge is itself a trap and you must always keep within the boundaries of the question in hand. It is very tempting to show the examiner the extent of your knowledge of your subject, but if this is outside the question, it is time lost and no marks earned. It is inevitable that some areas which you have studied and revised will not be the subject of questions, but under no circumstances attempt to adapt a question to a stronger area of knowledge at the expense of relevance.

When you are satisfied that you have grasped the full significance of the problem-type question, set out the fundamental principles involved.

You will then go on to identify the fundamental problem (or problems) posed by the question. This should be followed by a consideration of the law which is relevant to the problem. The source of the law, together with the cases which will be of assistance in solving the problem, must then be considered in detail.

Very good problem questions are quite likely to have alternative answers, and in advising a party you should be aware that alternative arguments may be available. Each stage of your answer, in this case, will be based on the argument or arguments considered in the previous stage, forming a conditional sequence.

If, however, you only identify one fundamental problem, do not waste time worrying that you cannot think of an alternative – there may very well be only that one answer.

The examiner will then wish to see how you use your legal knowledge to formulate a case and how you apply that formula to the problem which is the subject of the question. It is this positive approach which can make answering a problem question a high mark earner for the student who has fully understood the question and clearly argued their case on the established law.

Examination checklist

a) Read the instructions at the head of the examination carefully. While last-minute changes are unlikely – such as the introduction of a compulsory question or an increase in the number of questions asked – it has been known to happen.

b) Read the questions carefully. Analyse problem questions – work out what the examiner wants.

c) Plan your answer before you start to write.

d) Check that you understand the rubric before you start to write. Do not 'discuss', for example, if you are specifically asked to 'compare and contrast'.

e) Answer the correct number of questions. If you fail to answer one out of four questions set you lose 25 per cent of your marks!

Style and structure

Try to be clear and concise. Fundamentally this amounts to using paragraphs to denote the sections of your essay, and writing simple, straightforward sentences as much as

Revision and Examination Technique

possible. The sentence you have just read has 22 words – when a sentence reaches 50 words it becomes difficult for a reader to follow.

Do not be inhibited by the word 'structure' (traditionally defined as giving an essay a beginning, a middle and an end). A good structure will be the natural consequence of setting out your arguments and the supporting evidence in a logical order. Set the scene briefly in your opening paragraph. Provide a clear conclusion in your final paragraph.

Table of Cases

Adler v George [1964] 2 QB 7   20
American Cyanamid Co v Ethicon Ltd [1975] AC 396; [1975] 1 All ER 504   10
Anton Piller AG v Manufacturing Processes [1976] Ch 55; [1976] 1 All ER 779   5, 10
Anufrijera v Southwark London Borough Council [2004] 1 All ER 833   5
Arthur J S Hall v Simons [2000] 3 WLR 543   105, 107
Ashworth (Oliver) (Holdings) Ltd v Ballard (Kent) Ltd [2000] Ch 12   16
Atlan v United Kingdom (2001) The Times 3 July   199
Attorney-General v Associated Newspapers Ltd [1994] 2 WLR 277; [1994] 1 All ER 556   82, 95
Attorney-General's Reference (No 3 of 1999) [2001] 2 AC 91   165

Beckett (Alfred F) v Lyons [1967] 1 All ER 833   1
Black-Clawson International Ltd v Papierwerke Waldhof-Aschaffenburg AG [1975] AC 591; [1975] 1 All ER 810   18, 20, 24, 27, 69
Bulmer (HP) Ltd v J Bollinger SA [1974] Ch 401; [1974] 2 All ER 1226   24, 32
Bussone v Ministry of Agriculture [1978] ECR 2429   3

C v Director of Public Prosecutions [1995] 2 All ER 43 (HL); [1994] 3 WLR 888; [1994] 3 All ER 190 (QBD)   12, 36, 44, 45, 51, 53, 54, 57, 69
Caballero v United Kingdom (2000) 30 EHRR 643   144, 155, 189
Central London Property Trust v High Trees House Ltd [1947] KB 130   10, 13, 36, 39, 44, 45, 69
Chapman v DPP (1989) 89 Cr App R 190   177
Claims Direct Test Cases, Re [2003] 4 All ER 508   117, 127
Colchester Estates v Carlton Industries [1984] 3 WLR 693   42

Costa v ENEL [1964] CMLR 425   5
CR v United Kingdom (1995) The Times 5 December   53

Daniels v Walker [2000] 1 WLR 1382   135
Davis v Johnson [1979] AC 264   51, 57
Director of Public Prosecutions v Greene [1994] 3 All ER 513   171
Donoghue v Stevenson [1932] AC 562   13, 42, 44, 45, 46, 47, 69
Duke v GEC Reliance [1988] 1 All ER 626   32
Duport Steels Ltd v Sirs [1980] 1 WLR 142   27

Earl of Oxford's Case (1615) 1 Rep Ch 1   4, 9

Fisher v Bell [1961] 1 QB 394   26

Garland v British Rail Engineering Ltd [1983] 2 AC 751   32
Grey v Pearson (1857) 6 HL Cas 61   15, 26
Griffith v Jenkins [1992] 1 All ER 65   142
Grobbelaar v News Group Newspapers Ltd [2002] 1 AC 32   80, 84

Halloran v Delaney [2003] 1 WLR 28   117
Hedley Byrne & Co v Heller & Partners Ltd [1964] AC 465; [1963] 3 WLR 101   36, 39, 42, 69, 105
Heydon's Case (1584) 3 Co Rep 74   14, 18, 21
Holgate-Mohammed v Duke [1984] 1 All ER 1054   180
Hollins v Russell [2003] 4 All ER 590   117, 127

Inco Europe Ltd & Others v First Choice Distribution (A Firm) and Others [2000] 2 All ER 109   16, 18
IRC v Hinchy [1960] AC 748   26

Jasper v United Kingdom [2000] Crim LR 584   199

Table of Cases

John v MGN Ltd [1996] 2 All ER 35   80, 84
Jones v Secretary of State for Social Services [1972] AC 944   56

Kamann v Land Nordrhein-Westfalen [1984] ECR 1891   3
Keenan v United Kingdom (2001) The Times 18 April   144
Kingsley v United Kingdom (2001) The Times 9 January   144

Langley v North West Water Authority [1991] 3 All ER 610   41
Lawal v Northern Spirit Ltd [2004] 1 All ER 187   61, 64
Lees v Secretary of State for Social Services [1985] AC 930   15
Locobail (UK) Ltd v Bayfield Properties Ltd [2000] QB 51; [2000] 1 All ER 65   61, 64

McLeod v Commissioner of Police of the Metropolis [1994] 4 All ER 553   161, 171
Magor and St Mellons RDC v Newport Corporation [1952] AC 189; [1951] 2 All ER 839   15, 20, 26, 29–30
Mareva Compania Naviera SA v International Bulkcarriers SA [1975] 2 Lloyd's Rep 509   5, 10
Marleasing SA v La Comercial Internacional De Alimentacion SA Case106/89 [1992] 1 CMLR 305   32
Marshall v Southampton and South-West Hampshire Area Health Authority [1986] ECR 723   3

Nothman v Barnet London Borough Council [1979] 1 WLR 67; [1978] 1 WLR 220   24

O'Hara v Chief Constable of the Royal Ulster Constabulary [1997] 1 All ER 129   161–162, 180
O'Loughlin v Chief Constable of Essex [1998] 1 WLR 374   165, 173
Osman v DPP [1999] 1 FLR 193   160

Peach Grey & Co v Somners [1995] 2 All ER 513   112

Pepper v Hart [1992] 3 WLR 1033; [1993] 1 All ER 42   15, 17, 18, 21, 24, 25, 27, 28, 30, 31, 32
Powell v Kempton Park Racecourse Co [1899] AC 143   21
Practice Direction [1972] 1 All ER 608   104
Practice Direction [1976] Crim LR 561   204, 209, 211, 216
Practice Direction [1995] 4 All ER 379   202
Practice Note [1988] 3 All ER 1086   81, 82
Practice Note [1995] 1 All ER 234   16
Practice Note [1996] 3 All ER 383   111
Practice Note (Citation of Unreported Cases) [1996] 3 All ER 382   40
Practice Statement [1966] 1 WLR 1234   12, 36, 39, 41, 43, 44, 46, 47, 48, 49, 50, 56

R v Alladice [1988] Crim LR 608; (1988) 88 Cr App R 380   151, 168, 171
R v Allen (1872) LR 1 CCR 367   20, 23
R v Aspinall [1999] 2 Cr App R 115   165
R v Bournewood Community and Mental Health NHS Trust, ex parte L [1998] 3 WLR 107   18
R v Bow Street Metropolitan Stipendiary Magistrate, ex parte Pinochet Ugarte (No 2) [2000] 1 AC 119; [1999] 1 All ER 577   61, 64
R v Brent London Borough Housing Benefit Review Board, ex parte Khadim [2001] NPC 7   41, 43, 45
R v Central Criminal Court, ex parte Guney [1996] 2 All ER 705   188
R v Chief Constable of Lancashire, ex parte Parker [1993] 2 WLR 248   176–177
R v Chief Constable of the Royal Ulster Constabulary, ex parte Begley; R v McWilliams [1997] 4 All ER 33   17
R v Christou [1992] 3 WLR 228   179
R v Clegg [1995] 1 All ER 334   45, 53, 54
R v Commissioner of Police of the Metropolis, ex parte Blackburn [1968] 2 WLR 893   184
R v Cowan [1995] 4 All ER 939   165
R v Davies, Rowe and Johnson [2001] 1 Cr App R 8   199
R v Dossetter [1999] 2 Cr App R(S) 248   204, 209, 211

Table of Cases

R v DPP, ex parte Kebilene and Others [2000] 2 AC 326; [1999] 3 WLR 972   *184, 189*
R v Dunford (1990) 91 Cr App R 150   *152*
R v Farrow (1998) The Times 20 October   *153*
R v Ford [1989] 3 WLR 762; [1989] 3 All ER 445   *81, 86, 88*
R v Fulling [1987] 2 All ER 65   *181*
R v Gould [1968] 1 All ER 849   *42, 56*
R v Green [1992] Crim LR 292   *95*
R v Havering Magistrates' Court, ex parte Director of Public Prosecutions [2001] 1 WLR 805   *189*
R v Judge of the City of London Court [1892] 1 QB 273   *18, 20, 26*
R v Kensington and Chelsea Royal London Borough Council, ex parte Lawrie Plantation Services [1999] 3 All ER 929   *16*
R v Kansal (No 2) [2002] 1 All ER 257   *41, 43, 45*
R v Khan (Sultan) [1996] 3 All ER 289   *165*
R v Latif; R v Shahzad [1996] 1 All ER 353   *165*
R v Mandair [1994] 2 All ER 715   *143, 144*
R v Mason [1980] 3 All ER 777; [1981] QB 881   *82*
R v Miah; R v Akhbar (1996) The Times 18 December   *95*
R v Miller (1993) 97 Cr App R 99   *181*
R v Pitman [1991] 1 All ER 468   *204, 207, 209, 211, 217*
R v Preston [1993] 4 All ER 638   *204, 207, 209, 211*
R v R (Rape: Marital Exemption) [1991] 4 All ER 481   *12, 30, 36, 39, 44, 50, 52, 56, 69*
R v Samuel [1988] 2 WLR 920; [1988] 2 All ER 135   *151, 168, 171, 181*
R v Secretary of State for the Home Department, ex parte Al-Mehdawi [1989] 1 All ER 777   *48*
R v Self [1992] 1 WLR 476   *161, 174*
R v Sheffield Crown Court, ex parte Brownlow [1980] QB 530   *84*
R v Shivpuri [1986] 2 All ER 334   *39*
R v South Western Magistrates' Court, ex parte Cofie [1997] 1 WLR 885; (1996) The Times 15 August   *160, 176*

R v Thompson [1962] 1 All ER 65   *82*
R v Thompson (1995) The Times 6 February   *204, 207, 211, 217*
R v Turner [1970] 2 QB 321   *204, 207, 209, 211, 216*
R v Ward (Judith) [1993] 1 WLR 619; [1993] 2 All ER 577   *146, 156, 207*
R v Young (Stephen) [1995] 2 WLR 430   *82, 86, 91, 95*
R (On the Application of Joseph) v DPP [2001] Crim LR 489   *184*
Racz v Home Office [1994] 1 All ER 97   *80*
Rakhit v Carty [1990] 2 All ER 202   *48*
Rantzen v Mirror Group Newspapers [1993] 3 WLR 953; [1993] 4 All ER 975   *80*
Rickards v Rickards [1989] 3 WLR 749   *48*
River Wear Commissioners v Adamson (1877) 2 App Cas 743   *15*
Roberts Petroleum Ltd v Bernard Kenny Ltd [1983] 1 All ER 564   *40*
Rondel v Worsley [1969] 1 AC 191; [1967] 3 All ER 993   *105*

Saif Ali v Sydney Mitchell & Co [1980] AC 198; [1978] 3 All ER 1033   *105*
Sander v United Kingdom (2000) The Times 12 May   *81, 84*
Scandinavian Trading v Flota Petrolera [1983] AC 694   *5*
Sigsworth, Re [1935] Ch 89   *15, 18, 20*
Smith v Hughes [1960] 1 WLR 830   *15, 21*
Sport International Bussum BV v Inter-Footwear Ltd [1984] 1 WLR 776   *5*
Starrs v Procurator Fiscal 2000 SLT 42   *59, 64*
Swain v Hillman [2001] 1 All ER 91   *131, 141, 144*

Tanfern Ltd v Cameron-Macdonald [2000] 1 WLR 1311; [2000] 2 All ER 801   *131, 141, 144*
Tanistry Case, The (1608) Dav Ir 28   *1, 5*
Tempest v Kilner (1846) 3 KB 249   *21*
Thai Trading Co v Taylor [1998] QB 781; [1998] 2 WLR 893   *43*

Universal Corporation v Five Ways Properties [1979] 1 All ER 552   *21*

Table of Cases

Vinos *v* Marks and Spencer plc [2001] 3 All ER 784   *131*

Ward *v* James [1966] 1 QB 273; [1965] 1 All ER 563   *79, 85*
Webb *v* EMO Air Cargo Ltd [1992] 4 All ER 929   *32*
Westdeutsche Landesbank Girozentrale *v* Islington London Borough Council [1996] 2 All ER 961   *12, 36, 45, 50, 53, 69*

White *v* Jones [1995] 2 AC 207   *107*
Woolwich Building Society v IRC (No 2) [1992] 3 All ER 737   *8, 36*

Young *v* Bristol Aeroplane Co Ltd [1946] AC 163; [1944] KB 718; [1944] 2 All ER 293   *41, 43, 47, 56*

Table of Statutes and Other Materials

Arbitration Act 1996   *112, 114*
Access to Justice Act 1999   *64, 65, 66, 103, 104, 106, 107, 108, 116, 117, 119, 120, 123, 124, 125, 127, 140, 144, 183, 189*
    s1   *116, 120, 123*
    s2   *116, 120, 123*
    s3   *116, 120, 123*
    s4   *116, 121, 123*
    s5   *123*
    s8   *117*
    s10   *117*
    s11   *117*
    s12   *118, 121*
    s13   *118, 124*
    s15   *118*
    s16   *118*
    s17   *118*
    s29   *124*
    s55(1)   *141*
Act of Settlement 1701   *60*

Bail Act 1976   *163, 189, 192, 194*
    s3   *187*
    s4   *185, 193, 194*
    s5B   *189*
    s6(1)   *189*
    Schedule 1   *185, 186, 194*
        Sch 1, Part I   *186*
        Sch 1, Part II   *187*
Bail (Amendment) Act 1993   *189*
    s1   *188*

Children and Young Persons Act 1933
    s34(2)   *164*
    s42   *201*
Civil Procedure Act 1997   *128, 131, 132, 135*
    s1   *135*
    s6   *135*
Civil Procedure Rules 1998   *128, 131, 132, 135, 140, 144*
    Part 52   *140*
Civil Procedure (Amendment No 4) Rules 2003   *128*
Conditional Fee Agreements (Miscellaneous Amendments) Regulations 2003   *117, 119, 126*

Contempt of Court Act 1981
    s8   *82, 86, 91, 94, 95, 100, 102*
Contract (Rights of Third Parties) Act 1999   *35*
Courts Act 1971
    s12   *104*
    s17(4)   *60*
Courts Act 2003   *60, 63, 65, 71, 78, 84, 197, 200, 213*
    s19   *71*
Courts and Legal Services Act 1990   *65, 66, 72, 73, 84, 103, 104, 106, 107, 108, 112, 115, 119, 124, 126*
    s8   *80*
    s29   *108*
    s58   *108, 117, 125, 126*
    s58(2)   *108*
    s71   *64*
    s71(1)(a)   *59*
    s71(1)(b)   *59*
    s71(3)(b)   *59*
Crime and Disorder Act 1998   *13, 57, 183, 189, 195, 199, 207*
    s49(2)   *64*
    s51   *199, 213*
    s52   *213*
    s56   *186*
Criminal Appeal Act 1968   *145, 153*
    s2(1)   *153*
    s9   *143*
    s11   *143*
    s17   *145*
    s23   *143*
Criminal Appeal Act 1995   *35, 144, 145, 147, 148, 150, 151, 152, 153, 154, 155, 156*
    s1(1)   *142*
    s2   *143*
    s2(1)(a)   *145*
    s4   *143, 145, 153*
    s4(2)   *148*
    ss8–14   *143, 148*
    Sch 1   *148*
Criminal Defence Service (Advice and Assistance) Act 2001   *118, 124*

Table of Statutes and Other Materials

Criminal Justice Act 1967
    s9   *201*
    s11   *203, 207, 213*
    s22   *188*
Criminal Justice Act 1987   *96, 156*
Criminal Justice Act 1988   *199*
    s36   *143*
    s43   *143*
    s120   *81*
Criminal Justice Act 2003   *79, 84, 86, 89, 96, 100, 101, 102, 157, 163, 165, 173, 190, 193, 194, 198, 199, 202, 203, 206, 207, 213*
    s1   *157, 173*
    s2   *157, 173, 185*
    s3   *162*
    s4   *185*
    s14   *186, 187, 194*
    s18   *187, 188*
    s28   *184*
    s29   *198*
    s41   *80, 102, 198*
    s321   *81, 86, 92, 96, 102*
    Sch 3   *80, 198*
    Sch 33   *81, 86, 92, 96*
Criminal Justice and Public Order Act 1994   *150, 151, 152, 157, 159, 160, 165, 172, 173, 175, 177, 190, 200*
    s24   *163*
    s25   *163, 186, 194*
    s26   *187, 194*
    s27   *163, 176, 177*
    s28   *163*
    s30   *189*
    ss34–37   *164, 172, 174*
    s43   *82*
    s46(1)   *197*
    s48   *196, 204, 208, 210, 215, 217*
    s51   *83*
    s60   *159, 172, 173*
Criminal Law Act 1967
    s6(1)(b)   *203*
    s6(1)(c)   *203*
Criminal Law Act 1977   *199*
Criminal Procedure and Investigations Act 1996   *146, 147, 154, 155, 156, 199, 203, 207, 213*
    ss3–11   *202*
    s5(7)   *213*
    s29   *202*

Criminal Procedure and Investigations Act 1996 (*contd.*)
    s40   *202*
    s49   *88, 198*
    s54   *156*

Defamation Act 1996   *79, 84*

EC Treaty 1957   *5, 32*
    art 10   *3*
    art 249   *3*
European Communities Act 1972   *5, 8, 18, 24, 32*
    s2(1)   *3*
European Convention on Human Rights 1950   *4, 8, 14, 22, 30, 52, 54, 86, 89, 149, 151, 152, 169, 177, 195, 214*
    art 5   *155, 186, 189, 195, 203, 207*
    art 6   *64, 89, 135, 163, 189, 203, 207, 209, 211, 214*

Higher Rights Qualifications Regulations 2000   *104*
Human Rights Act 1998   *1, 4, 5, 8, 14, 16, 18, 22, 24, 30, 54, 59, 60, 65, 86, 87, 89, 111, 147, 155, 156, 163, 169, 186, 209*
    s2   *42, 54*
    s3   *14, 42, 54, 189*
    s6   *152*

Interpretation Act 1978   *16, 17, 29*

Judicature Acts 1873–75   *4, 5, 7, 10*
Judicial Pensions and Retirement Act 1993   *61*
Juries Act 1974   *84, 86, 88*
    s12(4)   *81*
Justices of the Peace Act 1997   *65*

Land Registration Act 2002   *139*
Law Commission Act 1965   *35*
Law Reform (Year and a Day Rule) Act 1996   *35*
Legal Aid Act 1988   *116, 120, 123*

Magistrates' Courts Act 1980   *200*
    s6(2)   *213*
    s12   *200*
    s105   *201*

Table of Statutes and Other Materials

Misuse of Drugs Act 1971   *178, 179, 180*

Occupiers' Liability Act 1984   *35*

Police and Criminal Evidence Act 1984
150, 151, 152, 157, 160, 165, 166, 167, 168, 169, 170, 172, 173, 174, 175, 176, 178, 179, 180, 190
- ss1–7   *170*
- s1   *157, 159, 167, 172, 173*
- s1(1)   *158*
- s1(3)   *157*
- s1(4)   *158*
- s1(5)   *158*
- s1(6)   *158*
- s1(7)   *158*
- s1(7)(a)   *158*
- s1(7)(b)   *158*
- s1(8)   *158*
- s2   *159, 172, 173*
- s8   *176*
- s8(3)   *160*
- s14   *176*
- s15   *160, 172, 173, 176*
- s16   *160, 172, 173, 176*
- s16(3)   *171*
- s17   *160, 161, 167, 172, 173, 176*
- s18   *161*
- s19   *161, 167, 172, 174, 179, 180*
- s22   *179, 180*
- s24   *161, 168, 171, 174*
- s25   *168*
- s25(3)   *162, 168*
- s28   *162, 168, 171, 180*
- s30   *162, 171*
- s32   *161, 179, 180*
- s40(1)   *163*
- s41   *163*
- s44   *163*
- s56   *163, 168, 171, 172, 174, 179, 181*
- s58   *168, 171, 176, 177, 179, 181*
- s58(1)   *164*

Police and Criminal Evidence Act 1984 (*contd.*)
- s60   *168, 193*
- s67   *172, 179*
- s76   *164, 169, 172, 174, 176, 177, 178, 179, 181, 216*
- s76(2)   *164*
- s76(2)(a)   *164, 168*
- s76(2)(b)   *164, 168*
- s76(4)   *182*
- s76(8)   *164*
- s78   *151, 164, 169, 172, 174, 179, 181*
- s82   *164*
- s116   *160, 173*
- s117   *162, 168, 171*
- Sch 5   *160*

Powers of Criminal Courts (Sentencing) Act 2000   *204, 207, 209, 210, 211, 215, 217*

Prevention of Terrorism Act 1984
- s12   *162*

Prosecution of Offences Act 1985   *190*
- s1   *184*
- s6   *184*
- s23   *184*

Rules of the Supreme Court   *140*

Solicitors Act 1974   *103*

Statute of Uses 1535   *7*

Supreme Court Act 1981   *60, 84*
- s69(1)   *79, 80*
- s69(3)   *79*

Theft Act 1968   *38, 158*
- s12   *188*
- s12A   *188*

Theft Act 1978   *38*

Treaty of Rome *see* EC Treaty 1957

Tribunals and Inquiries Act 1992   *110, 112, 113*

Unfair Contract Terms Act 1977   *35*

Chapter 1

Sources of Law

1.1 Introduction

1.2 Key points

1.3 Key cases and statutes

1.4 Questions and suggested solutions

1.1 Introduction

There are a variety of sources of English law. Each source has gained importance in a particular period of history. For example, the advent of law reporting increased the importance of case law. Sources are classified as formal sources, historical sources, legal sources and literary sources. European law is currently the most important source of law, particularly since the passing of the Human Rights Act 1998 by the English Parliament.

1.2 Key points

Custom (historical source)

a) All English law was at one time derived from custom; the law varied from area to area. The development of the royal courts, however, allowed the system to develop a 'common law' applicable across the country.

b) As a source of law, custom has a limited role in modern times because of its restrictive definition: see *The Tanistry Case* (1608) Dav Ir 28. A custom must:

   i) have been in existence from time immemorial, ie since 1189 or as long as living memory;

   ii) be reasonable: see *Beckett (Alfred F) v Lyons* [1967] 1 All ER 833;

   iii) be certain;

   iv) be obligatory;

   v) not have been interrupted.

A custom is therefore a practice which through the passage of time has obtained the force of law.

Primary legislation (legal source)

a) Legislation is seen as an important source of law as it expresses the will of a democratically elected Parliament and carries out legal and social reforms.

b) Most legislation is initiated by the Crown. A Bill must go through the relevant procedures in Parliament before it finally becomes law.

c) The main functions of legislation are as follows:

   i) reform and revision of the law – the Law Commission and Royal Commissions will generally review the law and make recommendations on reform;

   ii) social impact – legislation has a great impact on social areas of law, such as tax and landlord and tenant law;

   iii) consolidation – statutes are also a valuable means of consolidating various pieces of legislation and common law on a particular subject;

   iv) codification – legislation allows the codification of well developed areas of common law.

d) There are of course many criticisms of legislation: see 1975 *Renton Committee Report on the Preparation of Legislation* and the *Hansard Society Report, 1993*. In the main, the criticisms deal with the fact that statutes are too complex and over-elaborate. This can cause problems in understanding the law and difficulties in its interpretation by the courts.

Another criticism could perhaps be the fact that legislation appears to be inflexible because law never remains the same. As society evolves, so too must law. Hence, law is not susceptible to easy transition. Law can only be changed through an Act of Parliament.

Subordinate legislation (legal source)

Parliament itself is unable to legislate on all areas and will often delegate its legislative powers to ministers and inferior bodies. The legislation so produced has the same force of law as any produced by Parliament itself.

a) The reasons for delegation of legislative powers by Parliament are:

   i) lack of parliamentary time;

   ii) Parliament's inability to foresee all future contingencies that may require amendments of statutes;

   iii) insufficient expert knowledge for technical legislation;

   iv) to cope with emergencies.

b) Subordinate legislation is criticised on the basis that Parliament ought not delegate its power to create policy. Furthermore, delegation is made often in broad terms and can lead to abuse.

c) Subordinate legislation may be controlled in various ways:

i) Pre-drafting consultation with advisory and other bodies interested in the proposed legislation.

ii) The parent statute may require the subordinate legislation to be laid before Parliament. The subordinate legislation may then be subject to a negative or positive resolution. There also scrutiny committees in each House of Parliament to examine various types of delegated legislation.

iii) Judicial review by the courts where there is a challenge on the basis of procedural or substantive ultra vires.

iv) Publicity.

Case law (legal source)

The development of law reporting increased the importance of case law as a source of law. The Incorporated Council of Law Reporting was set up in 1865 and began to produce official Law Reports. Case law is particularly important in the development of the doctrine of precedent.

European Community law (legal source)

Section 2(1) of the European Communities Act 1972 incorporates European Community law into English law.

a) Article 249 of the EC Treaty outlines the different types of Community legislation:

i) regulations are binding and directly applicable in Member States (see *Bussone* v *Ministry of Agriculture* [1978] ECR 2429);

ii) directives are binding, but must be incorporated by national legislation (see *Marshall* v *Southampton and South-West Hampshire Area Health Authority* [1986] ECR 723);

iii) decisions are binding on those to whom they are addressed;

iv) recommendations and opinions hold no binding force.

b) Article 10 of the EC Treaty further imposes on the United Kingdom the duty of 'uniform interpretation': see *Kamann* v *Land Nordrhein-Westfalen* [1984] ECR 1891.

c) The decisions of the European Court of Justice are applicable in England. The ECJ sees Community law as supreme over national law and this affects the traditional doctrine of supremacy of the UK Parliament.

(The European Community is now known as the European Union.)

It is important to note that in order for international law to be binding in the United Kingdom, it must be part of English law, ie incorporated by Act of Parliament.

The European Convention on Human Rights is now part of the English legal system. It was incorporated through the Human Rights Act 1998. This means that the English courts are now bound by the jurisprudence of the European Court of Human Rights in Strasbourg.

Equity (legal source)

The principles of equity are a body of rules which developed in parallel with the common law. Despite their historic roots, they still remain an important source of law today.

The historical development of equity:

a) Norman conquest of 1066 and the creation of the common law applied by the royal courts and assizes.

b) Special petitions to the Chancellor as the 'Keeper of the King's Conscience'.

c) Development of a separate Chancery court applying principles of fairness and the creation of the 'maxims of equity'.

d) Conflict between common law and equity.

e) *Earl of Oxford's Case* (1615) 1 Rep Ch 1 decided in favour of equity.

Fusion of the administration of the two systems:

a) Judicature Acts 1873–75.

b) One set of courts and procedures applying common law rules and equitable principles.

c) Equity always prevails over common law.

d) Foundation of modern High Court system (post Woolf reforms)

Creations of equity:

a) Rights and remedies.

b) Mainly in property law.

c) Examples include the trust, mortgages and equitable remedies such as specific performance and injunctions.

Importance of equity today:

a) Continuing use of rights and remedies created.

b) Maxims of equity still apply in exercise of discretionary remedies.

c) Twentieth-century developments include promissory estoppel, Mareva injunctions (now known as freezing orders), Anton Piller orders (now known as search orders) and equitable rights for the deserted spouse.

See, recently, attempts to extend equitable jurisdiction in *Scandinavian Trading* v *Flota Petrolera* [1983] AC 694 and *Sport International Bussum BV* v *Inter-Footwear Ltd* [1984] 1 WLR 776.

1.3 Key cases and statutes

- *Anton Piller KG* v *Manufacturing Processes* [1976] 1 All ER 779
  Specifies the conditions for the granting of a search order

- *Anufrijera* v *Southwark London Borough Council* [2004] 1 All ER 833
  The Court of Appeal's power to award damages under the Human Rights Act 1998 was considered

- *Costa* v *ENEL* [1964] CMLR 425
  National law must give way to Community law

- *Mareva Compania Naviera SA* v *International Bulk Carriers SA* [1975] 2 Lloyd's Rep 509
  Specifies the conditions for the granting of a freezing order

- *Tanistry Case* (1608) Dav Ir 28
  Defines the characteristics of a custom

- European Communities Act 1972 – incorporated the Treaty of Rome into English law

- Human Rights Act 1998 – incorporated the European Convention on Human Rights into English law

- Judicature Acts 1873–1875 – fused practice and procedure relating to common law and equity

1.4 Questions and suggested solutions

QUESTION ONE

What is meant by a source of law? What sources of law have been recognised by the courts? To what extent is international law a source of law?

University of London LLB Examination
(for External Students) English Legal System June 1986 Q6

General Comment

A fairly simple question as long as the student does not yield to the temptation of merely writing a list of the different sources of law. Each part of the question must be answered directly and critically.

Skeleton Solution

Identification of sources – explanation of custom – legislation – precedent with case law as illustration – European Union law – textbooks – international law.

Suggested Solution

There are several meanings of the word 'source' as it is used in relation to law. Many writers divide the sources of law into categories; formal, historical, legal and literary sources, and naturally there is a certain amount of overlap between them. A formal source of law is that from which a system of law derives its validity and is a matter of jurisprudence which will not be dealt with here. The historical, legal and literary sources will be examined, especially insofar as they have been recognised by the courts.

Custom

The word custom may be used in several different senses and only in certain limited senses can it be said to have been recognised by the courts. The first use of the word describes the customs of Anglo-Saxon England which varied from village to village and town to town, and had grown up in response to frequently recurring problems. Most local customs governed the more important events in the community such as marriage, succession and how to deal with criminals. Such customs are no longer regarded as a separate source of law since they have either become part of the common law or been incorporated in statute. It is therefore only in this indirect sense that it can be said that Anglo-Saxon custom is recognised by the courts, and few survive today in a recognisable form.

It is possible to establish a local custom by proof of its uninterrupted enjoyment since time immemorial. Local custom is a term used to describe rules of law which apply only in a definite locality. Custom in this sense of the word is a separate source of law and must be settled by judicial decision. The type of local customary rights still existing are such things as rights of way or the right to dry fishing nets. If a local custom satisfies certain tests it will be recognised by the courts.

Legislation

Today, legislation is perhaps the most important source of law. It is recognised and followed by the courts and the courts must apply the law as laid down in statutes even if they do not agree with it. Of course one must not overlook the creative role of the judges in construing statutes which are ambiguous or uncertain, but the general rule is that the judges are the declarers of the law and not its makers.

Legislation is the principal legal source of law and it has its corresponding literary source in the various publications of statutes, notably the Queen's Printer's Copy.

Sources of Law

Public general Acts alone account for over 2,000 printed pages each year, supplemented by many thousands more of statutory instruments, Orders in Council and Circulars.

Legislation has not however always been accepted by the courts as absolutely binding. Before the sixteenth century judges enjoyed the same freedom in the application and interpretation of legislative acts as they had in applying and interpreting the common law of their own courts. As J H Baker puts it: 'In applying the spirit of the law, the medieval judges paid scant respect to the letter.' Sir Edward Coke in reporting a case of 1610 wrote: 'it appears in our books that in many cases the common law will control Acts of Parliament and sometimes adjudge them to be utterly void; for when an Act of Parliament is against common right and reason, or repugnant, or impossible to be performed, the common law will control it and adjudge such Act to be void.' There is some doubt, however, as to whether Sir Edward Coke reflected the views of his time. Many scholars feel that he was speaking of long-past ideas without authority. Indeed the Statute of Uses in 1535 gained immediate acceptance by the courts.

There is no doubt that today legislation is unquestioningly accepted by the courts, although the so-called rules of statutory construction do give judges a certain amount of flexibility in deciding what individual sections of statutes really mean.

Precedent

The doctrine of judicial precedent, whereby the decisions of certain courts are binding on other courts, is of comparatively recent origin and is certainly little more than a hundred years old. As early as the time of Edward I (1272–1307) the idea of judicial consistency can be seen in contemporary writings, but this is not the same thing as *binding* precedent. From the sixteenth century onwards cases were cited more frequently, a contributory factor being the development of printing and the improvement in the standard of reporting. In the nineteenth century Baron Parke gave his opinion that precedents must be regarded in subsequent cases and it was not for the courts 'to reject them and to abandon all analogy to them'. It was not until the reorganisation of the court structure by the Judicature Acts 1873–75 that the task of recognising a hierarchy of the courts became easier. Another major factor in the development of the doctrine of binding precedent was the establishment of the Council of Law Reporting in 1865. This raised the standard of reporting thus making law reports considerably more reliable.

Today precedents are accepted by the courts as being either binding or persuasive, depending partly on whether the legal principle in question was contained in the ratio decidendi or obiter dicta of the case, and partly on the court in which the judgment was given and its place in the hierarchy of the courts.

As a source of law, precedent has lost much ground to legislation in the past century, but still remains one of the primary legal sources of law with its corresponding literary source in the form of law reports.

European Union law

Since the accession of the United Kingdom to the European Communities on 1 January 1973, regulations, directives and decisions of the European Council or Commission are binding in England. Judges in court have to accept the authority of European Union law. The European Union has power to make law 'directly applicable' in Member States without the need for the legislatures of the states specifically to enact them into national law. This concept is contained in the European Communities Act 1972, and undoubtedly interferes with the doctrine of the sovereignty of Parliament. The law of the European Union is a legal source of law and its corresponding literary source are the texts of the Treaties themselves, the Official Journal of the European Communities and the decisions and principles of the European Court of Justice. The English courts are also bound by the decisions of the European Court of Human Rights since 2 October 2000 when the European Convention on Human Rights was incorporated into the English legal system by the Human Rights Act 1998.

Textbooks

Modern textbooks are an indirect literary source of all legal sources. Textbooks and articles in legal journals are used by practitioners for research and a lawyer may adapt the argument of the writer of an article or textbook, but the texts do not carry great authority in court although works such as *Chitty on Contracts* and *Archbold on Criminal Law* are frequently cited. In modern times, with reliable reports and detailed legislation, the scope for textbooks in court has greatly diminished. However, the case of *Woolwich Building Society* v *IRC (No 2)* [1992] 3 All ER 737 (HL) suggests that academic writers may provide a valuable authority when dealing with the scope of common law principles.

When talking of legal textbooks, of course, one had to be careful to distinguish between the ancient textbooks such as Glanvil's treatise *Tractatus de Legibus* written in about 1187, and books by Bracton and Littleton, which are commonly used as original sources of common law and as such are books of authority, and modern textbooks which are not.

International law

International law is the source of the rules accepted by civilised States as determining their conduct towards each other, and towards each other's subjects. In order to prove an alleged rule of international law it must be shown to have received the express sanction of international agreement or it must have grown to be part of international law by the frequent practical recognition of States in their dealings with each other. If international law is to be binding on the courts in this country it must have been adopted and made part of English law. The incorporation of the European Convention on Human Rights, for example, imports the European jurisprudence into English law through the Human Rights Act 1998, which gained force on 2 October 2000.

Sources of Law

QUESTION TWO

Assess the effects of equitable rights and remedies upon the English legal system. To what extent would you argue that there have been significant developments of equity since the early nineteenth century?

University of Wolverhampton LLB (Hons) by Distance Learning
English Legal System Examination June 1993 Q8

General Comment

Questions on equity always require essentially the same material and for that reason can be fairly straightforward. However, this makes it more important for the candidate to deal specifically with the issues the question raises, which here clearly requires something more than a historical discussion.

Skeleton Solution

History and origins – issues of conflict – development of rights and remedies – fusion – development post-1875 – evaluation of modern importance, with case law in support.

Suggested Solution

Although the foundations of equity can be traced back to the Norman conquest, its impact today remains as strong as ever. Its rights are the basis for many areas of modern law and its remedies are used daily by the legal practitioner of the 1990s. Its role in the English legal system is, therefore, one of both historical creation and modern development and usage.

That historical creation arose from the need to mitigate the harshness of the decisions of the common law developed after 1066. Whilst the royal courts and assizes produced the benefits of a widely available legal system applying a consistent set of rules and procedures, they also became rigid and inflexible, ignoring justice in the quest for legal certainty. By the thirteenth century, aggrieved litigants began to petition the Chancellor (at that time a clergyman), as the 'keeper of the King's conscience', in an effort to find a more just solution to their problem. As a consequence of the growth of these petitions, the Court of Chancery developed, where decisions were made on the basis of fairness and reason and so the notion of 'equity' was founded.

Initially, the two court systems operated in parallel, with equity being regarded as a gloss upon the common law. Where the law failed to provide a remedy, equity could operate to 'fill the gap'. However, as both systems became more developed, the situation became one of conflict rather than assistance. Equity began to be criticised by some for its unpredictability and it increasingly found a remedy opposing that offered by the common law. This culminated in the *Earl of Oxford's Case* (1615) 1 Rep Ch 1, in which James I decided in favour of equity as the prevailing rule in the case of conflict.

Equity was now free to develop. It created its own set of rights and remedies which are still in force today. The modern trust, now a core part of the English legal system, was an equitable development, along with many other areas of property law such as the equitable mortgage and the rules of probate.

Remedies were also created to support these rights. The injunction has its foundations in the early development of equity. It served then, as now, as an addition to the common law award of damages.

Alongside these developments, equity also created its own set of rules, the 'maxims of equity', to guide the judge in the use of his discretion in matters of equity. Whilst one of the attractions of equity was that it was based on the judge's discretion and therefore flexible, the maxims led some to criticise equity for becoming as rigid as the common law. Nevertheless, the work of the Chancery courts expanded as equity widened its scope through the late 1700s and early 1800s. By the middle of the nineteenth century it was realised that the two systems could no longer operate as separate bodies and a review of the system was needed.

This reform was achieved by the Judicature Acts 1873–75. This legislation provided for procedural fusion of the two systems into one court hierarchy, which is the basis of the modern divisions of today's High Court. Rather than eliminating equity, the Acts, it is submitted, strengthened and confirmed its place in the future. A litigant could now bring his proceedings in one court which would apply both the rules of common law and equity and the Judicature Acts confirmed that in the case of conflict, equity would prevail.

It would be easy to assume that having provided these foundations, the importance of equity as a developing body of law ceased after 1875. However, this is clearly not the case when one examines the many twentieth century developments of equity.

The rights and remedies created before 1873 continue to operate today. Furthermore, they have been refined and added to by modern judges and legal developments. The now established principle of 'promissory estoppel' in contract owes its existence to the judgment of Lord Denning in the *High Trees* case: *Central London Property Trust Ltd* v *High Trees House Ltd* [1947] KB 130. The contractual licence, constructive trust and doctrine of part performance are all creations of the judge's equitable discretion. The rights of the deserted spouse, an essential part of modern matrimonial property law, are the creations of equity, reinforced by statute.

The development of new and more complex remedies has been as active as that of rights. The order of specific performance is still vital. The injunction is perhaps more widely used than ever before, having a place in many areas of modern law, such as intellectual property rights, as well as its more traditional role. Anton Piller orders (now known as search orders) and Mareva injunctions (now known as freezing orders) have only been created in the last 30 years and they are an essential part of many legal proceedings: see *Anton Piller KG* v *Manufacturing Processes* [1976] Ch 55 and *Mareva Compania Naviera SA* v *International Bulkcarriers SA* [1975] 2 Lloyd's Rep 509. The appointment of receivers and orders to account are similarly important parts of modern legal practice which owe their existence to equity.

So the significance of equity in the modern legal system can be clearly illustrated. However, one concept that has perhaps changed is the historic notion of equity as flexible and fair. Whilst the reasoning behind many modern developments is the need to provide a solution which is appropriate to the facts and the changing demands of society, the wealth of guidelines that go with the discretion can be as rigid as any common law rules. For example, to be granted an injunction one must satisfy the complex requirements of the *American Cyanamid* rules: *American Cyanamid Co v Ethicon* [1975] AC 396. Search orders and freezing orders have been criticised by some judges as harsh and draconian and a set of rigid procedures aimed at safeguarding against abuse has developed alongside these two orders under the new civil procedure regime.

Therefore, equity as a source of law remains as current and as vital a part of the English legal system as ever, although the conscientious Lord Chancellors who first gave life to the idea may wonder at its role today.

QUESTION THREE

What do we mean when we speak of the 'common law'?

University of London LLB Examination
(for External Students) English Legal System June 2000 Q1

General Comment

This question requires students to consider the development of the law, particularly through judicial decision-making.

Skeleton Solution

Common law as a source of the English legal system – some interpretations – the traditional role of judges – *Practice Statement* – judicial law-making.

Suggested Solution

The law of England and Wales has been shaped by a variety of influences, and, of these, it can be argued that common law is one of the more significant sources as it can rightly be referred to as the system of law which is common to the whole country. Over the years, the phrase 'common law' has fallen victim to many interpretations, and a brief investigation of these interpretations is necessary before the mechanics of how common law develops is analysed.

One view is that common law can be described as the law of the land or the national laws, which are common to the whole country, and these have developed over time. Another perception is that common law is distinguishable with equity in that, where common law fails to satisfy the needs of a litigant, the principles of equity will fulfil it and make up for its defects. Equity is also the creation of judges and judicial activism. However, the most workable definition within the canvass of this question is that the term common law can be understood in the sense of the creation of legal principles which evolve from cases decided by the courts. This is otherwise known as judge-made laws or judicial law-making.

The modern role of a judge has recently become subject to debate. On the one hand, there is the argument that judges cannot make laws as that is the sole and exclusive role of the legislator. On the other hand, there is ample evidence to show that judges have created new legal principles from time to time. How, or why, is this so then? Well, the traditional role and function of a judge has always been seen to be that of declaring the law as it is. This is also known as the 'declaratory theory'. Hence, it is said to be that of 'jus dicere, non jus dare' (to say the law, not to give it). However, within this understanding there appears a startling limitation on the power of the judges to effect judicial discretion to change the law or reform it where it is evidently necessary or justified. So, it is with this arm of judicial activism that bold judges such as Lord Denning have created new areas or principles of law. By the same token, it must be borne in mind that judges are bound by the doctrine of judicial binding precedent, which means that when deciding cases, judges should aim to treat like cases alike, so as to maintain certainty and consistency with the application of the law and, for this purpose, they should observe the doctrine of precedent based on the hierarchy of the courts. Lord Denning, in his book *The Discipline of Law* ((1979) at p314), refuses to accept that the judges' hands are tied and declares that a rigid application of precedent would give rise to undesirable consequences, such as a bad precedent being followed blindly.

Perhaps this was the philosophy behind the *Practice Statement* [1966] 1 WLR 1234 which provided the House of Lords with the authority to deviate from adhering to the doctrine of precedent where it was justifiable to do so, and indeed their Lordships have shown or displayed a keen willingness to do this on many occasions.

One such instance is when the House of Lords were deciding the case of *R v R (Rape: Marital Exemption)* [1991] 4 All ER 481. In this case, the House overturned the rule that there was no offence of 'marital rape', a rule that had stood for well over 200 years. However, the *Practice Statement* is only used sparingly, and judges should (rightly so) perceive their role as one of application of existing laws rather than of evolution of new legal principles. It is these considerations that leave the senior judiciary in a predicament as to how far the doctrine of precedent should stand in the way of the sensible and just development of the law. Perhaps this view justifies the dissenting judgment of Lord Goff in the case *Westdeutsche Landesbank Girozentrale v Islington London Borough Council* [1996] 2 All ER 961, in which he presses the need to 'mould and remould' the authorities to ensure that 'practical justice is done'.

Another example of bold judicial activism came in the form of *C v Director of Public Prosecutions* [1995] 2 All ER 43, where the Queen's Bench Division removed the presumption of 'doli incapax' in criminal law affecting the age of responsibility, though the decision was eventually reversed by the House of Lords. But it must be stated that it was the bold step of the Queen's Bench Division that provided the impetus for Parliament to pass the Crime and Disorder Act 1998 which abolished the presumption of 'doli incapax' totally.

Within the sphere of tort law, for example, the celebrated case of *Donoghue v Stevenson* [1932] AC 562 shows that judges, namely Lord Atkin, created the 'neighbour principle', which effectively developed a new common law rule: that a manufacturer of a product can be liable to the ultimate consumer where the consumer is harmed by the manufacturer's negligence. Prior to this case, one could not sue if there was no contract in existence.

Similarly, Lord Denning developed the concept of 'promissory estoppel or equitable estoppel' in the *'High Trees'* case (*Central London Property Trust Ltd v High Trees House Ltd* [1947] KB 130). Lord Denning suggested, obiter dictum, where the conditions of promissory estoppel were satisfied, a creditor could not go back on a promise where it would be inequitable to do so.

In conclusion, it is submitted that a good number of judges, such as Devlin, Denning, Atkin and Diplock, have shown clear favouritism towards a creative role for the judge in developing common law principles to meet the needs of the times, but this should not contravene parliamentary supremacy and the basis on which the doctrine of precedent operates. This then, arguably, is the best definition of common law, for justice must not only be seen, but be seen to be done.

Chapter 2
Statutory Interpretation

2.1 Introduction

2.2 Key points

2.3 Key cases and statutes

2.4 Questions and suggested solutions

2.1 Introduction

The approach of the judiciary to interpretation of statutes is indicated by reference to the rules discussed below. The choice of approach depends on both the problem with the statute and the judge's conception of his own function.

The Human Rights Act 1998 became effective on 2 October 2000 and s3 authorises judges to use new methods of interpretation and statutory construction designed to ensure that, as far as it is possible to do so, Acts of Parliament and delegated legislation are compatible with the European Convention on Human Rights.

2.2 Key points

Main problems with statutes

a) Unexpressed words.

b) Broad terms.

c) Ambiguous words.

d) Unforeseeable developments.

The canons of interpretation

The mischief rule: Heydon's Case (1584) 3 Co Rep 74

Regard must be had to the four-stage analysis:

a) what was the common law before the making of the Act?;

b) what was the mischief or defect for which the common law did not provide?;

c) what remedy did Parliament provide?; and

d) the true reason for the remedy.

In the light of the above, the judge's task is to suppress the mischief and advance the remedy. This rule is used primarily where words are ambiguous. See also *Smith* v *Hughes* [1960] 1 WLR 830.

The literal rule

Words must be given their ordinary meaning (even if they lead to manifest absurdity): *Magor and St Mellons RDC* v *Newport Corporation* [1951] 2 All ER 839. This encourages precision drafting. See also *Lees* v *Secretary of State for Social Services* [1985] AC 930.

The golden rule

This approach allows the court to depart from the ordinary meaning of words where their application leads to an absurd result: *Grey* v *Pearson* (1857) 6 HL Cas 61; *River Wear Commissioners* v *Adamson* (1877) 2 App Cas 743. See also *Re Sigsworth* [1935] Ch 89.

Contextual approach

A progressive analysis which introduces a combination of elements of the established approaches. See the cases listed in section 2.3 for illustration.

Aids to interpretation

Internal aids

a) Other enacting words.

b) Long and short title.

c) Preamble.

d) Headings.

e) Side notes and punctuation – generally not to be used.

External aids

a) Historical setting.

b) Dictionaries.

c) Textbooks.

d) Statutes in pari materia (ie dealing with similar subject matters).

e) Statutory instruments.

f) Government publications – to discover the mischief.

g) Parliamentary materials – since the important case of *Pepper* v *Hart* [1992] 3 WLR

1032, courts may now refer to *Hansard* subject to the guidelines given in the decision: *Practice Note* [1995] 1 All ER 234.

h) Rules of language – such as ejusdem generis, expressio unius, exclusio atterius and noscitura sociis.

i) Presumptions.

2.3 Key cases and statutes

- *Ashworth (Oliver) (Holdings) Ltd v Ballard (Kent) Ltd* [2000] Ch 12 (CA)
  One Act can be read in conjunction with another to determine parliamentary intention

- *Inco Europe Ltd & Others v First Choice Distribution (A Firm) and Others* [2000] 2 All ER 109 (HL)
  Judges can add words to a statute to define parliamentary intentions

- R v *Kensington and Chelsea Royal London Borough Council, ex parte Lawrie Plantation Services* [1999] 3 All ER 929 (HL)
  Court drew a distinction in interpreting the meaning of words in planning law as opposed to normal contract law

- Human Rights Act 1998 – imposed the duty of compatibility in interpreting English law

- Interpretation Act 1978 – provided certain standard definitions of common provisions

2.4 Questions and suggested solutions

QUESTION ONE

'These rules and presumptions and maxims [concerning statutory interpretation] are inconsistent, and often flatly contradict each other, but they are treated in the textbooks and in judgments as having equal validity today, regardless of the differing social, political, and constitutional conditions under which they arose … The result is chaos. It is impossible to predict what approach any court will make to any case.' (D A S Ward, 1963.)

Is this a fair statement to make today?

University of London LLB Examination
(for External Students) English Legal System June 2001 Q1

General Comment

The statement is taken from a quote in 1963 and as such requires a comparative analysis

Statutory Interpretation

as to whether it remains valid today. Hence a historical appreciation of statutory interpretation is necessary.

Skeleton Solution

The legislative function and the traditional role of the judges – an examination of the literal rule, golden rule and mischief rule – the role of presumptions and other aids of interpretation – *Pepper* v *Hart* and its contribution – European influence and purposive approach – conclusion as to validity of Ward's statement today.

Suggested Solution

The ultimate resolution of a legal dispute must depend upon the meaning of a particular piece of legislation or statute. It is therefore usual for judges to provide a definitive interpretation of the meaning of the words used in the legislation. Whilst judges have the 'locus' to interpret, it is evident that they do not, and cannot, overrule legislation based on the traditional concept of parliamentary supremacy. Over time, rules, presumptions, maxims and other aids have been developed by judges to help them with the task of statutory construction in cases of ambiguity. This has been necessary because words and phrases have different facets and characteristics when used in differing contexts, and this may lead to confusion, technical distinctions and ambiguity. However, it is uncertain whether these 'innovative' rules of interpretation do contribute to the task of clarifying the law, and hence Ward argues that they are inconsistent and possess no actual value.

It is interesting to note that whilst Ward made this observation in 1963, another authority, namely Bennion, wrote in an article ((1997) 147 NLJ 684) that 'there are instead 1001 interpretive criteria'. It is also evident that Cross (Bell and Engle, *Cross on Statutory Interpretation* (3rd edn, 1995)) believed that there were no such 'rules'. It is, however, undeniable that judges have developed some common law rules known more passionately as the canons of interpretation. As Darbyshire (Eddey & Darbyshire, *English Legal System* (7th edn, 2001) observes: 'judges do not articulate the application of these "rules" but they do tend to apply them sequentially'. She further finds that the labels of these rules are now simply a construct for academic analysis. It is noteworthy, therefore, at this stage to appreciate the comment by Lord Browne-Wilkinson in *R* v *Chief Constable of the Royal Ulster Constabulary, ex parte Begley; R* v *McWilliams* [1997] 4 All ER 833:

> 'It is true that the House has power to develop the law, but it is a limited power. And it can be exercised only in the gaps left by Parliament. It is impermissible for the House to develop the law in a direction which is contrary to the expressed will of Parliament.'

The Interpretation Act 1978 was devised to provide judges with some guidelines on tactics of interpretation or statutory construction. But even that may engender problems as opposed to resolving them. Sometimes words are left undefined and it is the responsibility of the courts to determine their application. It is unsurprising, therefore, that the literal rule was created to give assistance to the judges. This rule simply states that words should be given their ordinary, everyday, literal meaning.

As Lord Reid observed in *Black-Clawson International Ltd* v *Papierwerke Waldhof-Aschaffenburg AG* [1975] AC 591: 'we are seeking the meaning of the words which Parliament used. We are seeking not what Parliament meant but the true meaning of what they said'. This rule may prove to be inflexible, because the literal meaning may cause absurd findings by the court, but as Lord Esher MR (as he then was) in *R* v *Judge of the City of London Court* [1892] 1 QB 273 said: 'if the words of an Act are clear, you must follow them even though they lead to a manifest absurdity. The court has nothing to do with whether the legislature has committed an absurdity'.

This might perhaps explain the philosophy behind the golden rule, which was to be applied in cases where the plain meaning of the words produced a manifest absurdity. Recently, in *Inco Europe Ltd and Others* v *First Choice Distribution and Others* [2000] 2 All ER 109, the use of the golden rule received approval from the House of Lords which stated that judges may add words from a statute to define parliamentary intentions. This is purely to avoid absurdity and give a fairer or more acceptable decision, as illustrated in *Re Sigsworth* [1935] Ch 89.

A third principle called the mischief rule is called upon in the event that the golden rule offers little or no assistance. This rule, which was first settled in *Heydon's Case* (1584) 3 Co Rep 74, allows the judge to examine existing legislation and case law before coming to a decision, with the intention that the ruling will 'suppress the mischief and advance the remedy'. In other words, this rules allows the judge to reflect on the purpose for which Parliament enacted a particular statute and then employ that purpose in delivering the judgment. This rule was recently applied by the House of Lords in *R* v *Bournewood Community and Mental Health NHS Trust, ex parte L* [1998] 3 WLR 107.

In 1993, the case of *Pepper* v *Hart* [1993] 1 All ER 42 further revolutionised the practice of interpretation of statutes, as their Lordships decided that they should have access to *Hansard* or reports of parliamentary debates in order to decipher parliamentary intention so as to be able to make a fair and acceptable decision. This practice is also known as the modern purposive or constructionist approach. It is arguable that this approach is in line with the European legal systems, which favour the purposive approach. With the advent of the European Communities Act 1972, and the passage of the Human Rights Act 1998, it has now been made certain that the English courts apply European jurisprudence in the interpretation of statutes so as to ensure that national law is compatible with European law.

Apart from the three main canons of interpretation, the court is often assisted by other principles of construction, such as presumptions, for example, innocent until proven guilty; and rules of language, such as 'ejusdem generis' which means where a list of words is followed by general words, then the general words are limited to the same kind of items as those on the list; and 'expressio unius est exclusio alterius' which means the mention of one thing excludes another. 'Noscitur a sociis' means that words

Statutory Interpretation

must be given their contextual meaning. Intrinsic aids (those found in the statute itself, such as long titles and short titles, preambles, schedules etc) also offer judges some help, as well as extrinsic aids (those found outside the statute, such as dictionaries, historical setting, Law Commission Reports, public inquiries etc).

Whilst Ward's statement is inclined towards a more traditionalist approach, over the years, and in the current climate of European governance, there is clear evidence of a move towards a more activist role. Whilst that is so, it appears that the House of Lords is still not prepared to take too creative an approach to statutory interpretation.

QUESTION TWO

You have been asked to make a presentation to a group of civil law lawyers on the approach to interpreting statutes used in the English legal system. Write a memorandum explaining the approaches adopted, illustrating your argument with actual cases and contrasting the English approach with that in civil law jurisdictions.

University of London LLB Examination
(for External Students) English Legal System June 2000 Q2

General Comment

A relatively direct question on the various approaches used in interpreting statutes, with a slight twist in that students are required to compare the English approach with that of other civil law jurisdictions.

Skeleton Solution

Role of the courts – role of Parliament – literal, golden and mischief approaches – traditional English approach compared with the purposive 'European' approach.

Suggested Solution

In answering this question, the traditional role of the judge is once again subject to examination, as the concept of an impartial judiciary has always been seen as the cornerstone of the English legal system. Traditionally, convention dictates that while it is the exclusive prerogative of Parliament to legislate and make laws, the role of the judge is to interpret and apply the law, not to create it. However, this may be easier said than done. The function of the court in interpreting and construing statutes is an important one, since it is the judges who must 'make sense' of the statute which is the subject matter of interpretation. Therefore, conventionally, it is evident that interpretation does not leave scope for much judicial discretion but has always been perceived as a scientific process.

Because judges are dealing with words, this may sometimes give rise to problems in that a word may have more than one meaning, and this leads to ambiguities in the process of interpretation. Therefore, when words are unclear or are not instantly susceptible to a clear interpretation, it falls on the judge to resolve the ambiguity and deliver an acceptable decision. When judges embark on this exercise, it is known as statutory construction. Obviously, the parliamentary draftsmen cannot be expected to foresee or envisage every possible eventuality in the framing of a statute.

Hence, some degree of judicial discretion is implicit and necessary to make sense of the intentions of Parliament in giving effect to a particular statute. As Lord Reid stated in *Black-Clawson International Ltd v Papierwerke Waldhof-Aschaffenburg AG* [1975] AC 591:

> 'We are seeking the meaning of the words which Parliament used. We are not seeking what Parliament meant but the true meaning of what they said.'

In aid of this, judges have devised several canons of interpretation, and other intrinsic and extrinsic aids, to assist them to fulfil the arduous task of interpretation. The first of these rules is called the 'literal rule', where the words or phrases in issue are given their ordinary literal meaning. In the words of Lord Esher MR (as he then was) in the case of *R v Judge of the City of London Court* [1892] 1 QB 273:

> 'If the words of an Act are clear, you must follow them even though they lead to a manifest absurdity. The court has nothing to do with the question whether the legislature has committed an absurdity.'

The literal rule can therefore be described as a 'strict adherence' rule, and this description would firmly rebut the proposition that statutory interpretation is essentially a personal matter.

Concurrent with the development of the literal rule in the nineteenth century is the development of the second canon of interpretation, namely the 'golden rule'. This is applied in cases where the plain meaning of the words produce a 'manifest absurdity'. In such circumstances, the golden rule provides the judges with a basis to modify the grammatical and ordinary sense of the words, so as to avoid the absurdity and inconsistency, but no further. Lord Denning in a dissenting judgment in *Magor and St Mellons Rural District Council v Newport Corporation* [1952] AC 189 opined as follows:

> 'No patience with an ultra-legalistic interpretation which would deprive them of their rights together ... we sit here to find out the intention of Parliament ... and carry it out, and we do this better by filling in the gaps and making sense of the enactment than by opening it up to destructive analysis.'

Professor Zander has described this rule as: 'an unpredictable safety valve to permit the courts to escape from some of the more unpalatable effects of the literal rule'. The golden rule has been applied in cases such as *Adler v George* [1964] 2 QB 7, *R v Allen* (1872) LR 1 CCR 367 and *Re Sigsworth* [1935] Ch 89.

The question then arises: what if the utility of both the literal and the golden rule proves futile? Herein comes the third rule of interpretation, known as the 'mischief rule'. This rule is a departure from the other two rules in that it concentrates not solely on the words of the statute, but on the purpose for which Parliament enacted the statute. It is

Statutory Interpretation

derived from *Heydon's Case* (1584) 3 Co Rep 74, where the Court of Exchequer resolved that four matters must be considered:

1. the common law prior to the Act in question;
2. what was the mischief and defect for which the common law did not provide;
3. what remedy had Parliament resolved to 'cure the disease'; and
4. the true reason for the remedy.

Judges must consider all these reasons in giving due importance to the intentions of Parliament. They must suppress the mischief and advance the remedy. An example of the application of this rule can be seen in the case of *Universal Corporation* v *Five Ways Properties* [1979] 1 All ER 552, wherein Buckley LJ stated:

> '... that doctrine (viz the mischief rule) ... does not entitle the court to disregard the plain and natural meaning of wide general terms in a statute. If the language is equivocal and requires construction, then the doctrine is a proper one to refer to; but if the language is quite plain then the duty of the court is to give effect to what Parliament has said.'

The case of *Smith* v *Hughes* [1960] 1 WLR 830 provides another illustration of the use of the mischief rule.

Apart from these rules, the courts have often invoked rules of language in interpreting certain formats of words. One rule is 'ejusdem generis', where a list of words is followed by general words, then the general words are limited to the same kind of items as those on the list, as seen in *Powell* v *Kempton Park Racecourse Co* [1899] AC 143. Another such rule is called 'expressio unius exclusio alterius', the mention of one thing excludes another, as seen in *Tempest* v *Kilner* (1846) 3 KB 249. Additionally, intrinsic aids, such as long and short titles, schedules, headings and marginal notations, have also been used by judges in interpreting. The use of extrinsic aids were, however, rather limited but in recent years the rules have been more relaxed. This is perhaps partly encouraged by the teleological approach used for the interpretation of European law, and in *Pepper* v *Hart* [1993] 1 All ER 42, the House of Lords permitted the use of *Hansard*. Lord Griffiths stated:

> 'The courts now adopt a purposive approach which seeks to give effect to the true purpose of legislation and are prepared to look at much extraneous material that bears on the background against which the legislation was enacted.'

It is submitted that the purposive approach allows for more judicial difference of opinion than the literal approach and provides a greater scope for subjective judicial opinion of policy and intention. This type of purposive approach has long been familiar to continental lawyers. In civil law jurisdictions, and especially to the judges of the European Court of Justice, this broad and general approach (technically described as a 'teleological' approach) has been frequently used when interpreting the treaties and instruments of European law. The English legal system, on the other hand, is more akin to a literal approach, but some constitutional experts have suggested that it is possible to identify a 'ripple effect' in which principles expounded by the European Court of Justice, and thereafter applied by the domestic courts in respect of European matters, have also begun to influence judicial decision-making on purely domestic issues. This view is compounded by the recent passage of the Human Rights Act 1998, which incorporates into English law the European Convention on Human Rights and subjects the English courts to the European jurisprudence.

QUESTION THREE

'European Community legislation is drafted in a way that requires a purposive approach to its interpretation. This requirement, however, runs counter to the literal approach that is dominant in the English system.'

Discuss.

University of London LLB Examination
(for External Students) English Legal System June 1999 Q2

General Comment

This question requires a discussion of the literal method of statutory interpretation in the context of the dichotomy between it and the teleological approach adopted for the interpretation of the treaties and instruments of European Union law. Source material can be found not only in textbooks on English legal system but also in textbooks on constitutional law. Loveland's *Constitutional Law – a Critical Introduction* (3rd edn, 2003) is recommended. Also recommended is Zander's *The Law-Making Process* (5th edn, 1999).

Skeleton Solution

Definition of traditional literal approach to statutory interpretation and the constitutional reasons for that approach – definition of the European teleological method of interpretation, its contrast with English methods and the constitutional implications of European Union membership – recent moves to a more purposive approach and the 'ripple effect' of the European Union teleological approach on the role of English judges as interpreters of legislation.

Suggested Solution

The time-honoured view of the English judiciary has been that their duty lies with giving effect to what Parliament has said, not what it may have meant to say. Judicial respect for parliamentary sovereignty has traditionally persuaded the majority of judges to follow a literal approach to statutory construction. It is an approach that demands that words be given their ordinary literal meaning as far as possible, even though in some cases a strict literal interpretation may result in what the judge regrettably regards as hardship or injustice in the particular case. Such a view may be seen as harsh but is considered by many jurists to be a necessary evil in order to maintain the benefits conferred by parliamentary sovereignty and the separation of powers. Justification of it is in part based on the belief that judges should not become partners in the creation of new law because of the unrepresentative and unaccountable character of the judiciary. Permitting the judiciary to add to or detract from the stated provision of an Act of Parliament, to achieve a result on the grounds that Parliament would have preferred it if it had considered the issue in question at the time of passing the statute, turns the judge into a legislator. Adherence to the literal approach protects the impartiality and independence of the judges by directing criticism of 'bad law' at Parliament and, in affording the judiciary a stabilising function rather than a reforming one, it promotes certainty and consistency in the law.

The 'purposive' approach adopted across most of mainland Europe has little similarity to any approach yet adopted in the United Kingdom. It operates in relation to loosely drafted codes of law which openly invite the judges to become partners in the process of declaring law. In their interpretation of the treaties and instruments of European Union law, the judges of the European Court of Justice, most of whom are continental lawyers, have used a very broad and generous approach technically described as a 'teleological' approach. Since an overriding priority of the European Union is the ensuring of harmonisation and effectiveness of European law in all Member States, it has been ruled by the European Court of Justice that the teleological approach must be used within the member states in their interpretation of European Union law in domestic courts and it was adopted by the English judiciary for this purpose as early as 1974.

The traditional literal approach of English statutory interpretation is wholly different to the purposive or teleological approach. Parliamentary draughtsmen demonstrate the intention of Parliament by a very detailed and precise language which encourages literal interpretation. The objective of the court is to discover the intention of Parliament as expressed in the words used. These must be given their plain, ordinary or literal meaning and, if that meaning is clear, it must be applied even though the result is absurd, or even though the interpretation may inflict hardship on those affected by the legislation. 'Manifest absurdity' is the only exception. It may be avoided at the discretion of the judge by the deployment of the 'golden rule' which, in its narrow application, modifies the literal rule to the extent that an alternative meaning is constructed which achieves consistency with the rest of the statute and a sensible result: *R v Allen* (1872) LR 1 CCR 367. Where the words used can have only one literal meaning, a second broader application of the rule might be used in preference to the literal rule. This is especially so where considerations of public policy intervene to discourage the adoption of an obnoxious interpretation. A precondition of the use of the golden rule is the rejection of the literal rule. Unless it can be shown that the statutory framework or the legal context in which the words are used require a different meaning, the words of the statute should be assigned their natural and ordinary meaning.

There has been judicial reluctance to apply the golden rule both in its narrow and its broader applications and in *Nothman* v *Barnet London Borough Council* [1979] 1 All ER 42 Lord Denning promoted a more activist role saying: 'Whenever the strict interpretation of a statute gives rise to an absurd and unjust situation, the judges can and should use their good sense to remedy it'. In *Discipline of Law* (Butterworths (1979)) Lord Denning argues that the actual words used in the statute are merely the starting point and not the finishing point and in *Nothman* he suggests that 'The literal method is now completely out of date'. This accords with the views he expressed in *Bulmer* v *Bollinger* [1974] Ch 401, an action involving European Union law, in which he advocated the adoption of a more purposive approach for the interpretation of all UK statutes. There has been gradual recognition that, in order to reconcile English statutory law with European law (as required by the European Communities Act 1972), United Kingdom judges might be justified in radically modifying the words of an English statute to achieve consistency. Lord Diplock defended the approach on the ground that the 1972 Act had introduced a new rule of statutory interpretation requiring a United Kingdom court to construe all domestic legislation in a manner respecting European obligations 'however wide a departure from the prima facie meaning of the language of the provision might be needed in order to achieve consistency'.

Some constitutional experts have suggested that it is possible to identify a 'ripple effect' in which principles espoused by the European Court of Justice, and thereafter applied by the domestic courts in respect of European Union matters, have also begun to influence judicial decision-making on purely domestic issues. For example, the use extrinsic material, including travaux preparatoires, as an aid to statutory interpretation had traditionally been restricted, but over time those rules have been relaxed. In *Black-Clawson International Ltd* v *Papierwerke Waldhof-Aschaffenburg AG* [1975] AC 591 it was recognised that reference could be made to reports of law reform bodies which contributed to the making of the Act to ascertain the 'mischief' that Parliament had intended to remedy. Loveland in *Constitutional Law – a Critical Introduction* suggests that the 'ripple effect' may explain why the House of Lords permitted the use of *Hansard* in *Pepper* v *Hart* [1993] 1 All ER 42) and thereby supported a more purposive approach to statutory construction. Such a change was not strictly required by European Union law but was perhaps influenced by our membership in the sense that the constitutional principles of the Union, and the thinking of the judges of the European Court of Justice, have become sufficiently firmly established in the minds of United Kingdom judges to begin to merge into the courts' constantly evolving conceptions of the contemporary role of the common law. The rules of statutory interpretation are rules of common law and, consequently, legitimate targets for change by activist judges in the event of changing political conditions. The Human Rights Act 1998 provides a perfect example of this.

Statutory Interpretation

QUESTION FOUR

'Statutory interpretation is essentially a personal matter. No rules can bind the process since any such rules must themselves be subjects of interpretation.'

Discuss.

University of London LLB Examination
(for External Students) English Legal System June 1998 Q2

General Comment

It is important to note the emphasis given to a question and to address this in the answer. This question works from the premise that there are no rules and that judicial discretion can abound. It demands a discussion of the rules of statutory interpretation that explores the nature and the effectiveness of self-imposed judicial restraint and the extent to which different approaches to statutory interpretation are recognised.

Skeleton Solution

The constitutional role of the courts and the traditional function of judges – the presumption of parliamentary intention and the extent to which it curbs judicial discretion – judicial adherence to the literal rule and the limited application of the golden rule with emphasis on the nature of the self-imposed restraint this entails – the mischief rule, the effect of the decision in *Pepper* v *Hart* and the extent of change to judicial discretion that may result from a purposive approach.

Suggested Solution

The concept of an impartial judiciary is the cornerstone of the English legal system. The traditional role of the judge is to interpret and apply the law, not to create it. The function of the courts in interpreting and construing statutes is, however, a vital one, since it is the courts which must 'give life' to the provisions by considering and applying them. For the greater part of the time, this is a process that turns on the application of clear provisions to the disputed facts of the case. Interpretation of the statute then takes the form of a formal, scientific process that neither gives rise to, nor leaves scope for, much judicial discretion. The position is altered when statutory words are unclear, or at least not instantly susceptible to a clear interpretation, and the court must resolve uncertainties and, occasionally, resolve ambiguities in the language used. Here the court becomes concerned with the construction of the statute and, in deference to the sovereignty of Parliament, the traditional approach of the judiciary has been the careful consideration of 'the intention of Parliament'.

The concept of the 'intention of Parliament' as the underlying theme for purposes of statutory construction provides a constitutional basis by which to limit what would otherwise be very wide, possibly absolute, judicial discretion in the application of statute law. It acts as a buffer that helps to protect the impartiality and independence of the judges by directing criticism of 'bad law' at Parliament and, at its simplest level, dictates that the resolution of the defect is for the legislature and not a matter of creative law-making to be left to the discretion of the judge. But here there lies a divergence of opinion as to what the proper function of the judge is when faced with uncertainties in statutory provision. It is a debate that turns on the extent to which the traditional restrictive, literal approach to statutory interpretation should be replaced by a more permissive, purposive one. The literal approach holds that the judge should look primarily to the words of the legislature in order to construe the meaning of any statutory provision. The purposive approach looks to the reason for the enactment of the statute and affords the judge the power to look beyond the words of the statute.

By its nature, the literal approach permits a departure from a literal interpretation only in very limited circumstances. The objective of the court is to discover the intention of Parliament as expressed in the words used. These must be given their plain, ordinary or literal meaning and, if that meaning is clear, it must be applied even though the result is absurd, or even though the interpretation may inflict hardship on those affected by the legislation. The court does not consider the result of the application of the rule and this was stated as early as 1892 by Lord Esher MR in *R v Judge of the City of London Court* [1892] 1 QB 273 when he said:

> 'If the words of an Act are clear, you must follow them even though they lead to a manifest absurdity. The court has nothing to do with the question whether the legislature has committed an absurdity.'

If this were the final word on the matter, the proposition that statutory interpretation is essentially a personal matter would be firmly rebutted. However, it is not the final word precisely because the 'canons of interpretation' are not rules as such and are 'subjects of interpretation'. Concurrent with the nineteenth-century development of the literal rule there was the development of the so-called golden rule. This is applied in cases where the plain meaning of the words produce a 'manifest absurdity' but, in its narrow application, it is restricted to being a means of modifying the operation of the literal rule to prevent an interpretation 'that would lead to some absurdity, or some repugnance or inconsistency with the rest of the instrument, in which case the grammatical and ordinary sense of the words may be modified, so as to avoid the absurdity and inconsistency but no farther': per Parke B (later Lord Wensleydale) in *Grey v Pearson* (1857) 6 HL Cas 61. The rule is not entirely clear in its extent and is rarely invoked and cases such as *IRC v Hinchy* [1960] AC 748, *Fisher v Bell* [1961] 1 QB 394 and *Magor and St Mellons Rural District Council v Newport Corporation* [1952] AC 189 indicate that 'odd' literal constructions do not automatically lead to use of the rule. A precondition of its use is the rejection of the literal rule. Unless it can be shown that the statutory framework or the legal context in which the words are used require a different meaning, the words of the statute are to be given their ordinary and grammatical meaning.

The literal rule was the product of the nineteenth century and reached its most extreme expression during that time. The twentieth century saw the emergence of what came to known as the purposive approach, though not without considerable controversy, and the boundaries of the judicial latitude it offers still remain undecided. In *Black-Clawson International Ltd* v *Papierwerke Waldhof-Aschaffenburg AG* [1975] AC 591 Lord Wilberforce noted that the frequently repeated statement 'that it is the function of the courts to ascertain the intention of Parliament' can, if too 'unreflectingly' repeated, lead to 'neglect of the important element of judicial construction' which is not confined to a 'mechanical analysis' of words, but should be related to matters such as:

> 'Intelligibility to the citizen, constitutional propriety, considerations of history, comity of nations, reasonable and non-retroactive effect and, no doubt, in some contexts, to social needs.'

A judge may only give consideration to these factors within the confines of an acceptable framework of judicial activism. For statutory interpretation, this framework is closely tied to the concept of parliamentary sovereignty and the separation of powers. Judicial activism cannot amount to 'a naked usurpation of the legislative function under the thin disguise of interpretation': per Lord Simmonds, in *Magor and St Mellons*. These words were levelled as criticism of the view expressed by Lord Denning in the Court of Appeal in the same case, that 'we sit here to find out the intention of Parliament ... and we do this better by filling in the gaps and making sense of the enactment than by opening it up to destructive analysis'. Lord Simmonds, and the majority of the House, was of the view that 'If a gap is disclosed the remedy lies in an amending Act'. The constitutional objections to judicial creativity surfaced again in the House of Lords' hearing in *Duport Steels Ltd* v *Sirs* [1980] 1 WLR 142 when Lord Denning drew strong condemnation from Lord Diplock and Lord Scarman in particular on the ground that he had failed to give effect to the plain words of the provision in order to avoid a parliamentary policy that he found 'unjust'. Lord Scarman said that 'in the field of statute law the judge must be obedient to the will of Parliament as expressed in its enactments ... Unpalatable statute law may not be disregarded or rejected merely because it is unpalatable.'

Departure from a literal interpretation in cases of ambiguity may be accomplished under the 'mischief rule' which allows the judge to search for the intention of Parliament by looking at the history of the Act in question, and in the *Black-Clawson* case (above) this was held to include reports of law reform bodies which contributed to the making of the Act. Until recently the use of other extrinsic material, including travaux preparatoires, as an aid to statutory interpretation has been restricted, but over time the rules have been relaxed. This is perhaps partly encouraged by the teleological approach used for the interpretation of EU law and in *Pepper* v *Hart* [1993] 1 All ER 42, in which the House of Lords permitted the use of *Hansard*, Lord Griffiths felt able to say:

> 'The courts now adopt a purposive approach which seeks to give effect to the true purpose of legislation and are prepared to look at much extraneous material that bears on the background against which the legislation was enacted.'

The purposive approach allows for more judicial difference of opinion than the literal approach and provides a greater scope for subjective judicial opinion of policy and

English Legal System

intention. However, the purposive approach we have adopted is not the European version of purposive construction under which judges may fill in gaps in relation to loosely drafted codes of law which openly invite the judges to become partners in the process of declaring law. Thus, whilst *Pepper* v *Hart* may signify a welcome relaxation of the inflexible literal approach, it falls well short of a metamorphosis in judicial attitudes. Our domestic legislation continues to be written in detailed and precise language that intends to demonstrate the 'intention of Parliament' in a clear and unambiguous way. This does not lend itself to any rapid departure from the traditional methods of statutory interpretation and for so long as the parliamentary draughtsmen continue to draft statutes in such awesome detail, the more likely it will be that judges will adhere to their self-imposed restraint against filling in omissions in statutes.

QUESTION FIVE

'The rules and principles of statutory interpretation do little or nothing to solve problems. They simply justify solutions usually reached on other grounds.'

Discuss.

University of London LLB Examination
(for External Students) English Legal System June 1997 Q2

General Comment

The question is obviously easier to tackle if one recognises the source and context of the quotation, which in this case is Zander's *The Law-Making Process* (5th ed, 1999). Since this book is usually recommended reading for those studying English legal system at undergraduate level, it is not unfair of examiners to expect students to demonstrate some familiarity with that text. Even though Zander is an eminent and respected academic, a good student should be able to contest the proposition in question through serious minded and thoughtful argument.

Skeleton Solution

Why the rules of statutory interpretation are not 'rules' at all – the character of judicial policy choices which lie behind the fiction of interpretation – comparison with the declaratory theory as a useful fiction to protect the judiciary – Lord Diplock's views on the fiction of statutory interpretation in the context of taxation appeals – the literal rule as a constitutional restraint upon flagrant judicial law-making – the effects of *Pepper* v *Hart* on the use of presumptions of legislative intent – conclusion upon the accuracy of Zander's proposition.

Suggested Solution

The proposition in question is put forward by Professor Michael Zander in *The Law-Making Process* (5th ed, 1999). It is based on the view that the literal, golden and mischief rules of interpretation are not rules in the ordinary sense since they all point to different solutions to the same problem. Nor is there any indication, either in the so-called rules or elsewhere, as to which to apply in any given situation. The same is true of all the other principles of and guides to interpretation. Therefore, the choice of appropriate principle in a particular case becomes one of subjective policy preference often totally unrelated to the substance of the principle selected.

In support of this controversial assertion Professor Zander quotes an example of a bear trainer who comes to a railway station with his bear and reads a notice, 'No dogs allowed on the train'. By applying the maxim 'expressio unius exclusio alterius' (the expression of a single category excludes similar other categories) he would claim to be entitled to board the train with the bear. The competing argument is that, as a matter of logic and common sense, if dogs are not allowed, bears are not either. It follows that the solution to the problem does not depend on the deployment of maxims of interpretation but on some notion as to what the rule is intended to achieve and the application of whatever interpretation best suits this objective. Hence Zander concludes that it is the judge and not the rule or principle that determines the outcome. The principles may suggest an answer but there will usually be a counter-principle to suggest the opposite result.

Zander's conclusion may be accurate but it is controversial because it reveals the character of judicial law-making which lies behind the fiction of statutory interpretation. Just as the declaratory theory is a useful fiction in protecting the judge from the charge of political selection or disregard of precedents, so the principles of statutory interpretation (contained in the common law and the Interpretation Act 1978) provide an indispensable shield for the judges compelled to work in a constitution based on parliamentary sovereignty and the separation of powers.

Few judges have openly acknowledged that statutory interpretation is as much a fiction as the declaratory theory. One exception is Lord Diplock in a 1965 lecture, quoted in Zander's book. Discussing tax appeals, Lord Diplock observes that whenever the court decides that kind of dispute it legislates about taxation:

> 'Do not let us deceive ourselves with the legal fiction that the court is only ascertaining and giving effect to what Parliament meant. Anyone who has decided tax appeals knows that most of them concern transactions which Members of Parliament and the draftsman of the Act had not anticipated, about which they had never thought at all ... The court may describe what it is doing in tax appeals as interpretation. So did the priestess of the Delphic oracle. But whoever has final authority to explain what Parliament meant by the words that it used makes law as much as if the explanation it has given were contained in a new Act of Parliament.'

With respect to both Professor Zander and Lord Diplock the above views cannot be allowed to pass without challenge. The literal rule compels the judge to respect the limits of language, and Lord Denning's attempts to do 'justice' by a perverse interpretation of plain statutory words were frequently rebuffed by the House of Lords for being a usurpation of parliamentary sovereignty, eg *Magor and St Mellons Rural*

District Council v *Newport Corporation* [1952] AC 189. Judicial manipulation of statutory language, even with the best of motives, would risk provoking parliamentary anger, with consequent dangers for the independence of the judiciary.

The decision of the House of Lords in *Pepper* v *Hart* [1993] 1 All ER 42 to revoke the rule forbidding judicial reference to *Hansard* as an aid to interpretation may also limit the scope for judicial law-making. This may seem curious since the decision is generally portrayed as an adoption of a purposive approach and therefore more liberal than the old strict literalist approach. Lord Griffiths stated ([1993] 1 All ER 42 at 50):

> 'The courts now adopt a purposive approach which seeks to give effect to the true purpose of legislation and are prepared to look at much extraneous material that bears on the background against which the legislation was enacted.'

Prior to *Pepper* v *Hart* judges could choose from a variety of presumptions of legislative intent, but that becomes impossible if *actual* legislative intent can be deduced from a reading of *Hansard*. Whereas previously a judge could, if he or she desired, protect basic human rights through the presumption against oppressive use of state power, today such a judge may be defeated from giving such protection by discovering from *Hansard* that the relevant lawmakers had a narrow and illiberal intention! Indeed, if the House of Lords had been able to look at *Hansard* in *R* v *R (Rape: Marital Exemption)* [1991] 4 All ER 481 it would have seen that the relevant legislation was probably intended to preserve a husband's ancient common law immunity from prosecution for 'marital rape'!

However, since the judges are not obliged to give priority to statements made in Parliament there remains the potential for them (if they feel so bold) to continue, where possible, to seek to construe an ambiguous statute in a manner which best advances desirable social goals, such as the protection of fundamental human rights. Subject to political reality, Zander's proposition is essentially correct since judges have the last word on the proper interpretation of a statute. This of course is subject to the conformity requirement as is evident from the European Communities Act 1972 and more recently the Human Rights Act 1998 which incorporated into English law the European Convention on Human Rights.

QUESTION SIX

Will the increased importance of the law of the European Union entail a radical change in the way that judges in the UK interpret statutes?

University of London LLB Examination
(for External Students) English Legal System June 1996 Q2

General Comment

This question is a departure from the usual kinds of question on statutory interpretation because it lays the emphasis on the constitutional implications of

Statutory Interpretation

membership of the European Union. It follows that the source material for this question can be found not only in textbooks on English legal system but also in textbooks on constitutional law, eg Loveland's *Constitutional Law – a Critical Introduction* (3rd edn, 2003). The precise issue raised by this question is also dealt with in Zander's *The Law-Making Process* (5th edn, 1999).

Skeleton Solution

Definition of traditional literal approach to statutory interpretation and the constitutional reasons for that approach – recent moves to a more purposive approach, notably the landmark decision of *Pepper* v *Hart* – definition of the European teleological method of interpretation and the contrasts with English methods – the constitutional implications of EU membership: the 'ripple effect' on the role of judges as interpreters of legislation.

Suggested Solution

Traditionally judges in the English legal system have preferred to give statutes their ordinary literal meaning as far as possible, even though in some cases a strict literal interpretation may result in what the judge may regard as hardship or injustice in the particular case in which the statute is being applied. This preference was based on judicial respect for parliamentary sovereignty and the separation of powers. It was felt that it would undermine sovereignty and turn the judge into a legislator if, for example, he added words to a statute to achieve the result he thought Parliament would have preferred if Parliament had considered the policy issue in question at the time of passing the statute. It was believed to be dangerous for judges to become partners in the creation of new law because of the unrepresentative and unaccountable character of the judiciary. The literal approach therefore protected the impartiality and independence of the judges by directing criticism of 'bad law' at Parliament rather than at those who were delivering the message. Other advantages of the literal approach were said to be its easy application and its promotion of certainty and consistency in the law. It gave the judge a stabilising function rather than a reforming one.

However, in the landmark decision of *Pepper* v *Hart* [1993] 1 All ER 42 the House of Lords held that there were no longer objections of principle to the use of *Hansard* as an external aid to statutory construction, and there was judicial endorsement of a more purposive approach to construction under which a judge looks beyond the strict literal meaning to try to discern either Parliament's true intentions when passing the legislation in question or Parliament's wishes in the event of an unforeseen event arising, ie the judge must decide what Parliament would have done if it had thought of the matter. The consequence of such an approach may well be to 'put words into Parliament's mouth' by altering the statutory text and reading in words so as to achieve this outcome.

Such an approach has long been familiar to continental lawyers, and especially to the judges of the European Court of Justice who have used a very broad and generous approach (technically described as a 'teleological' approach) when interpreting the treaties and instruments of European Union law. As long ago as 1974, barely a year after the United Kingdom's accession to the European Communities, it had been recognised by United Kingdom judges that they should adopt the teleological approach when required to interpret EC treaties and instruments in United Kingdom courts: per Lord Denning in *Bulmer v Bollinger* [1974] 3 WLR 202 at 216, who said that the United Kingdom judges must forgo the literal approach and

> '... follow the European pattern. No longer must they examine the words in meticulous detail. No longer must they argue about the precise grammatical sense. They must look to the purpose or intent ... They must divine the spirit of the Treaty and gain inspiration from it. If they find a gap they must fill it as best they can'.

It was not appreciated at first that this approach might also be adopted in the interpretation of domestic legislation, but gradually the argument was accepted that, in order to reconcile English statutory law with European law (as required by the European Communities Act 1972), United Kingdom judges might be justified in radically modifying the words of an English statute to achieve such consistency. In *Garland v British Rail Engineering Ltd* [1983] 2 AC 751, especially at p935, Lord Diplock defended the new approach on the ground that the 1972 Act had introduced a new rule of statutory interpretation requiring a United Kingdom court to construe all domestic legislation in a manner respecting European obligations 'however wide a departure from the prima facie meaning of the language of the provision might be needed in order to achieve consistency'.

However, this approach was not adopted by the House of Lords in *Duke v GEC Reliance* [1988] 1 All ER 626 because in that case the domestic law predated the relevant EC Directive and the Law Lords took the view that only traditional interpretative theory could be invoked: it was impermissible to 'distort' such domestic legislation in order to achieve consistency with subsequent European law. This setback was temporary, however, because in *Marleasing SA v La Comercial Internacional De Alimentacion SA* Case 106/89 [1992] 1 CMLR 305 the European Court of Justice ruled that the teleological approach must be used in such a situation because the overriding priority was to ensure the harmonisation and effectiveness of European law in all Member States. The House of Lords has accepted the implications of this ruling: *Webb v EMO Air Cargo Ltd* [1992] 4 All ER 929.

Some constitutional experts have suggested that it is possible to identify a 'ripple effect' in which principles espoused by the ECJ, and thereafter applied by the domestic courts in respect of EU matters, have also begun to influence judicial decision-making on purely domestic issues: see for example Loveland's argument (*Constitutional Law – a Critical Introduction*). He suggests this 'ripple effect' may explain why the House of Lords lifted the ban on *Hansard* in *Pepper v Hart* and thereby supported a more purposive approach to statutory construction. Such a change was not strictly required by EU law but was perhaps influenced by EU membership in the sense that the constitutional principles of the EU, and the thinking of the judges of the ECJ, have become sufficiently firmly established in the minds of United Kingdom judges to begin to merge into the courts' constantly evolving conceptions of the contemporary role of the common law. The rules of statutory construction are rules of common law and, consequently, legitimate targets for change by activist judges in the event of changing political conditions.

Chapter 3

Law Reform and Agencies

3.1 Introduction

3.2 Key points

3.3 Question and suggested solution

3.1 Introduction

The concept of law reform involves the consideration of how changes in the law are brought about and the adequacy of our system. It requires discussion of both legislative reform and the role of the judiciary. Students should, however, check whether law reform is on their syllabus as this varies from one examining board to another.

3.2 Key points

Ideas for reform

These can come from many sources:

a) Pressure groups such as JUSTICE, Liberty, Shelter and Legal Action often call attention to 'gaps' in the law.

b) The legal profession – the Bar Council, the Law Society or the judiciary – may call for change.

c) Events and the media may highlight problems especially where an apparent failing in the law has failed to adequately deal with a tragic disaster, eg the Dunblane shootings (March 1996) which led to tighter legislative controls over the use of handguns.

d) Politicians and public opinion may provide a call for change in miscarriage of justice cases.

e) Government often gives the impetus for reform and may appoint the Law Commission as and when the need for law reform arises.

Official reform bodies

Law Commission

a) The Law Commission (for England and Wales) and the Scottish Law Commission are the only permanent bodies dedicated to law reform in the United Kingdom. They consider changes in the law and codification of existing laws. The Law Commission was set up by the Law Commission Act 1965.

b) Issues are referred to it by the Lord Chancellor, who now holds the position of Secretary of State for Constitutional Affairs. The Commission then thoroughly researches the issue and consults with interested parties before issuing a final report and draft Bill to place before Parliament.

c) It is regarded as a very capable body but has not enjoyed huge success in getting its proposals introduced due to lack of political impetus and parliamentary time.

d) Examples of parliamentary enactments initiated by the Law Commission include: the Unfair Contracts Terms Act 1977, the Occupiers' Liability Act 1984, the Law Reform (Year and a Day Rule) Act 1996 and the Contract (Rights of Third Parties) Act 1999.

e) The Law Commission has recently produced two reports which intend to effect changes within the English legal system. They are:

   i) *Partial Defences to Murder* (Consultation Paper No 173, October 2003);

   ii) *Renting Homes* (Consultation Paper No 284, November 2003).

Law Reform Committee

Part of the Department of Constitutional Affairs (previously known as the Lord Chancellor's Department), this committee is made up of academics, lawyers and members of the judiciary. It is not a permanent body and has been little used in recent years.

Criminal Cases Review Commission (CCRC)

Set up as a result of the Criminal Appeal Act 1995. Primarily responsible for correcting miscarriages of justice and in that context plays an influential role in reforming criminal law.

Ad hoc committees

a) Royal commissions are formed to investigate and suggest reform in a particular area of the law. The most recent was the Royal Commission on Criminal Justice which reported in July 1993. Royal commissions are made up of both practitioners and academics and produce comprehensive reports and proposals into their area of inquiry.

b) Internal Government procedures such as departmental committees and the civil service have been used increasingly in recent years. They are a much quicker and cheaper way of investigating proposals but are not regarded as the most comprehensive method of review.

Criticisms of the present system

The temporary nature of all but the Law Commission.

a) The failure of Parliament to discuss valuable Law Commission proposals due to lack of time or political interest.

b) The lack of a body dedicated to a systematic review of the law.

However, in March 2003 a report on the workings of the Law Commission was prepared for then Lord Chancellor's Department (now the Department for Constitutional Affairs) which stated that the Law Commission's independent position is indeed secure. The report can be viewed at: ww.dca.gov.uk/majrep/lawcom/halliday.htm.

Role of the judiciary

Whilst the judiciary claim to merely apply and not create the law, they do have a role in law reform.

a) The use of the doctrine of precedent allows the judges to create binding law for future decisions.

b) The *Practice Statement* [1996] 1 WLR 1234 gives the House of Lords greater scope.

c) The role of the higher courts as an appellate body allows the law to be amended.

d) There are many examples where the courts have been responsible for major developments in the law, eg *Hedley Byrne* v *Heller* [1964] AC 465; *Central London Property Trust Ltd* v *High Trees House Ltd* [1947] KB 130, and *R* v *R (Rape: Marital Exemption)* [1991] 4 All ER 481 which revised the law on marital rape.

Nevertheless, the judges claim to be reluctant to act as a creative body and will often steer away from it. They have also been known to make many errors: see the debates over judicial law reform conducted by the Law Lords in such cases as *Woolwich Building Society* v *IRC (No 2)* [1992] 3 All ER 737, *C* v *DPP* [1995] 2 All ER 43 and *Westdeutsche Landesbank Girozentrale* v *Islington LBC* [1996] 2 All ER 961.

Alternatives

a) Codification of the law and/or consolidation

Whilst this might 'simplify' the law and provide certainty, it would of course, be at the expense of flexibility. Many areas of English law have proved too complex to be codified.

b) A 'fast route' through Parliament for uncontroversial or 'technical' reform. This would overcome the problem of pressure upon parliamentary time.

c) A commitment by Government to put before Parliament a certain number of Law Commission proposals per year. This suggestion arises out of the fact that the Government approves of many Law Commission drafts but only some are placed before Parliament as Government Bills.

3.3 Question and suggested solution

'The official law reform agencies have failed to meet the need to reform the law.'

Discuss the effectiveness of these agencies and whether they are the only source of legal change.

> University of Wolverhampton LLB (Hons) by Distance Learning
> English Legal System Examination June 1993 Q6

General Comment

This question requires special care because students must consider some alternative sources, as well as the need for reform.

Skeleton Solution

Sources of ideas and 'need' – official bodies; their existence and success – alternatives; judiciary – conclusions.

Suggested Solution

The issue of reform of the law does not generally attract media attention, nor is it considered controversial. Nevertheless, law reform is an essential part of the English legal system. Generally, one thinks of change coming through Acts of Parliament, but the process begins long before and may not reach fruition in a statute.

When one examines the origins of the process of reform that the real need can be clearly seen. As society evolves and new situations arise socially, morally and technically the law must change to keep pace with those changes, eg the need to protect against criminal damage and theft of computer programmes or to change the law on marital rape. The pressure for change may come from various sources. Pressure groups such as JUSTICE, Liberty, Legal Action, Shelter and environmental lobbies often draw attention to gaps in the law. Media people and Members of Parliament may provide a vociferous source of pressure, especially where a controversial issue or tragic event needs to be dealt with. The legal profession, the judiciary and academics have been known to highlight changes required. These are just examples which show that the pressure and need for reform undoubtedly exists.

Having identified this need, one must consider how far it is being met: it is in examining this area that the inadequacies of the system can be clearly identified.

The official reform bodies are various. The most important, and only permanent, body is the Law Commission for England and Wales which was founded in 1965 in response to calls for a Ministry of Justice. Issues are referred to the Commission by the Department for Constitutional Affairs (formerly the Lord Chancellor's Department). The permanent, specialist staff then investigate the law and consult interested bodies before submitting a fully-informed report and draft Bill to the Government. The next stage of the process should be presentation to Parliament for debate. However, despite receiving Government approval, many reports are simply shelved due to the pressures on parliamentary time. This is especially true of technical or legalistic reforms (eg patent legislation or land law) which do not attract the political interest for the Government or MPs, although they may be vital.

The quality of the Commission's reports and Bills is widely agreed to be excellent and where a proposal does eventually get put into practice it is usually well drafted and workable. But unless some way can be found to get these draft Bills through Parliament they will fail to meet the need for change no matter how carefully considered and created they are. One proposal has been a special 'fast track' through Parliament, making greater use of the House of Lords, for non-controversial legislation. However, this idea has not received Government backing.

Over the years, there have been various other types of non-permanent reform agencies. The Law Reform Committee, made up of academics, lawyers and judges, has not been used in recent years. The Criminal Law Revision Committee of leading academics and practitioners has been very successful in the past, having been instrumental in producing the Theft Acts. Various ad hoc committees may be used, the most well known of which are probably the Royal Commissions, the most recent being the Phillips Commission on Criminal Justice (2003). There have been several Royal Commissions over the past decades which have dealt with matters such as changes in the law of tort and reform of the legal profession. Their composition usually provides wide representation of interests with members from the legal profession, academics, judges and experts in the relevant subject matter. Their failing lies not in the quality of their investigation and proposals, but in their lack of power to persuade Government to adopt their ideas.

In the past decade or so increasing use has been made of Government department reviews to propose reform. These are favoured because they are quicker and less expensive than the other bodies. However, they have been criticised for a lack of clarity in their proposals, especially where a Bill is rushed through Parliament against a backdrop of political and media attention.

Frequently attempts at reform are made through the use of Private Member's Bills, which may be introduced by any Member of Parliament in the limited parliamentary time allocated. These rarely achieve first reading and often lack clarity or completeness because the Members of Parliament have no immediate access to parliamentary draftsmen. Their best chance of success is if they are adopted as a Government Bill, as happened in the case of the abolition of the solicitors' monopoly on conveyancing, originally proposed by a Labour back bencher.

There are, then, many official ways to introduce change. Many of them fail to receive the necessary backing to become law, though they may have dealt very thoroughly and efficiently with the original need at draft stage. One route for reform that is not subject to the uncertainties of political life is via the judiciary's use of precedent.

Although not an 'official body' the judiciary are an active agency for change. Whilst judges generally claim to be declaring the law, not creating it, in practice they are responsible for many changes and developments. This is especially true of the common law with the use of the doctrine of precedent allowing the higher courts to bind future decision makers. The 1966 *Practice Statement* ([1966] 1 WLR 1234) gave the House of Lords considerable scope and over the years they have been responsible for many changes in all areas of law. Even persuasive authorities have provided a valuable source of change, eg *Hedley Byrne v Heller* [1964] AC 465 establishing a new area of negligence and *High Trees* (*Central London Property Trust Ltd v High Trees House Ltd* [1974] KB 130) establishing a new principle of contract law. Arguably, they have sometimes been responding to a social need, such as reforming the law on marital rape in *R v R (Rape: Marital Exemption)* [1991] 4 All ER 481, even though their response might be said to be rather slow! Often, however, they have simply been amending a mistake, for example in criminal law with the case of *R v Shivpuri* [1986] 2 All ER 334, and often their decisions have attracted a great deal of criticism from academics for the lack of specific expertise.

How far the judges meet the need for reform is therefore debatable, and they certainly would not regard themselves as a reform agency. They do, however, provide a sometimes useful alternative to the official bodies.

The lack of a consistent review of the law and the inability of the Law Commission to force its proposals through show that the system often fails to respond to the demand for change. Proposals to reform this aspect of the law have ranged from relatively minor changes in parliamentary procedure through to the introduction of a Ministry of Justice. None, however, has yet been adopted and so the problem remains and the need is unmet.

Chapter 4

The Doctrine of Precedent

4.1 Introduction

4.2 Key points

4.3 Key cases

4.4 Questions and suggested solutions

4.1 Introduction

The doctrine of stare decisis (binding judicial precedent) applies within the hierarchical structure of the courts. The basis of the doctrine is that decisions of higher courts bind those of lower courts. This practice allows the treatment of like cases alike. The modern doctrine emerged in the nineteenth century with the development of a formal system of law reporting. This does not mean that an unreported case may not be cited as a precedent: see *Roberts Petroleum Ltd v Bernard Kenny Ltd* [1983] 1 All ER 564. However, leave to cite unreported cases will not usually be granted unless the transcript contains a relevant statement of legal principle not found in reported authority: *Practice Note (Citation of Unreported Cases)* [1996] 3 All ER 382 (CA, Civil Division).

4.2 Key points

Reasons for upholding the doctrine

a) Fairness.

b) Predictability.

Ingredients of a decision

a) Findings of fact.

b) Statements of principles of law.

c) Judgment based on applying law to facts ie the ratio decidendi.

d) Statements made obiter dicta.

The Doctrine of Precedent

The operation of the doctrine

The European Court of Justice

a) On matters of Community law, the decisions of this court are binding on UK courts.

b) The ECJ is not bound by its own previous decisions, but generally tends to follow them.

The House of Lords

a) The decisions of the House of Lords are binding on all other courts within the UK.

b) Since the *Practice Statement* [1966] 1 WLR 1234 the House of Lords is no longer bound by its own previous decisions, but will generally follow them.

In this respect, see the decision of the House of Lords in *R v Kansal (No 2)* [2002] 1 All ER 257 where despite finding that their earlier decision was wrong, the House of Lords nevertheless refused to depart from it because of the need to maintain consistency.

The Court of Appeal (Civil Division)

a) The decisions of the Court of Appeal are binding on all lower courts.

b) The Court of Appeal (Civil Division) is bound by decisions of the House of Lords.

c) The Court of Appeal is also bound by its own previous decisions except in very limited circumstances. In *Young v Bristol Aeroplane Co* [1946] AC 163 the Court of Appeal made clear the exceptional circumstances in which it would not be bound by its own previous decisions. Firstly, where there are two previous conflicting Court of Appeal decisions. Secondly, where the previous Court of Appeal decision conflicts with a later House of Lords decision, and finally where the previous Court of Appeal decision was made per incuriam ie without due care, eg in ignorance of a binding authority. In *Langley v North West Water Authority* [1991] 3 All ER 610, the Court of Appeal said that departure from a previous Court of Appeal decision should only be considered if the earlier one was manifestly wrong.

In this respect, see the recent decision on the Court of Appeal in *R v Brent London Borough Housing Benefit Review Board, ex parte Khadim* [2001] NPC 7, where the Court of Appeal set down certain rules in relation to modification of an earlier decision.

The Court of Appeal (Criminal Division)

a) The decisions of this court are binding on all lower courts.

b) The Court of Appeal (Criminal Division) is bound by the decisions of the House of Lords.

c) The Criminal Division of the Court of Appeal is not required to follow its own previous decisions, where to do so would cause injustice to the appellant: *R v Gould* [1968] 1 All ER 849. With the introduction of ss2 and 3 of the Human Rights Act 1998 this practice is further reaffirmed.

The High Court

a) All divisions of the High Court are bound by the decisions of superior courts.

b) Where the court sits as a court of first instance, it is not bound by its own decisions, but will tend to follow them: *Colchester Estates* v *Carlton Industries* [1984] 3 WLR 693. Again, where to do so will cause injustice, then the court of first instance is allowed to deviate so as to preserve justice.

Other courts

a) Are bound by the decisions of the superior courts.

b) Are not bound by their own previous decisions.

Persuasive authorities

a) Privy Council decisions are highly persuasive.

b) Ratio of Scottish courts.

c) Ratio of Commonwealth courts.

d) Ratio of foreign courts.

e) Obiter dicta statements. *Donoghue* v *Stevenson* [1932] AC 562 and *Hedley Byrne & Co* v *Heller & Partners* [1964] AC 465 are both examples of cases with influential obiter dicta.

Avoiding awkward precedents

At times a court may feel that it does not wish to adhere strictly to the doctrine of precedent and may therefore seek to avoid the application of a precedent. It may do to in a number of ways.

Distinguishing

Cases ought only to be distinguished where it is 'reasonable' to do so, generally upon dissimilar facts.

Overruling

This is allowable within the hierarchical structure of courts. It is an important means by which a degree of flexibility is maintained within an inherently rigid doctrine. Consider also the concept of prospective overruling.

Statements made 'per incuriam' (literally 'through want of care'), eg without the court having considered relevant cases.

4.3 Key cases

- *Practice Statement* [1966] 1 WLR 1234
  Their Lordships are no longer bound by their previous decisions

- *R v Brent London Borough Housing Benefit Review Board, ex parte Khadim* [2001] NPC 7 (CA)
  Certain rules were set down in relation to modification of an earlier decision

- *R v Kansal (No 2)* [2002] 1 All ER 257
  Their Lordships are not readily inclined to depart from earlier decisions

- *Thai Trading Co v Taylor* [1998] QB 781; [1998] 2 WLR 893
  Per incuriam decisions have no binding effect

- *Young* v *Bristol Aeroplane Co* [1946] AC 163
  Exceptionally, the Court of Appeal may not be bound by its previous decisions

4.4 Questions and suggested solutions

QUESTION ONE

'Within the present system of precedent in the English legal system, judges have very little discretion in their decision-making.'

Discuss.

University of London LLB Examination
(for External Students) English Legal System June 2001 Q2

General Comment

Whilst this is a short question, it is suggestive and provocative. The entire fundamentals of the doctrine of precedent require analysis. The traditional role of judges under the umbrella of common law should be compared with the requirement of judicial activism and the need to adapt and adopt changes as public defenders. Examples of cases and instances where new 'law' or 'principles' have been enunciated must therefore be discussed.

Skeleton Solution

The rationale of 'stare decisis' – its necessity and role within common law – a brief note on its hierarchical operation – 'ratio' and 'obiter' – the tussle between law (Parliament) and discretion (judges) – instances where judicial activism has prevailed

– *R v R (Rape: Marital Exemption)*; *C v Director of Public Prosecutions*; *Donoghue v Stevenson*; *Central London Property Trust Ltd v High Trees House Ltd* and other examples.

Suggested Solution

Traditionally, the role of the judge has been one of 'jus dicere, non jus dare' (to say the law, not to give it) and this is compounded by the doctrine of parliamentary supremacy. Judges have always been perceived as interpreters of law as opposed to legislators. Certainly, the attitude of the courts has been no less passive, in a sense that they tend to let the legislature correct or remedy 'defective' legislation or ambiguous laws. However, with the passage of time coupled with the dawn of the European influence, a clear sway towards a more activist and purposive role has emerged. It is arguable, therefore, that the conventional declaratory theory has now been abandoned in favour of proactive judicial law-making.

Whilst the doctrine of precedent dictates that like cases should be adjudged alike so as to bring certainty and consistency to the application of the law, it must be borne in mind that this is a flexible doctrine and therefore subjects itself to changes as and when necessary. If applied strictly, this theory of 'stare decisis' leaves no scope for judicial discretion or creativity in developing common law principles to meet the needs of a changing society. Clearly, the law should reflect the time, and judges who are seen as 'public defenders' should see to this. It is not surprising, therefore, that the radical and unorthodox Lord Denning, in his book (*The Discipline of Law* (1979)), stated that 'the hands of judges are never tied'. It is perhaps this view that is reflected in the *Practice Statement* [1966] 1 WLR 1234 in which the House of Lords recognised that too rigid an adherence to precedent may lead to injustice in a particular case, and also unduly restrict the proper development of the law.

The judicial change in the law relating to marital rape is a good example, not only of the abandonment of the declaratory theory but also of the controversy concerning judge-made law. In *R v R (Rape: Marital Exemption)* [1991] 4 All ER 481, the Law Lords overturned the rule that there was no offence of 'marital rape', a rule that had stood for 200 years. The House of Lords perceived the old law to be anachronistic and offensive, and that it did not reflect the change of time and society. Lord Keith stated that the common law should evolve in the light of changing social, economic and cultural developments.

As Lord Reid observed in an article ((1972) 12 JSPLT 22–28), legal principle and public policy must be complimentary. If the law is to keep in step with movements of public opinion, the judges must know how ordinary people of all grades of society think and live. This, however, does not deter some senior judges from continuing to perceive their role as one of application of existing law rather than of evolution of new legal principles. The Law Lords are no doubt sensitive to the threat to the rule of law inherent in the retrospective character of judicial overruling. Considerations such as these leave the senior judiciary (at times!) in a difficult position as to how far the doctrine of precedent should stand in the way of the sensible and just development of the law. In

Westdeutsche Landesbank Girozentrale v *Islington London Borough Council* [1996] 2 All ER 961, Lord Goff, dissenting, gave an eloquent plea for the need to 'mould and remould' the authorities to ensure that 'practical justice is done'.

In *R* v *Clegg* [1995] 1 All ER 334, for instance, Lord Lloyd said, obiter, that he was not averse to judges developing law, or indeed making new law, when they can see their way clearly, even where questions of social policy are involved, but that judicial law reform should be avoided if the wider policy issues arising from a proposed change in the law were clearly of a character suitable only for parliamentary debate and decision. This perhaps explains why some judges lower down in the hierarchy are determined to effect changes in the law. For example, in *C* v *Director of Public Prosecutions* [1995] 2 All ER 43, the Queen's Bench Division was bold enough to remove the presumption of 'doli incapax' in criminal law affecting the age of responsibility, though the decision was eventually reversed by the House of Lords. It is interesting, however, to note that subsequently, Parliament in 1998 passed the Crime and Disorder Act 1998 abolishing the presumption of 'doli incapax'.

The House of Lords' attitude to maintaining consistency and uniformity was recently illustrated in *R* v *Kansal (No 2)* [2002] 1 All ER 257 where despite finding that their earlier decision was wrong, their Lordships refused (by three to two) to depart from it for reasons of consistency. Lord Denning MR tried without success to alter the convention that the Court of Appeal is bound by its own previous decisions. In *Davis* v *Johnson* [1979] AC 317, it was argued that in many cases, the Court of Appeal is the last resort for the penurious litigant and that, since justice should be done in each individual case, the Court of Appeal, as a matter of principle, should be able to depart from its own previous decisions if they were wrong. Recently, in *R* v *Brent London Borough Council Housing Benefit Review Board, ex parte Khadim* [2001] NPC 7, the Court of Appeal set down certain rules in relation to modification of an earlier decision made by itself.

There are other cases which clearly illustrate judicial activism. For example, Lord Atkin's 'neighbour principle', which developed the tort of negligence in *Donoghue* v *Stevenson* [1932] AC 562. The concept of equitable estoppel was created by Lord Denning in his judgment in *Central London Property Trust Ltd* v *High Trees House Ltd* [1947] KB 130. Another famous case which exemplifies how the common law can be continually extended by the influence of obiter dicta is the case of *Hedley Byrne* v *Heller & Partners Ltd* [1963] 3 WLR 101.

In conclusion, therefore, whilst judicial activism should be encouraged, particularly to avoid the undesirable consequences resulting from too rigid an application of precedent, over enthusiasm in the form of dynamism should be discouraged, since it endangers the judge's appearance of impartiality and can be seen as usurping parliamentary authority. Perhaps Lord Denning's plea in his book *The Discipline of Law*, that is: 'to keep the path to justice clear of obstructions which would impede it', aptly reflects the current situation.

QUESTION TWO

Could the Court of Appeal depart from its own previous decisions? What would be the advantages and disadvantages of such a course?

University of London LLB Examination
(for External Students) English Legal System June 1999 Q1

General Comment

This topic is commonly examined and it is important to notice the thrust of the question in the second sentence. It is necessary to decide what should be discussed in this part of the answer. The first part of the question requires a straightforward discussion of the role of precedent and the structure of the appeals process. The answer should include discussion of the problem of overlap with the powers of the legislature.

Skeleton Solution

Changing attitudes – the role of the Court of Appeal in the appeal system – scope and impact of the 1966 *Practice Statement* – reasons why the *Practice Statement* is confined to the House of Lords – arguments for and against a similar system for the Court of Appeal.

Suggested Solution

When Lord Denning MR tried without success in *Davis* v *Johnson* [1979] AC 264 to alter the convention that the Court of Appeal is bound by its own previous decisions there was general agreement that such a step would introduce too much uncertainty into the appeals process and upset the delicate balance that has to be maintained for the successful operation of a common law system. Treating like cases alike brings certainty and consistency to the application of the law and adherence to binding judicial precedent based on the hierarchy of the courts is a carefully guarded tradition. There is, however, a sea change in thinking. In recent years there has been much debate about the need for increased judicial activism and this has found practical expression in the willingness of the judiciary to take a more creative role in the law-making process within the boundaries imposed by the constitutional sovereignty of Parliament. There has been concurrent movement toward a system of justice that is accessible to all persons who need to use it and flexible in its operation. The implementation of the reforms proposed in Lord Woolf's *Access to Justice* report, published in July 1996, was intended to introduce 'a new landscape for civil justice for the twenty-first century' and much of the philosophy underpinning this was based on the notion that judges should be pro-active not reactive, that parties should move from being aggressive to co-operative and that the cost of the proceedings should be proportionate to the nature of the disputes. Lord Woolf in his report and Sir Richard Scott in his implementation of the proposals emphasised that changes in attitude of the judiciary and the legal professions are as important as changes in the procedure.

This all amounts to change that affects thinking about all parts of the legal system and which can be expected in time to influence the attitude taken as to the role of the Court of Appeal in the appeals process. In *Davis* v *Johnson* (above) Lord Denning MR argued that in many cases the Court of Appeal is the last resort for the penurious litigant and that since justice should be done in each individual case the Court of Appeal, as a matter of principle, should be able to depart from its own previous decisions if they were wrong. The House of Lords rejected this view in a way that Lord Denning later described as a 'crushing rebuff', but there is something to be salvaged from the sympathy for his view expressed by Lord Salmon that may become important to the shaping of the brave new landscape of modern justice. Lord Salmon agreed with Lord Denning on the point of the inherent right of a court to regulate its own activity but argued that total agreement of all the Lord Justices was necessary in order to change such a practice. At the time, it seemed unlikely that such unanimity would ever be reached among the members of the Court of Appeal and even less likely that such a step would be countenanced by the House of Lords. Certainty was seen as being more important than flexibility in respect of the role of the Court of Appeal within the appeals system. It was felt, and by many is still felt, to be important to maintain the role of the Court of Appeal as a second tier of judges that serves as a quality control on the judgments of the lower courts, assuring litigants of a high quality of justice at moderate cost. The Court of Appeal should play the strict constitutional role of applying the law as it exists and leave the quasi-legislative development of the law permitted by the 1966 *Practice Statement* ([1966] 1 WLR 1234) to the House of Lords. Many would argue that this is arrant nonsense. The Lord Justices are experienced lawyers accustomed to setting precedents that are well reasoned and long lived and in reality the careful distinguishing of authorities and the malleability of legal principles allow the Court of Appeal to make law in all but name. If this view is accepted then giving the Court of Appeal the right to depart from its own decisions avoids deception and increases clarity in the law.

The debate comes down to the view that is taken of the correct balance between certainty and flexibility in an appeals system. Those that favour certainty as the controlling factor do so because they see it as allowing all relations to be conducted in a sure knowledge of the consequences. Those that favour increased flexibility work from the recognition that life can never be perfectly forecast and situations will arise that require changes in the legal rules governing relations between people and with the state. The three exceptions laid down in *Young* v *Bristol Aeroplane Co Ltd* [1944] KB 718 can be seen as providing for the delicate balance that must be maintained between certainty and flexibility in respect of the discretion of the Court of Appeal to depart from its own decisions. First, where two decisions of the Court of Appeal are in conflict, the Court may choose between them. Second, where the Court of Appeal has chosen not to follow a decision of the House of Lords, for example, because it thought the House of Lords' decision was reasonably distinguishable, it is for the Court of Appeal to decide at its discretion whether its apparently conflicting precedent should be followed. Clearly, if the House of Lords' decision was not reasonably distinguishable, the Court of Appeal must disregard the conflicting precedent. However, if the Court of Appeal believes that the conflicting decision involved only a general consideration of the issues raised by its own earlier decision and has not substantially undermined its authority, the Court of Appeal may choose to follow its own prior decision. If this is not the case it would appear that the Court of Appeal must treat its conflicting decision as impliedly overruled by the later House of Lords' decision: *R v Secretary of State for the Home Department, ex parte Al-Mehdawi* [1989] 1 All ER 777. If the conflicting decision of the decision of the House of Lords was made later in time and had been overlooked this would be covered by the third exception which states that the Court of Appeal may disregard a decision of its own reached per incuriam, that is, without due care, for example as a result of overlooking a relevant binding authority: *Rakhit v Carty* [1990] 2 All ER 202 and *Rickards v Rickards* [1989] 3 WLR 749.

The 1966 *Practice Statement* (see above) adjusted the balance in favour of flexibility for the House of Lords in certain circumstances but it also reflected the conservative view of the need to maintain the hierarchy of the courts and confine any activist role in changing the law to the court of last resort by stating: 'This announcement is not intended to affect the use of precedent elsewhere than in this House'. The accompanying press notice indicated that the power would be sparingly used and it has been. Perhaps the debate about increased activism and the development of a more flexible system should focus more on the role of the House of Lords than the Court of Appeal. The *Practice Statement* gives the Lords considerable discretion in departing from its own decisions when 'it is right to do so'. Critics argue that the Lords take too conservative a view and are motivated more by the desire not to admit that their own previous decisions are wrong but this is probably untrue and in any case far too simplistic a view to take. The Law Lords are no doubt sensitive to the threat to the rule of law inherent in the retrospective character of judicial overruling. An overruled decision is treated as if it had never been made and the effect of this may be serious so far as it concerns the legality of actions taken by citizens in reliance upon the earlier decision. This is more likely to be why the House of Lords does tend to reverse a decision of the Court of Appeal rather than overrule a House of Lords' decision. Lord Salmon has suggested that power be given to the Court of Appeal to refer cases to the House of Lords where they disagree with the decision they were bound to make by precedent and that such appeals would be paid for from public funds. This system still envisaged argued submissions before the Lords, preparation and research and all the procedure of a proper appeal and it is suggested that it is unlikely that the public purse will be used to finance it. A more efficient method could be devised whereby the Lords review the arguments and evidence adduced in the lower courts and give their judgment in writing when they are satisfied. This could even be done as 'pro bono' work by their Lordships, giving them an active role in initiating the reviews as guardians of the growth of law. Such an approach would clarify the three-tier appeals system that we have without inhibiting the Court of Appeal or making the House of Lords redundant.

Alternatives such as these are the practical solution. The idea that the Court of Appeal should be allowed to depart from its own previous decisions stems from the need to recognise a more active role for a court of last resort. That court is, and should remain as, the House of Lords. Extending the wide power of the *Practice Statement* to the Court of Appeal, even for conservative use in special circumstances, would overbalance the system towards uncertainty and injustice. It is access to the House of Lords in their role as lawmakers that should be improved.

QUESTION THREE

' ... there was never a more sterile controversy than that upon the question whether a judge makes law. Of course he does. How can he help it?' (Lord Radcliffe.)

Discuss.

University of London LLB Examination
(for External Students) English Legal System June 1998 Q1

General Comment

This broad question offers the opportunity to discuss theoretical questions about the role of the judiciary within the common law system and their function in the development of the common law. The essential theme is that of whether a judge makes law. This raises some difficult issues concerning their true role and the theoretical and practical limits on that function.

Skeleton Solution

The traditional role of the judge and the declamatory theory of precedent justice – the notion of judicial activism compared to the 'disinterested application of known law' – views expressed by members of the judiciary and notably those of Lord Devlin and Lord Denning – the 'activist' elements and the 'traditional' elements of the 1966 *Practice Statement* and an evaluation of the dilemma facing the judiciary in respect of the overruling of precedent – the argument for increased activism in the lower courts and particularly the Court of Appeal.

Suggested Solution

The modern role of a judge has become a much debated problem. It is questioned whether it is still that of 'jus dicere, non jus dare' (to say the law, not to give it). A significant but increasing minority of the judiciary, and a good proportion of lawyers and other jurists, take the view that the function of a judge is not simply a disinterested application of known law but a function that requires a more activist judicial law-making approach.

The traditional view sits with the declamatory theory of English common law: the function of a judge is to declare what has always been the correct legal position at common law. In carrying out this task judges should aim to treat like cases alike so as to bring certainty and consistency to the application of the law and, for this purpose, they should observe a doctrine of precedent based on the hierarchy of the courts. Since constitutionally the task of legislating is for Parliament this doctrine should be one of binding judicial precedent (stare decisis) so as to limit the scope of judicial discretion to change or reform the law. If applied strictly, this theory leaves no scope for judicial creativity in developing common law principles to meet the needs of changing society. It can be argued that even under a rigid system of precedent there ought to be, and is, room for 'activist judicial law-making' because the function of a judge is to render a social service, namely the removal of a sense of injustice, and sometimes too rigid an adherence to precedent might perpetuate rather than remove a perceived wrong. Lord Denning when he was Master of the Rolls pointed out that a judge might be faced with the problem that a just solution of a dispute would involve abrogating an apparently established rule of law. The application of the latter to a changed set of social conditions and values might perpetuate injustice in individual cases and Parliament may not have the time to pass appropriate remedial legislation. In this situation Lord Denning refused to accept that the judges' hands were tied and in his book *The Discipline of Law* (Butterworths (1979) p314) he declares himself against 'too rigid application' of precedent where such an approach insisted that a bad precedent must be followed.

These sentiments are reflected in the *Practice Statement* [1966] 1 WLR 1234 in which the House of Lords recognised that too rigid an adherence to precedent may lead to injustice in a particular case and also unduly restrict the proper development of the law. The House has shown willingness to do this. For example, in *R v R (Rape: Marital Exemption)* [1991] 4 All ER 481 the House overturned the rule that there was no offence of 'marital rape', a rule that had stood for 200 years. The sparing use of the 1966 *Practice Statement*, however, indicates that senior judges continue to perceive their role as one of application of existing law rather than of evolution of new legal principles. The Law Lords are no doubt sensitive to the threat to the rule of law inherent in the retrospective character of judicial overruling. An overruled decision is treated as if it had never been made. The effect of this may be serious so far as it concerns the legality of actions taken by citizens in reliance upon the earlier decision. For example, the legality of taxation arrangements or contractual dealings may be undone. In criminal law overruling might 'criminalise' activity which was not criminal at the time it was committed and for this reason would be a breach of the rule of law. Considerations such as these leave the senior judiciary in a difficult position as to how far precedent should stand in the way of sensible and just development of the law. In *Westdeutsche Landesbank Girozentrale v Islington London Borough Council* [1996] 2 All ER 961 Lord Goff, dissenting, gave an eloquent plea for the need to 'mould and remould' the authorities to ensure that 'practical justice is done'. However, the House of Lords was divided three to two, with the three in the majority preferring the certainty of sticking to precedent and the two in the minority preferring bold judicial activism.

The *Practice Statement* also reflected the conservative view of the need to maintain the hierarchy of the courts by emphasising that any activist role in changing the law should be confined to the court of last resort, namely: 'This announcement is not intended to affect the use of precedent elsewhere than in this House'. This has not deterred determined judges lower down in the hierarchy from 'developing the different principles of cases into a coherent whole'. For example, in C v *Director of Public Prosecutions* [1995] 2 All ER 43 the Queen's Bench Division was bold enough to remove the presumption of 'doli incapax' in criminal law affecting the age of responsibility, though the decision was eventually reversed by the House of Lords. Lord Denning MR tried without success to alter the convention that the Court of Appeal is bound by its own previous decisions. In *Davis* v *Johnson* [1979] AC 264 it was argued that in many cases the Court of Appeal is the last resort for the penurious litigant and that since justice should be done in each individual case the Court of Appeal, as a matter of principle, should be able to depart from its own previous decisions if they were wrong.

Lord Radcliffe's words 'Of course he does. How can he help it?' should not be construed as necessarily implying liberal activism. Within the confines of a conservative view of the doctrine of judicial precedent there is scope for some judicial discretion to shape and mould common law principles to meet changing times. Activism does not deny that following precedent is desirable. Instead, it seeks to rebut the contention that the judge's role is purely formal in following precedent and merely involves applying the law to the facts of each case. Activism is defensible in democratic terms on the ground that it keeps the common law reasonably up to date, in touch with changing social conditions and humane. It is a task requiring the exercise of sensitive judicial discretion, perhaps involving the weighing of competing public or private interests. Activism is, nonetheless, controversial and many judges have denied its legitimacy as usurping the sovereignty of Parliament. Lord Devlin sought to deal with this constitutional objection by drawing a distinction between 'activism' and 'dynamism'. Activist law-making is permissible in that it is taken from a consensus found by the judge to exist at the time in question and which commands his or her sympathy. Dynamism takes an idea for reform from outside this consensus and requires judicial enthusiasm for its propagation. Enthusiasm cannot be considered a judicial virtue since it endangers the judge's appearance of impartiality and can be seen as usurping parliamentary authority. Dynamism, therefore, is impermissible whereas activism is more in the nature of an 'escape route' that enables the judge in a particular case to avoid any undesirable consequence resulting from too rigid an application of precedent. Lord Denning in *The Discipline of Law* (Butterworths (1979) p314) describes the process as being akin to a path through the woods: 'You must follow it certainly so as to reach your end. But you must not let the path become too overgrown. You must cut out the dead wood and trim off side branches, else you will find yourself lost in thickets and brambles. My plea is simply to keep the path to justice clear of obstructions which would impede it.'

Both Lord Denning and Lord Devlin clearly favour a creative role for the judge in developing common law principles to meet the needs of the times but this is an 'activist' role carried out within the framework of parliamentary sovereignty and precedent justice. They are not advocating a dynamic role in which judges would behave as legislators. Their view of the role of a judge has an outcome that is similar to the sentiment expressed by Lord Radcliffe but expressed in different terms. Whichever way it is phrased, the gist of it becomes that precedent justice should not be used as an excuse for the blind application of principles but as a means of finding the best solution within the framework of a number of competing considerations.

QUESTION FOUR

'English judges should discard any remnants of the declaratory theory of judging and freely admit that they make law. The question then should become under what conditions and for what purposes they make law.'

Discuss.

> University of London LLB Examination
> (for External Students) English Legal System June 1997 Q1

General Comment

The question puts the emphasis on a conceptual approach to the issue of judicial law-making. Accordingly, the suggested solution concentrates on the general evidence of such law-making, using it to detect the conditions under which, and the purposes for which, such law-making occurs. Use is made of various judicial expressions of attitude on this topic and the (sometimes) hostile critical reactions they provoke. A mere narrative of the mechanical operation of the doctrine of precedent has been avoided in favour of a livelier and more stimulating conceptual sketch.

Skeleton Solution

The abandonment of the declaratory theory – the judicial change in the law relating to marital rape – the justification given by the judges for such change – academic criticism of judicial law-making – reconciling irreconcilables: making the law certain but also up to date – recent judicial observations: have the judges become cautious again? – effect of incorporation of the European Convention on Human Rights into English law.

Suggested Solution

English judges no longer assert that they simply discover and declare what the common law is and always has been. Indeed, as long ago as 1972 Lord Reid observed that the judges no longer believed in fairy tales and no longer pretended that 'in some Aladdin's cave there is hidden the common law in all its splendour and that on a judge's appointment there descends on him knowledge of the magic words "Open Sesame" ': (1972) 12 JSPTL 22–28.

The judicial change in the law relating to marital rape is a good example, not only of the abandonment of the declaratory theory but also of the controversy concerning judge-made law. In *R v R (Rape: Marital Exemption)* [1991] 4 All ER 481 the House of Lords concluded that the ancient common law principle that a husband could not be convicted of 'raping' his wife (because marriage always implied her consent to sexual intercourse) was anachronistic and offensive. Lord Keith said that the common law is capable of evolving in the light of changing social, economic and cultural developments. Accordingly, the husband's conviction for rape was upheld and the husband's subsequent attempt to challenge the ruling in the European Court of Human Rights failed because the European Court held that the retrospective change to the criminal law was a progressive and foreseeable evolution of the common law: *CR v United Kingdom* (1995) The Times 5 December.

It follows that some of the conditions under which, and the purposes for which, judges may freely admit to making law can be detected from these judgments: that it should be reasonably foreseeable that the judges will make such a change in the law; and that such change accords with common sense, legal principle and public policy. As Lord Reid said in his 1972 article (above), if the law is to keep in step with movements of public opinion the judges must know how ordinary people of all grades of society think and live. Clearly the five elderly law Lords in R v R were confident that they were accurately reflecting the mood for change, but their decision did not pass without criticism from some learned quarters.

In a letter to *The Times* (26 October 1991) Professor A T H Smith pointed out that the constitutional implications of abandoning the declaratory theory included the possibility of judicial extension of the law of blasphemy so that it protected those other than the Christian community. It can be argued that all such contentious changes to the criminal law are best left to the elected and accountable legislature, particularly as the adjudicatory nature of the legal system prevents the courtroom from becoming a debating chamber reflecting all points of view.

Lord Reid in his 1972 article summed up the dilemma for the judges as follows: 'people want two inconsistent things; that the law shall be certain, and that it shall be just and shall move with the times'. He thought that it was the business of the judges to keep both objectives in view: 'Rigid adherence to precedent will not do. And paying lip service to precedent while admitting fine distinctions gives us the worst of both worlds. On the other hand too much flexibility leads to intolerable uncertainty'.

In *R v Clegg* [1995] 1 All ER 334 Lord Lloyd said, obiter, that he was not averse to judges developing law, or indeed making new law, when they can see their way clearly, even where questions of social policy are involved, but that judicial law reform should be avoided if the wider policy issues arising from a proposed change in the law were clearly of a character suitable only for parliamentary debate and decision.

Similar sentiments were expressed by Lord Lowry in *C v DPP* [1995] 2 All ER 43. Lord Lowry emphasised that judicial caution should prevail if Parliament has rejected opportunities of clearing up a known difficulty, or has legislated while leaving the difficulty untouched.

In *Westdeutsche Landesbank Girozentrale v Islington London Borough Council* [1996] 2 All ER 961 five Law Lords were divided on the issue of whether to develop the equitable law of restitution so as to award compound interest to the plaintiff bank. The majority (Lords Browne-Wilkinson, Slynn and Lloyd) held it would not be appropriate to develop the law so as to award this remedy. Lord Browne-Wilkinson said that such development would usurp the function of Parliament and was also surrounded by unresolved questions. This 'leave it to Parliament' attitude was not shared by the two dissenting Law Lords (Lords Goff and Woolf), who thought that the need to award a just remedy overrode the need for certainty in commercial transactions. Lord Goff was particularly eloquent:

> '... it is the great advantage of a supreme court that, not only does it have the great benefit of assistance from the judgments of the courts below, but also it has a greater freedom to mould, and remould, the authorities to ensure that practical justice is done within a framework of principle ... No genetic engineering is required, only that the warm sun of judicial creativity should exercise its benign influence rather than remain hidden behind the dark clouds of legal history.'

Nevertheless, the majority views expressed in this case, together with the cases of *C v DPP* and *R v Clegg*, above, confirm the impression that most judges will always have difficulty in discarding the remnants of the declaratory theory so long as they are confined by traditional notions of parliamentary sovereignty and the separation of powers. Indeed, the absence of a general judicial power to alter the common law explains the failure to develop a general right of privacy in English civil and criminal law. The present position is that since the European Convention on Human Rights came into force in the United Kingdom on 2 October 2000 via the Human Rights Act 1998, our judges are duty bound to take into account the jurisprudence of the European Court of Human Rights in Strasbourg: s2. By virtue of s3, the courts are obliged to interpret existing and future legislation in conformity with the Convention.

QUESTION FIVE

'Judging cannot be described as an art or a craft since all a judge does is follow precedent and apply the law to the facts of the case.'

Discuss.

University of London LLB Examination
(for External Students) English Legal System June 1996 Q1

General Comment

A traditional kind of question calling for discussion of the purposes of the doctrine of precedent and the ways in which the functions of a judge are affected by the operation of that doctrine. The essential theme is on whether judging is (or should be) an art or a science. Judges have differed on this question and reference should be made to the divergent views as expressed in caselaw and extra judicially in books, lectures and articles. A useful source of judicial views on the conceptual basis of precedent and the role of the judge is Zander's *The Law-Making Process* (5th edn, 1999).

The Doctrine of Precedent

Skeleton Solution

The declaratory theory of common law, the doctrine of precedent, and the functions of a judge should be defined and inter-related – the constitutional overtones of precedent and the judicial role should be touched on – the limited scope for discretion under the doctrine of precedent should be examined – any movements or trends away from the orthodoxy of precedent should be explored, notably Lord Denning's attitudes to precedent – there should be a critical attempt at evaluating whether the job of judging has become more of an art than a science.

Suggested Solution

According to the declaratory theory of English common law the function of a judge is to declare what has always been the correct legal position at common law. Judges should also aim to treat like cases alike so as to bring certainty and consistency to the application of the law. For this purpose they should observe a doctrine of precedent based on the hierarchy of the courts. Since constitutionally the task of legislating is for Parliament this doctrine should be one of binding judicial precedent (stare decisis) so as to limit the scope of judicial discretion to change or reform the law. As a result the function of a judge becomes, at least in formal terms, scientific: 'the disinterested application of known law', as Professor Jaffé described it in *English and American Judges and Lawmakers* (1969).

By contrast, in his famous work *The Judge* (1979), Lord Devlin argued that even under a rigid system of precedent there ought to be, and is, room for 'activist judicial lawmaking' because the function of a judge is to render a social service, namely the removal of a sense of injustice, and sometimes too rigid an adherence to precedent might perpetuate rather than remove a perceived wrong. Such activism is defensible in democratic terms on the ground that it keeps the common law reasonably up to date, in touch with changing social conditions, and humane. It is a task requiring the exercise of sensitive judicial discretion, perhaps involving the weighing of competing public or private interests. If Lord Devlin was correct this would rebut the contention under discussion that the judge's role is purely formal in following precedent and merely involves applying the law to the facts of each case.

Yet the notion of an 'activist' judge is a controversial one and many judges have denied its legitimacy, even though, as explained above, it may have a rational and democratic basis. The doctrine of parliamentary sovereignty, which nowadays is largely confined to the UK's unwritten and idiosyncratic constitution, may help to explain judicial sensitivity to any possible accusation of judicial law-making. Lord Devlin attempted to deal with constitutional objections by distinguishing between 'activism' (permissible) and 'dynamism' (impermissible). Activist law-making is taken from a consensus found by the judge to exist at the time in question and which commands his/her sympathy. On the other hand, dynamism takes an idea for reform from outside this consensus and requires judicial enthusiasm for its propagation. Lord Devlin argued that enthusiasm was not a judicial virtue because it endangered the judge's appearance of impartiality and might provoke a jealous reaction from a sovereign Parliament. It appears that the doctrine of stare decisis contains a number of safeguards or 'escape routes' to ensure that a judge at an appropriate level of the court hierarchy can perform the activist function of which Lord Devlin spoke. If a judge chooses to use one of these escape routes he/she will be choosing to exercise a greater discretion than is normally exercised and may find himself/herself 'up to his/her neck' in policy as a result – a conclusion reached by Professor Griffith in his celebrated work *The Politics of the Judiciary* (5th edn, 1995).

Among the most important of the escape routes from precedent is the power of the House of Lords to overrule one of its own previous decisions where it thinks it right to do so (*Practice Statement* [1966] 1 WLR 1234), and the power of the Court of Appeal (Civil Division) to depart from one of its own previous decisions in the three situations set out in *Young v Bristol Aeroplane* [1944] 2 All ER 293, namely:

1. where there are conflicting Court of Appeal precedents on the issue;

2. where a Court of Appeal decision is inconsistent with a House of Lords' decision; and

3. where a Court of Appeal decision appears to have been decided 'per incuriam', without due care, and is consequently erroneous.

It may be added that the Court of Appeal (Criminal Division) may follow the same guidelines as the Civil Division, but is also entitled to exercise a more generous discretion to depart from one of its own decisions where it is convinced that such a decision was wrongly decided and would cause hardship if followed in a case where a citizen's liberty is at stake: *R v Gould* [1968] 1 All ER 849. At first sight the House of Lords would appear to have a generous discretion to depart from precedent under the 1966 *Practice Statement* but in fact it has always been cautious in the use of the discretion. Indeed, it could be argued that in a series of decisions since the *Statement* was issued the Law Lords have attempted to 'structure' the exercise of the discretion by laying down formal guidelines, thereby attempting to resurrect a more scientific, disinterested approach. This was important because of the sensitive policy background to many of the changes in the law which the House was invited to make. For example, Lord Reid advised that the power should be used 'sparingly' and not whenever the House considered a previous decision to have been wrongly decided; there should, he said, be additional reasons to justify an overruling, such as where it has become manifestly unjust to apply the precedent as a result of new social conditions or modern conceptions of public policy: *Jones v Secretary of State for Social Services* [1972] AC 944 at 966. Such justification was found to exist in *R v R (Rape: Marital Exemption)* [1991] 4 All ER 481 where the House set aside the ancient common law principle that a husband could not in law be capable of raping his wife. The decision did not pass without some controversy and criticism, but can be defended as a classic example of Lord Devlin's 'judicial activism' concept by reforming the law so as to ensure that the common law would continue to command public confidence. Nevertheless, the criticisms probably reminded the Law Lords of the wisdom of cloaking policy changes behind a formal legal structure because in a more recent case the House, in declining to change the law of doli incapax (the presumption that a child between the ages of ten and14 does not know his criminal act to be seriously wrong), agreed on the formulation of the following principles upon which judicial law reform should be based:

1. to beware of imposing a new remedy if the solution is doubtful;
2. to be cautious if Parliament has already had opportunities to deal with the problem;
3. to leave disputed matters of social policy to parliamentary reform;
4. not to lightly set aside fundamental legal doctrines; and
5. not to make a change unless it can be achieved with finality and certainty: *C v DPP* [1995] 2 All ER 43, especially per Lord Lowry at p52g–j.

However, since the passing of the Crime and Disorder Act 1998, the presumption of doli incapax has been abolished. Judges can now freely interpret on the basis of this Act, without which the above situation would still apply.

Such structuring of discretion is indicative of a scientific approach in that it tries to eliminate or minimise subjective judicial decision-making which might otherwise become arbitrary and undemocratic. When Lord Denning was Master of the Rolls (1962–1982) he was robust in arguing that the function of the judge was to do justice in the case before him, and that the doctrine of precedent should not be applied so rigidly as to stand in the way of modernisation and humanisation of the common law.

Occasionally this led him to break the rules of precedent by behaving as though the 1966 *Practice Statement* extended to the Court of Appeal. It did not, and he was reminded of that fact by the Law Lords in *Davis v Johnson* [1979] AC 264. Nevertheless, the many occasions on which Lord Denning got away with naked judicial law reform (eg, the invention of promissory estoppel) make it nonsense to contend that a judge is confined to the purely mechanical role of applying established precedents to new cases.

Indeed, the modern expansion of judicial review as a weapon to curb misuse of executive power may be cited as another example where formal legal doctrines have failed to prevent judicial activism in using the law for social or political purposes. An art, or a craft, call it what you will, but it is there as plainly as the sun shines in the sky. Even at the lowest levels, such as the lay magistracy, no amount of structuring of discretion has eliminated the inevitable subjectivity of the assessment of such matters as sentencing or family/youth civil matters, where indeed no system of precedent can operate even at a purely formal level.

Fundamentally, it must be borne in mind that the courts' essential task is interpretation, and it is the job of Parliament to legislate. This can never be compromised on any basis.

Chapter 5

The Judiciary and Magistrates

5.1   Introduction

5.2   Key points

5.3   Key cases and statutes

5.4   Questions and suggested solutions

5.1 Introduction

The modern judiciary can be traced back to the twelfth century, although judges were appointed from the ranks of royal clerks. By the fourteenth century a professional judiciary began to emerge. There was until the seventeenth century great political influence over the judiciary. By the eighteenth century, this political influence extended only to appointment and removal. As part of its plan to ensure the composition of the Bench better reflects society generally, the Government published a 'National Strategy for the Recruitment of Lay Magistrates' (October 2003: see www.dca.gov.uk). Another recent development is the creation of the Judicial Appointments Commission, headed by Lord Falconer, the new Lord Chancellor and Secretary of State for Constitutional Affairs. This Commission will act as an independent body to select new judges. Lord Faloner will continue as the Lord Chancellor until the position is abolished by legislation which is currently going through Parliament.

5.2 Key points

Appointment

Judges in England and Wales are usually chosen from practising lawyers, mainly barristers, although some circuit judges are solicitors. Lawyers working in the Government Legal Service are also eligible for appointment (since September 1994). In June 2003 the Government announced the creation of a new Department for Constitutional Affairs (DCA), replacing the Lord Chancellor's Department. The DCA will have broadly similar responsibilities to its predecessor. The newly formed Judicial Appointments Commission headed by Lord Falconer will now oversee the recruitment and appointment of judges.

a) Lord Falconer currently holds two positions, namely that of the Lord Chancellor and the Secretary of State for Constitutional Affairs.

b) The Lord Chief Justice, the Master of the Rolls, the President of the Family Division, the Vice-Chancellor, the Lords of Appeal in Ordinary and the Lord Justices of Appeal are appointed by the Queen on the advice of the Prime Minister. Note that the number of Lord Justices of Appeal is 37.

c) Puisne judges of the High Court, circuit judges and recorders are appointed by the Queen on the advice of the Lord Chancellor, who is now known as the Secretary of State for Constitutional Affairs.

d) Justices of the peace (lay magistrates) are appointed directly by the Secretary of State for Constitutional Affairs. District judges (formerly stipendiary magistrates) are appointed by the Queen on the advice of the Secretary of State for Constitutional Affairs. Note also the other changes effected by the Access to Justice Act 1999. In this respect, the National Recruitment Strategy will examine not only how to raise the profile of the magistracy generally, but also develop a framework to target the recruitment and retention of magistrates from under-represented groups.

e) The formal requirements are as follows:

   i) A Lord of Appeal in Ordinary must have held high judicial office for two years or a Supreme Court qualification (ie, a right of audience there) for not less than 15 years.

   ii) A Lord Justice of Appeal must have a ten-year High Court qualification or be a judge of the High Court: s71(1)(a) Courts and Legal Services Act 1990.

   iii) A puisne judge of the High Court must have a ten-year High Court qualification or have been a circuit judge for at least two years: s71(1)(b).

   iv) Section 71(3)(b) defines High Court qualification as being a right of audience in relation to all High Court proceedings.

f) The Secretary of State for Constitutional Affairs has introduced advertisements for specific vacancies for assistant recorders and circuit judges. The advertisments contain 'job descriptions' of the qualities expected from a judge, eg intellectual ability, sound judgment, integrity and fairness.

g) With the passing of the Human Rights Act 1998 it is arguable that the Act can be used to challenge the process of judicial appointments. See the impact of the Scottish decision in *Starrs v Procurator Fiscal* 2000 SLT 42 in the United Kingdom.

Training

a) The Judicial Studies Board (JSB) is responsible for training the judiciary. Many have criticised the lack of training and continuing education for judges.

b) Initial training consists of induction courses for new appointees and time spent sitting with more experienced judges. Short residential courses are also provided.

c) Judges are invited to attend periodic refresher courses once in every three years. The JSB also runs annual one day seminars and occasional specialist seminars.

d) The Phillips Royal Commission on Criminal Justice (2003) has proposed the following changes:

   i) More resources should be allocated to judicial training generally.

   ii) More specialist training should be given on race and gender issues.

   iii) Judges' performance during training should be properly monitored.

   iv) There should be shorter intervals between the refresher courses and attendance should be made compulsory.

   v) More use should be made of 'mixed' training seminars where all judges attend (whatever their level of appointment) with members of the profession.

e) The Judicial Studies Board has been given an independent budget and separated from the Department for Constitutional Affairs. It is expected that increased Government resources will be provided for 'human awareness' training following the report of a special working party for the Board under the chairmanship of Potter J. The training will cover gender awareness, and sensitivity to unrepresented parties, witnesses, jurors, victims and their families, children and persons under physical and mental disability. Training for judges as trial managers will also be needed in the light of the recent reforms in civil justice. Some of these have been put in place – for example, ethnic awareness courses within the judiciary. Training for judges as trial managers commenced in 2000.

   There are additional special training schemes for new areas of law, such as the introduction of the Human Rights Act 1998.

f) The Courts Act 2003 contains provisions to improve and underpin the appraisals and training of magistrates.

Removal

a) Judges of the High Court and above hold office during good behaviour subject to a power of removal by Her Majesty on an address presented by both Houses of Parliament: Supreme Court Act 1981. The power of removal is also subject to the doctrine of security of tenure held by all superior court judges through the Act of Settlement 1701.

b) Circuit judges and recorders may be removed from office by the Secretary of State for Constitutional Affairs on grounds of incapacity or misbehaviour: s17(4) Courts Act 1971.

c) Magistrates may be removed by the Secretary of State for Constitutional Affairs for good cause.

d) The Royal Commission (2003) has suggested that there should be better monitoring arrangements with a system of performance appraisal by fellow judges and members of the Bar.

e) The Judicial Pensions and Retirement Act 1993 introduced a general compulsory retirement age of 70 for Lords of Appeal in Ordinary, judges of the Court of Appeal and High Court, circuit judges, district judges, recorders and district judges (formerly stipendiary magistrates). Extensions of service, a year at a time, up to the age of 75 (but not beyond that age) may be made by the Secretary of State for Constitutional Affairs if desirable, except in respect of Lords of Appeal in Ordinary and judges of the Court of Appeal and High Court. The retirement rules introduced by the Act do not apply to the Secretary of State for Constitutional Affairs.

Immunity, independence and impartiality

a) A judge may not be sued for anything he says or does in the exercise of his judicial office.

   i) This immunity applies to judges of superior courts even if they act with malice or in bad faith.

   ii) Judges of lower courts are subject to the same immunity so long as they are acting within their jurisdiction. This also applies to district judges in the magistrates' court.

   iii) Magistrates may only be made liable if acting outside their jurisdiction and in bad faith.

b) The judiciary is said to be independent because of its separation from the legislature and executive. Of course, the Secretary of State for Constitutional Affairs is a political appointee; however, as a matter of convention he keeps his political activities separate from his judicial responsibilities.

c) One of the more fundamental requirements is that a judge is free from bias and is impartial at all times. The case involving Lord Hoffmann illustrates the principle: see *R* v *Bow Street Metropolitan Stipendiary Magistrate, ex parte Pinochet Ugarte (No 2)* [1999] 1 All ER 577. See also *Locobail (UK) Ltd* v *Bayfield Properties Ltd* [2000] 1 All ER 65. Also see *Lawal* v *Northern Spirit Ltd* [2004] 1 All ER 187 (HL) which provides another illustration of the care with which the judiciary avoid the perception of bias.

Background

Research has indicated that the judiciary has been dominated by the upper and middle classes: see J A G Griffith, *The Politics of the Judiciary* (5th ed, 1995). This dominance stems from the fact that the Bar has always attracted the Oxbridge educated and the wealthy. The position appears to be changing albeit at a very slow pace. There is now greater participation of women and racial minorities. In July 1993 the then Lord Chancellor stated that applications for judicial posts from women and black and Asian lawyers would be encouraged. However, he rejected measures to ensure a certain proportion of the judiciary are from the ethnic minorities. A later survey by the Labour Research Magazine (1999) found that the majority of judges in the High Court and above were from public schools and Oxbridge educated. From the new appointments between 1997 and 1999, 73 per cent had been to public school and 79 per cent to Oxbridge.

As at December 2003, a survey by the Department of Constitutional Affairs (DCA) (see *Women and Ethnic Minorities in the Judiciary* (2003); www.dca.gov.uk/judicial/ethmin) there were no women among the 12 Law Lords (although in January 2004 Hale LJ became the first female member in the House of Lords); three women out of 37 Court of Appeal judges; seven women out of 107 High Court judges; 60 women out of 610 circuit judges; and 181 women out of 1,409 recorders. The Equal Opportunities Commission in January 1995 called for more women judges as part of an overhaul of the judicial appointments system. In his Annual Report 2000–2001, then Lord Chancellor, then Lord Irvine, pointed out that ethnic minority judges represent 4.2 per cent of the group from which most judges are appointed. In the same report Lord Irvine stated that 26.9 per cent of those appointed through open competition were women compared to 23.5 per cent in the previous year. It is also interesting to note that the Lord Chancellor's Department judical appointments group staged a recruitment event at the Lesbian and Gay Law Conference 2000. The Commission would also like to end the reliance on 'word of mouth' references from senior judges which it believes represents a serious obstacle to many women. The number of ethnic minority judges is very small – less than 1 per cent in the county court and virtually none in the High Court and above. In the 2003 DCA survey (see above) it was disclosed there is one ethnic minority sitting in the Court of Appeal and another in the High Court. Hence, slowly but surely, the judicial structure is changing.

In December 1999, at the Government's request, Sir Leonard Peach was commissioned to carry out an inquiry into the system for judicial appointments. One of the key recommendations of the Peach report was that a Commissioner for Judicial Appointments should be appointed to provide independent monitoring of the procedures for appointing judges and Queen's Counsel. Accordingly, the then Lord Chancellor appointed the first Commissioner in 2001. The Peach report was generally happy with the status quo and did not make any change to the system of secret soundings, in particular. However, since its inception, the Department for Constitutional Affairs has been compiling monthly judicial statistics, as well as conducting investigations into the selection and appointment of judges, with a particular focus on women and ethnic minorities. The DCA has acceded to the Government's wish of creating an independent Judicial Appointments Commission. This is currently being addressed by the Government, the judiciary and the legal profession.

The functions of the judge

a) Supervision of the conduct of the trial.

   i) The recent Royal Commission has proposed that all Crown Court procedures should be supervised by a resident Crown Court judge to speed up the pre-trial process.

   ii) The Commission also suggested that judges should intervene more readily and quickly during the trial to expedite the proceedings.

b) Arbiter of legal issues.

c) In most civil cases, the judge is the sole arbiter of fact, law, and quantum of damages. Where there is a jury, eg in defamation cases, the judge may give guidelines to the jury in assessing quantum of damages.

d) In criminal cases, the judge must explain the law and sum up the facts to the jury.

The Royal Commission suggested that consideration should be given to the role of the judge in summing up and whether it is always appropriate for him to comment upon the facts.

e) In criminal cases the judge is also responsible for sentencing the defendant.

f) The interpretation and clarification of the law. Sometimes this involves law reform by the judge but because of the political sensitivity of such reform the scope for it is extremely limited: see Chapters 2, 3 and 4.

Magistrates

a) Appointments are now the responsibility of the Judicial Appointments Commission led by the Secretary of State for Constitutional Affairs.

b) The Department for Constitutional Affairs has been entrusted with the task of achieving a more socially-balanced Bench.

c) In relation to lay justices, the Courts Act 2003 provides as follows:

   i) Every attempt is made to appoint a fair mix of sexes, political parties, social classes and races.

   ii) The main requirement is that the magistrate is over 21 and below 60 on appointment.

   iii) A lay justice must normally live or work in the area.

   iv) Lay justices are not required to be legally qualified, but do undergo training.

   v) The services of a lay magistrate are unpaid except for expenses.

English Legal System

- d) District judges (formerly stipendiary magistrates)
    - i) Following the Access to Justice Act 1999, there are currently 96 professional judges who sit in the magistrates' courts. They are known as district judges.
    - ii) These professional judges must have a seven-year general advocacy qualification within s71 Courts and Legal Services Act 1990.
    - iii) They are appointed by the Queen on the Secretary of State for Constitutional Affairs' recommendation. They work full time, receive a salary in excess of £75,000 and belong to the professional judiciary.
- e) The justices' clerk
    - i) The main function of a clerk is to advise magistrates as to law and practice, although they cannot influence the decision of the magistrates: s49(2) of the Crime and Disorder Act 1998.
    - ii) Section 71 Courts and Legal Services Act 1990 requires a clerk to have a five-year magistrates' court qualification.
    - iii) The clerk's role is vital as lay magistrates can only sit if there is a qualified clerk present.
    - iv) The clerk is also responsible for court administration and organisation of training of magistrates. There are currently about 250 justices' clerks who are employed by the Magistrates' Courts Committee.
- f) Number of magistrates or justices of the peace

    As at April 2003, there were a total of 28,344 justices of the peace in England and Wales, nearly 16 per cent moer than the previous year. On these 51 per cent were men. There are currently (December 2003) 106 district judges and 173 deputy district judges at the magistrates' court.

5.3 Key cases and statutes

- *Lawal* v *Northern Spirit Ltd* [2004] 1 All ER 187 (HL)
  Illustrates the extent of care with which the judiciary avoid the perception of bias

- *Locobail (UK) Ltd* v *Bayfield Properties Ltd* [2000] QB 451
  Challenge to the impartiality of a judge

- *R* v *Bow Street Metropolitan Stipendiary Magistrate, ex parte Pinochet Ugarte (No 2)* [2000] 1 AC 119
  Raises the issue of bias within the judiciary

- *Starrs* v *Procurator Fiscal* 2000 SLT 42
  A judge who had no security of tenure was not 'independent' within the meaning of art 6 of the European Convention on Human Rights

The Judiciary and Magistrates

- Access to Justice Act 1999 – introduced changes affecting the work of the magistrates' courts
- Courts Act 2003 – deals (inter alia) with the training and appraisal of magistrates
- Court and Legal Services Act 1990 – sets out the qualification criteria for judges throughout the court hierarchy
- Human Rights Act 1998 – arguably, it can be used to challenge the process of judicial appointments
- Justices of the Peace Act 1997 – consolidated earlier legislation

5.4 Questions and suggested solutions

QUESTION ONE

What, if any, do you see as the weaknesses of the current system for making appointments to the higher judiciary? How could the system be improved?

University of London LLB Examination
(for External Students) English Legal System June 2000 Q7

General Comment

This question requires an evaluation of the appointments system affecting the higher judiciary. Students are asked to discuss the weaknesses of the current system and accordingly suggest reforms.

Skeleton Solution

An outline of the current appointments system – distinction between the junior judicial and senior judicial posts – the weaknesses – the pressure for reforms – the Peach Report.

Suggested Solution

In *The Politics of the Judiciary* (5th edn, 1995), J A G Griffith launches a seething attack on perhaps what is perceived to be one of the most frequently heard criticisms of the English judiciary, that being its unrepresentative character, in that it is made up of predominantly white, public school, oxbridge educated, middle aged or elderly males. This narrow social and educational background of judges has come under constant attack, and the fairly recent research conducted by the Labour Research Department in 1999 is no exception.

It is argued that such a character of the judiciary results in an establishment-minded outlook, and produces out-of-touch comments on the values of society. Rightly or wrongly, this perception seems to have resulted in a drop of public confidence in the judiciary. This was one of the major problems which the then Lord Chancellor, Lord

Irvine, inherited from the former Conservative Lord Chancellor, Lord Mackay (1987–1997).

Essentially, the judiciary can be classified into two main types: inferior judges and superior judges. These categories obviously affect the way in which each type of judge is appointed, and which courts they sit in. As far as inferior judges are concerned, since the autumn of 1994 there has been a system of job advertisements for junior judicial posts, such as circuit judges, district judges and Crown Court recorders. The advertisements set out a person specification which, apart from the professional qualifications (which are set out by the Courts and Legal Services Act 1990), places emphasis on legal skills, judicial experience, intellectual ability and sound judgment, humanity and courtesy, oral and written communication skills, ability to act in an independent manner, administrative skills, integrity, honesty and uprightness, community experience and contacts and collegiality. It was stressed that the primary consideration was to select the best candidate on merit regardless of sex, race, religion or political outlook. This greater openness in specifying criteria for judicial appointments was designed to alleviate fears and criticisms of an 'old boy network', under which candidates were chosen because they shared the same background, character and outlook as those already on the bench, and from whom the Department for Constitutional Affairs (formerly the Lord Chancellor's Department) obtains confidential soundings and references.

Appointments in the High Court have followed a similar system of advertisements and interviews since February 1998. This replaced the old system of 'invitation' by the Lord Chancellor. As a result of the Access to Justice Act 1999, there is now a duty to consider solicitor-advocates who have had at least two years of circuitry experience. However, the appointment discretion is by nature wide and subjective in relation to those who are eligible. For many years (and still so) there has been a 'secrecy' surrounding the appointments of Queen's Counsel, from whom usually the bulk of appointments are made at the High Court level. This secrecy is compounded by the secrecy of the decision-making process concerning the appointments themselves — no reason is given for why an apparently suitable candidate is passed over. The files on candidates kept by the Department for Constitutional Affairs are strictly private and confidential.

Arguably, the weaknesses of the appointments system can be said to be the perpetuation of the 'old boy network' appointment system perceived by many critics as being the controlling force behind the 'soundings' appointments. Proposals have been made for a more formal system of appointments which includes the use of psychometric tests to assess character and detect undesirable prejudices.

Another constant criticism levelled at the appointments system is the distinct lack of judicial positions filled by females and ethnic minorities. As at December 2003, there were no women Law Lords. However, in January 2004 Hale LJ became the first female member of the House of Lords. The first and only female head of division was Dame Elizabeth Butler-Sloss, who was appointed in 2000. There were three female Lord

Justices of Appeal (of 37), seven female High Court judges (of 107), and 60 female circuit judges (of 610). As far as ethnic minorities are concerned, there is now one member of the Court of Appeal from an ethnic minority (but not black or Asian) and one High Court judge. This, therefore, reveals that women and members of the ethnic minorities are not reflected in the judiciary in the proportions in which they populate the legal profession. Whilst this issue has received a lot of attention, restoring the proper balance in the judiciary is likely to take some time. The Department for Constitutional Affairs is actively developing schemes to make the judicial system more sympathetic and responsive to the needs of women and ethnic minorities, for example by enabling prospective applicants to spend time 'shadowing' a judge so as to obtain knowledge of, and confidence in, the discharge of judicial functions. Creating a system of permanent part-time judges in the High Court and on circuit is another idea that might prove attractive for women who are combining a judicial career with the responsibility of bringing up a family. Perhaps this explains the rationale behind the creation of the new post of a Judicial Appointments Commissioner (first appointed in 2001), whose role will be to keep the appointment process under review.

Another radical reform suggested is the inclusion of pure academic lawyers, since there is a good proportion of women and ethnic minorities among the teachers of law. This, it is argued, would clearly tend towards the appointment of women and ethnic minorities. The traditional view that only advocates make good judges is being increasingly challenged, but opening up appointments to solicitors, and indeed to persons like academic lawyers, requires a more advanced scheme of selection and training.

The Department for Constitutional Affairs is committed to modernise the appointments system so as to promote fairness and equality of opportunity. This was achieved partially through the Peach Report in 2000, which incidentally recommended the Office of a Commissioner for Judicial Office. Be that as it may, the Peach Report was generally happy with the status quo, and did not make any changes or recommendations in respect of the 'soundings' practice. However, the Department for Constitutional Affairs is in the process of making judicial appointments more open and accessible and it is in this context that the Government, the judiciary and the legal profession are committed to establishing the new and independent Judicial Appointments Commission to oversee judicial appointments.

QUESTION TWO

'My root belief is that the proper role of the judge is to do justice between the parties before him. If there is any rule of law which impairs the doing of justice, then it is the province of the judge to do all that he legitimately can to avoid the rule – or even to change it – so as to do justice in the instant case before him.' (Lord Denning.)

Critically assess this statement.

University of London LLB Examination
(for External Students) English Legal System June 2001 Q7(b)

General Comment

A very general question which may confuse the student, as it does not disclose any specific area of discussion. Rather, the question calls for a discussion of the work of a judge, which essentially is an issue of common law jurisprudence. It is therefore necessary to distinguish between judicial discretion and notions of the constitutional position of the judiciary. A thorough, overall appreciation of the entire English legal system is required to do well in a question of this nature.

Skeleton Solution

The traditional role of a judge – what it represents – distinction of their role as interpreters of parliamentary intention and as public defenders – what does a judge do in a case? – what are the motivations or inspirations behind a decision? – has justice been served in the end?

Suggested Solution

If judges are perceived as public defenders and protectors of civil liberties, then they should be endowed with powers to effect changes in the law when the law conflicts with notions of fairness and justice and does inequity to the litigant or the accused. If the law is not reflective of changing times and society, then it is the duty of the judge to correct this and put things in order. But is this the case, and this seems to be the question raised by Lord Denning within the context of the quotation.

The question raises several issues, such as the value of judicial decision-making or judicial discretion, and the constitutional position of the judiciary. Of course, at the core of both these issues lies the question 'can justice be value free?'

As far as the English law is concerned, the constitutional position of the judiciary can be examined through the doctrine of the separation of powers, where it is stated that the three primary organs of the state are the legislature, the executive and the judiciary. They are distinct and exclusive in nature and functions, although arguably they overlap in many ways. The legislature, or Parliament, legislates or makes law; the executive or the Government implements and administers those laws; and the judiciary or the courts and judges declare, adjudicate, determine and enforce those laws. Hence, in a strict sense, the traditional role of the judge has always been seen to be that of declaring the law as it is. This is also known as the 'declaratory theory'. Therefore, it is akin to 'jus dicere, non jus dare' which means to state the law, not to give it. Judges have shown support for this stance, by stating in cases that it is their duty to give effect to the intention of Parliament by declaring the law as it is, and that it is not within their remit to correct legislative deficiencies or inaccuracies. That, they say, is the sole and exclusive prerogative of Parliament.

Whilst this argument can be accepted on the one hand, on the other, does it not pose a startling limitation on the powers, jurisdiction and discretion of a dynamic judiciary? Lord Denning's quote seems to suggest a proactive instead of a reactive judiciary in operation. Judicial activism is absolutely necessary in these times. We live in a world which is constantly undergoing changes and transformations, and Parliament cannot be expected to cope with changes by effecting laws which reflect the adapting and adopting of these changes. It simply has not the time. This, in fact, is one of the justifications for delegated or subordinate legislation. By invoking the same argument, can it not be argued that if Parliament could delegate to lesser bodies, such as ministerial departments, ministers and local authorities, to make law, then why should not judges be given similar powers to add, amend or apply the law as is suitable, fair and acceptable to the case before them?

Perhaps it is thoughts such as this that justify judicial activism. Radical and unorthodox judges such as Lord Denning have shown clear favouritism towards this practice, by creating new principles or extending the arm of the law, as it were. In this respect, it must be stated that one of the hallmarks of the English legal system is the common law, which simply means that many of our primary legal principles have been made and developed by judges from case to case. An example of this is the crime of murder. There is no statute telling us or defining murder as a crime. It is a common law creation. Another example of common law would be the development of the law of negligence by Lord Atkin, who created the 'neighbour principle' in the case of *Donoghue* v *Stevenson* [1932] AC 562. This laid the foundation for subsequent cases in the law of tort.

Judges, whilst being bound by the doctrine of precedent, can and do nevertheless effect quite dramatic changes in the law through the medium of statutory interpretation and reinterpretation of the common law. This happened in 1991, when the lower courts (initially) and finally the House of Lords abolished the rule that a husband cannot be guilty of raping his wife in *R* v *R (Rape: Marital Exemption)* [1991] 3 WLR 767. The law prior to this had stood for almost 250 years. Ostensibly, judges are not concerned with law reform, but it is not uncommon for them to draw attention to anomalies and to call for change. As Lord Reid stated in *Black-Clawson International Ltd* v *Papierwerke Waldhof-Aschaffenburg AG* [1975] AC 591):

> 'We are seeking the meaning of the words which Parliament used. We are seeking not what Parliament meant but the true meaning of what they said.'

Another instance where judicial discretion has prevailed over parliamentary intention, or has resulted in the passing of legislation, is the case of *C* v *Director of Public Prosecutions* [1995] 2 All ER 43 in which the Queen's Bench Division was bold enough to remove the presumption of 'doli incapax' in criminal law affecting the age of responsibility. Although the House of Lords subsequently reversed this decision, it led to the passing of the Crime and Disorder Act 1998, which abolished the presumption of doli incapax. Cases such as *Hedley Byrne* v *Heller & Partners Ltd* [1963] 3 WLR 101 and *Central London Property Trust Ltd* v *High Trees House Ltd* [1947] KB 130 illustrate that judges have been instrumental and responsible for major developments in the law.

Nevertheless, judges have also shown reluctance to act as a creative body and will often steer away from it. For example, in *Westdeutsche Landesbank Girozentrale* v *Islington*

London Borough Council [1996] 2 All ER 961, the House of Lords showed a clear inclination towards sticking to precedent rather than preferring bold judicial activism.

Clearly, a judge has to be bold and creative to meet the needs of the times, and it is submitted that this reason should not be used blindly, but as a means of finding the best solution within the framework of a number of competing considerations. Lord Denning was, as ever, right in his contention.

QUESTION THREE

Critically discuss the English system for selecting and training the judiciary.

University of London LLB Examination
(for External Students) English Legal System June 1998 Q3

General Comment

In answering a question such as this it is important to provide a discussion of the current situation and not a lengthy report of the old appointment methods which should only be referred to where appropriate to illustrate the extent of a reform or to develop an argument for further reform. It should also be remembered that a discussion of the work of the Judicial Studies Board and the Department for Constitutional Affairs is vital.

Skeleton Solution

Identification of the pressure for a substantial review of the role of the modern judiciary – greater openness and fairness in the appointments system found in the introduction of advertisement for judicial posts and the new interview systems – identification of the differences between the processes for appointment to the junior judicial posts and appointment to the High Court bench – reasons for the continuing concern over the new style of consultations used by the Department for Constitutional Affairs in respect of appointments; the low representation of minorities and women; the call for an independent judicial appointments body – the improvement to training provision; new schemes to open up training opportunities for members outside of the Bar.

Suggested Solution

It is only in recent years that attention has been given to the issues of the suitability of the process by which our judiciary are selected and the adequacy of their training for judicial office. Concern over both these matters arose from evidence of a public lack of confidence in the judiciary caused by the belief that it had become unrepresentative of the diverse needs of modern society. Pressure mounted for a substantial review of the role of the modern judge and this was undertaken as part of a major programme of review and reform embracing most aspects of the legal system initiated by Lord Mackay of Clashfern, who took office as Lord Chancellor in 1987. During the period of his office a number of changes were introduced in respect of the appointment and the training of the judiciary. The former Lord Chancellor, Lord Irvine, continued the initiatives for reform and this led to the creation of the post of Commissioner for Judicial Appointments. However, the newly formed Department for Constitutional Affairs (DCA) under the present Secretary of State for Constitutional Affairs, Lord Falconer, is currently looking into fresh ideas and initiatives in the selection and appointment of the judiciary.

Disquiet over the unrepresentative character of the judiciary centred on the method of appointment to the bench used by the former Lord Chancellor's Department which was seen as being class-ridden and discriminatory. Decisions on appointments were conducted in secret and relied on 'soundings' obtained in confidence from serving judges and senior practising lawyers. The then Lord Chancellor responded to the call to open up competition for judicial posts and demystify the appointment process in the autumn of 1994 by introducing advertisement for the junior judicial posts of circuit judge, district judge and recorder in the Crown Courts and county courts. In the case of circuit judge, this replaced the 'application' system that previously pertained. Short-listed applicants were interviewed by a panel including a serving judge, a lay person and an official of the Lord Chancellor's Department. Recommendations were then made to the Lord Chancellor. At present, the DCA is in the process of making judicial appointments more open and accessible and it is in this context that the Government, the judiciary and the legal profession are committed to establishing the new and independent Judicial Appointments Commission to oversee judicial appointments.

In February 1998 a system of advertisements and interviews was instituted for vacancies on the High Court bench to replace the system of invitation previously used. Candidates were interviewed by a panel consisting of a judge, a civil servant from the Lord Chancellor's Department and a lay person. The panel then gave advice to the Lord Chancellor but he still used a form of 'sounding' in that he made his final decision not solely on the advice from the interview panels but also on the results of confidential consultations about prospective candidates. Proposals have been made for a more formal system with the use of such as psychometric tests to assess character and detect undesirable prejudices. This perhaps will be one of the criteria exercised by the newly formed Judicial Appointments Commission, an independent body entrusted with the task of appointing new judges. In this respect it is worth noting that the Courts Act 2003 (at s19) deals with changes to the training and appraisal of magistrates.

The profession were particularly hostile to the lack of disclosure of information that used to pertain under the old system. 'Soundings' were taken in strict confidence and the subject of a file had no opportunity to check the accuracy of the information nor to challenge recommendations that may have been made. It was widely believed that the Lord Chancellor's Department took into account very subjective criteria relating to a candidate's 'standing' and 'temperament'. Lord Irvine, when he was Lord Chancellor, and others who have been involved in the selection process, emphatically denied that this was the case, and in an attempt to allay concerns Lord Irvine instructed that any adverse allegations made about a candidate must be disclosed to that candidate, who should then be given an opportunity to rebut them.

Advertisement necessitated the publication of criteria for appointment and for the first time the Lord Chancellor's Department revealed the kind of qualities looked for in candidates for judicial office. In addition to the legal and administrative skills demanded by the post, the list includes qualities such as: fairness, humanity and courtesy, integrity and honesty, community experience and contacts. Published criteria tend to amount to an awesome list of attributes that no doubt have as much to do with restoring public confidence in the judiciary as they do with setting criteria for appointment. All advertisements contain a pledge that applications will be considered 'regardless of ethnic origin, gender, marital status, sexual orientation, political affiliation, religion or (subject to the physical requirements of the office) disability'. Both the former Lord Chancellors, Lord Mackay and Lord Irvine, stressed that their appointments were made 'on merit' and are not influenced by factors such as these and both rejected 'quick fix solutions' aimed at tackling the low representation of women and ethnic minorities among the judiciary – for example, the use of positive discrimination, fast track methods of promotion and quotas – on the grounds that they would undermine the fundamental principle that the best qualified candidates must be appointed regardless of gender or race.

Lord Irvine encouraged more applications for judicial positions from female and ethnic minority lawyers but restoring a balance on the judiciary is likely to take some time. The statistics produced for 1998 record a very low percentage of representation of ethnic minorities for junior judicial posts and none at all for the High Court bench and higher posts. Whatever the merits of the old 'soundings' system might have been, it had the unfortunate result of favouring Queen's Counsel who belonged to the 'right social group' and the 'elite' chambers. Our judiciary comprises mainly white, middle-aged and establishment-minded men who share the same background of a public school education followed by Oxford or Cambridge and belong to the same social clubs. In the face of this, the claim that the 'soundings' system had 'built-in head winds' which, in particular, obstructed the advancement of women and ethnic minorities does seem to have some credibility. The DCA is now actively developing schemes to make the judicial system more sympathetic and responsive to the needs of women and minorities, for example, by enabling prospective applicants to spend time 'shadowing' a judge so as to obtain knowledge of, and confidence in, the discharge of judicial functions. Creating a system of permanent part-time judges in the High Court and on circuit is another idea that might prove attractive for women in combining a judicial career with the responsibility of bringing up a family.

Whilst there has been general support for changes to date, critics continue to argue that more radical reforms are required. The Courts and Legal Services Act 1990 widened the pool of persons from which the judiciary may be appointed but it is argued that it should be widened further. The inclusion of pure academic lawyers, for example, would help to increase the appointment of women and ethnic minorities since there is a good proportion of both among the teachers of law. The traditional view that only advocates make good judges is being increasingly challenged but opening up appointment to solicitors, and indeed to persons like academics lawyers, requires a more advanced scheme of training than that currently offered by the Judicial Studies Board under the watchful eye of the DCA. The Judicial Studies Board was established in 1979 'to determine the principles on which judicial studies should be planned, to approve the proposed forms of the study programmes and to observe them in operation': Lord Chancellor's Department, 1998. Originally, the Board was responsible only for the full- and part-time training of the Crown Court judiciary. In 1985, the role expanded to include the training of: full- and part-time judiciary of the county courts; lay and stipendiary magistrates; and judicial chairmen and members of tribunals. It has introduced longer and more detailed courses of training but there is a reluctance to introduce too much 'education' and 'monitoring' in the fear that it might undermine the independence of the judiciary, and that it may lead to a professional career judiciary of the sort found in continental legal systems. There is, however, some evidence of continuing public disquiet about the competency of the judiciary which the Secretary of State for Constitutional Affairs is seeking to address in a way that both balances the need to restore public faith in the representative character of the judiciary and the need to maintain an independent judiciary to safeguard the rule of law.

In a series of speeches during 1998 Lord Irvine reiterated his intention to modernise the appointments system so as to promote fairness and equality of opportunity. This was partially achieved through the Peach report in 2000 which recommended the office of a Commissioner for Judicial Appointments. The Peach recommendation was accepted and the Lord Chancellor appointed the first Commissioner in 2001 to oversee the whole system of appointment of judges. As mentioned above, the DCA is in the process of establishing the new and independent Judicial Appointments Commission, and is working closely with the Government, the judiciary and the legal profession in this respect.

QUESTION FOUR

To what extent do you believe that recent changes to the rules concerning eligibility and appointment to judicial office will overcome the criticisms that have been made of the judiciary in recent years? What more needs to be done?

University of London LLB Examination
(for External Students) English Legal System June 1995 Q3

General Comment

The appointment of judges seems to be becoming a favourite with examiners and, consequently, knowledge of the changes to eligibility requirements made by the Courts and Legal Services Act 1990, and by the Secretary of State for Constitutional Affairs' exercise of discretionary powers under the Act, is essential. Recent developments such as job advertisements and the appointment of a Commissioner for Judicial

Appointments need to be analysed, and students who have kept abreast of these developments by taking a lively interest in current affairs, or by reading the main law journals, will be well enough informed to make critical comment on these changes. The case for and against a Judicial Appointments Board should also be examined.

Skeleton Solution

Recent innovation of job advertisements and descriptions – continued secrecy over appointments to the High Court bench – the dangers of an 'old boy network' – the danger of too much openness – lessons of the USA system – problems of under-representation of women and ethnic minority candidates – academics as judges – the case for and against a Judicial Appointments Board, as recommended by the Peach report in 2000 – the current initiatives of the Department for Constitutional Affairs.

Suggested Solution

Until fairly recently there were no advertisements for vacancies on the bench and no objective job descriptions. Advertisements for posts in the county courts and Crown Courts were initially introduced by the former Lord Chancellors, Lord Mackay and Lord Irvine, and have been maintained by the present Secretary of State for Constitutional Affairs, Lord Falconer, but appointment to the High Court bench and above remains by invitation of the Secretary of State, and is at his personal discretion. The process remains largely secret and there is still a suspicion of an 'old boy network' which relies heavily on personal recommendations from existing judges. The danger that white males will recommend other white males is apparent, even though the establishment denies it is real. However, the creation of an independent Judicial Appointments Commission is bound to impact against this 'ancient' practice.

The files kept on candidates for judicial office are strictly confidential and there is no opportunity for those affected to check on the accuracy of the information, and no opportunity to challenge the good faith of referees who may have given a poor recommendation. Indeed, the names of referees will usually be withheld from the candidate. It could be argued that 'openness in Government' requires open and public interviews in which adverse material and its sources are disclosed, either to the candidate or to an independent reviewer so as to permit an opportunity for challenge. The problem with too much openness is that it might deter able people from putting themselves forward for fear that a 'glamorous' private life will be revealed: in the USA the screening of judicial candidates in the full glare of television cameras has been said to result only in the dull and mediocre coming forward.

The current emphasis is on the candidate's legal knowledge and judicial experience, intellectual ability, sound judgment, integrity, fairness, understanding of people and society, humanity, courtesy and ability to communicate. It replaces such concepts as 'standing' and 'sound temperament' which were said to discriminate in favour of establishment candidates. The new changes relate to the skills required for a trial judge, but there remains the problem of dealing with the under-representation of women and ethnic minorities on the bench. The former Lord Chancellor, Lord Irvine, had rejected solutions based on affirmative action, on quotas, or even fast tracks, on the ground that these would be 'quick fixes' and damage the integrity and standing of the bench. In his Annual Report 2000–2001, the then Lord Chancellor reiterated the fact that judicial appointments are now made on merit, regardless of ethnic origin, gender, marital status, political affiliation, sexual orientation, religion or disability.

However, it could be argued that an apparent drop in public confidence in the judiciary needs more than a pious hope that in a few years' time more women and ethnic minorities will appear on the bench. The Courts and Legal Services Act 1990 provided a starting point by allowing solicitors to become eligible for appointment to the High Court bench, since the proportion of women and ethnic minorities is much higher in the solicitors' profession than in the world of the barrister. But the former Lord Chancellor, Lord Irvine, had discretionary power to do much more. For example, the appointment of Hale J (Brenda Hoggett) gave hope that those who have spent time as academic lawyers or Law Commissioners will be given more sympathetic treatment in regard to appointment to the bench than previously. The concept of the academic as a judge may be controversial, but it would at least widen the pool from which judges are chosen and again open a door for more women and ethnic minority candidates. In January 2004, Hale LJ was appointed as the first woman into the House of Lords. The first and only female Head of Division was Dame Elizabeth Butler-Sloss who was appointed in 2000. In December 2003 there were three female Lord Justices of Appeal (of 37), seven female High Court Judges (of 107) and 60 female circuit judges (of 610). There is one new member of the Court of Appeal from an ethnic minority (but not black or Asian) and one High Court judge.

Perhaps the most radical reform to the way judges are chosen would be the establishment of a Judicial Appointments Board, as recommended by the Peach report in 2000, to act as an independent advisory body to the Secretary of State for Constitutional Affairs. Its members would be chosen from a responsible cross-section of society, eg some lawyers, but with a lay majority, such as laymen with experience of the administration of justice – probation workers, social workers, and the like. The Board would bring more openness into selection procedures and give reasons for recommending or rejecting candidates. The aim of the Board would be to control the political influences that may affect the Lord Chancellor's decisions, and the Board would try to restore public confidence in the impartiality and fairness of selection procedures. The recent appointment of a Judicial Appointments Commissioner in 2001 goes to some extent to achieve this aim. However, the fact that the Commissioner plays no role in the appointment of judges seems somewhat an irony. This task is now borne by the newly created (June 2003) Judicial Appointments Commission, led by Lord Falconer, the Secretary of State for Constitutional Affairs. This body will oversee the appointment and recruitment of new judges.

The problem with such reform is that a lay majority might not be competent to assess the qualities required of a good judge: we do not have laymen choosing hospital consultants, for example. There would also be the danger of political lobbying of the Board for particular candidates, or possibly against particular candidates, resulting in the recommendation only of 'compromise candidates', ie not the best ones but the ones to whom there is least objection. Finally, the Board might undermine the concept of individual responsibility to Parliament for the administration of justice, currently discharged by the Secretary of State for Constitutional Affairs in the House of Lords and by his junior Minister in the House of Commons. It was this latter risk that Lord Mackay, the former Lord Chancellor, relied on in announcing his rejection of the concept of a Judicial Appointments Board in his 1993 Hamlyn Lecture, 'The Administration of Justice' (Mackay, *The Administration of Justice* (Sweet & Maxwell, 1994), esp pp7–8). Conversely, the Peach report seems to advocate this approach. Some of the Peach recommendations were put into force by the then Lord Chancellor, Lord Irvine.

QUESTION FIVE

'The biggest obstacle to the just deciding of cases by lay magistrates is the human element. Lay magistrates are selected from a narrow group of people and are inadequately trained.'

Discuss.

University of London LLB Examination
(for External Students) English Legal System June 1994 Q6

General Comment

The question invites specific critical analysis of two issues concerning the lay magistracy: its representative character and the training given to lay magistrates. Students must be careful to concentrate on these issues and to avoid a general narrative of the general advantages and disadvantages of the lay magistracy. References to empirical research and statistical illustrations are useful in this kind of detailed critique.

Skeleton Solution

Outline introduction to the character of the lay magistrate – the concept of the 'gifted amateur' – a breakdown of the composition of the lay magistracy in terms of race, sex, age, class and political affiliation – recent attempts to broaden recruitment – criticism of inadequate training of magistrates – recent improvements in training – assessment of their value – conclusions.

Suggested Solution

The representative character of the lay magistracy has certainly been challenged in recent years and this is worrying not only from the point of whether it impedes the just deciding of cases but also from the point of sustaining public confidence in the system. As for training, the very concept of the lay magistrate or 'gifted amateur' seems to stand in the way of attempts to formalise the system or to ensure greater consistency in the application of the law where discretion may be available, eg in the area of sentencing. The issues of composition and training will be considered in turn, though it is suggested that other matters are also relevant to the administration of justice in the magistrates' courts, eg the role and influence of the magistrates' clerk.

The lay magistracy is predominantly white, middle-aged, middle-class and the great majority support the Conservative Party. There are more men than women, though the disparity is not as great as among the judiciary and only about 5 per cent of JPs are from ethnic minorities. Only about 15 per cent of JPs have a manual labour background; the vast majority are from 'white-collar' professions or are well-off housewives. On political bias one study in St Helens, Lancashire, showed that where Labour took 60 per cent of the votes cast in the 1992 general election, more than half the local magistrates were Conservative supporters; only 26 per cent supported Labour (*The Times* (1992) 9 December). Since 1997 there is a tilt towards an increased support for Labour.

Such statistics are said to undermine public confidence in the lay magistracy, which is generally suspected of class and race bias and a pro-police prejudice in the dispensation of justice. The present Secretary of State for Constitutional Affairs, Lord Falconer, has responded to these fears by requiring the local advisory committees which advise him on appointments to operate more openly and to be more positive in recruiting people from under-represented sections, eg by advertising vacancies in ethnic minority newspapers and by persuading local employers to give paid time off to employees who wish to serve as JPs. There are attempts being made to 'demystify' the position of a JP by informing the public of the nature of the job and that applicants need not have legal knowledge or legal skills. It has been argued that a national recruitment drive, which goes to the factory shop floor, might help attract working-class applicants.

Turning to the issue of training, the amateur nature of most benches is said to result in inefficient handling of cases and a reluctance to challenge delaying tactics of defence counsel in particular. James Morton, editor of the New Law Journal, has argued that research shows that a stipendiary magistrate can get through the work of three benches. 'Stipes' make up their minds more quickly; they can point advocates to issues which trouble them; they need not retire to consider whether they should grant an adjournment. He argues that the consequent saving in time allows court clerks to get on with administration. The saving in money, when balanced against legal aid costs, and the cost of heating, lighting, adjournments and the like, must be enormous. Morton contends that there is considerable empirical evidence that advocates and defendants alike do not fool around as much with a stipe as they do with a lay bench. Time and costs are saved and justice is seen to be done swiftly. The Courts Act 2003 addresses the issue of training and appraisal of magistrates.

Of course the logic of such an argument points to the abolition of the lay magistracy and its replacement by a professional and salaried stipendiary system. However, if it is desired to retain a lay element in the administration of justice in courts which deal with approximately 98 per cent of criminal cases as well as an important civil jurisdiction in such matters as licensing and family law, then improved training may be the solution rather than outright abolition.

There are at present introductory training and voluntary refresher courses for all JPs, but in 1991 Lord Mackay, the then Lord Chancellor, admitted their inadequacy and introduced a new training programme during which all new and serving JPs receive much more extensive training in sentencing, as well as communication and chairmanship skills. All chairmen-magistrates must now undergo compulsory refresher courses every five years. Both basic and refresher courses contain compulsory assessments by judges, justices' clerks and fellow lay magistrates.

It remains to be seen whether such improvements in training lead to a fairer and more consistent handling of cases by lay magistrates. It is suggested that abolition of the lay element would deprive the administration of justice of valuable citizen participation which, although human and prone to mistake, is important in offsetting the case-hardened professionalism of lawyers and law enforcement agencies such as the police. JPs come and go and this fluidity also offsets the permanence and rigidity of the rest of summary jurisdiction. Even the sentencing discretion of JPs, which has been the subject of savage criticism of its inconsistent treatment of similar cases, has a value in ensuring a truly 'local' system of justice in which, for example, heavier penalties than the national average might be imposed in order to stamp out a particular kind of crime which has become more prevalent in that locality than in society generally.

At present the Secretary of State for Constitutional Affairs, Lord Falconer, is considering increasing the powers of magistrates in the lower courts, with particular emphasis on powers of sentencing. Whether this will materialise is, of course, another question altogether. This is one of the issues addressed by the Courts Act 2003.

Chapter 6

The Jury System

6.1 Introduction
6.2 Key points
6.3 Key cases and statutes
6.4 Questions and suggested solutions

6.1 Introduction

Although of much earlier origin, by the beginning of the nineteenth century the concept of jury trial was safely entrenched into the English legal system and considered to be an important safeguard for the individual. Lord Denning MR in *Ward* v *James* [1966] 1 QB 273 regarded the jury as the 'bulwark of our liberties'. The participation of lay persons in criminal trials may also be seen as giving credibility to the criminal justice system. However, trial by jury is now increasingly limited to serious criminal cases, as a majority of criminal cases are tried by magistrates' courts. The Auld LJ review (2001) recommended that juries should not be used in complicated fraud cases. Some of the recommendations have been codified through the Criminal Justice Act 2003. The 2003 Act introduces several radical changes affecting the jury system.

6.2 Key points

Jury trial in civil cases

The vast majority of civil cases are tried by a judge alone. There are, however, some civil cases in which there may be trial by jury.

a) Section 69(1) of the Supreme Court Act 1981 allows a right to jury trial in cases of fraud, defamation, malicious prosecution and false imprisonment. Even in these cases there is a possibility of refusal especially where there are long and complex documents to be considered. The Defamation Act 1996 has abolished the right to trial by jury in defamation cases where the claim is for £10,000 or less.

b) In all other civil cases, the decision to allow a jury trial rests with the court's discretion: see s69(3) of the 1981 Act, and, eg, *Ward* v *James* [1966] 1 QB 273. The reasons for refusing trial by jury are bound up with the need to:

   i) assess fair compensation;

ii) maintain uniformity in awards;

iii) encourage predictability, allowing for settlement out of court.

It has been said that there is a presumption against jury trial in all cases other than those available under s69(1) above: *Racz v Home Office* [1994] 1 All ER 97 (HL).

See the case of *Grobbelaar v News Group Newspapers Ltd* [2002] 1 AC 32.

c) Jury awards of damages

If a civil jury is summoned it will have the function of determining both liability and damages (quantum). There has been concern about excessive awards of compensation, especially in some defamation cases. As a safeguard, s8 of the Courts and Legal Services Act 1990 allows the Court of Appeal to substitute a fresh award of damages in a defamation case where it regarded the jury's award as 'excessive'. This power has been interpreted so as to give the Court of Appeal a broad discretion to interfere with jury awards, particularly if there is a need to protect freedom of the press, which might otherwise be threatened by huge awards of damages for incidents of defamation: *Rantzen v Mirror Group Newspapers* [1993] 3 WLR 953; [1993] 4 All ER 975 (CA).

As an additional safeguard against excessive awards the common law has been developed to allow judges to give guidance to defamation juries on appropriate levels of compensation: *John v MGN Ltd* [1996] 2 All ER 35 (CA).

Jury trials in criminal cases

The only criminal cases in which trial by jury is now used are those triable on indictment in the Crown Court. As most cases are tried summarily, trial by jury is only used for more serious offences. Section 41 and Sch 3 of the Criminal Justice Act 2003 amend the allocation procedure in the magistrates' court, which affects the right to jury trial in criminal cases.

Qualifications

a) Any person between the ages of 18 and 70 may serve on a jury provided that person:

i) is registered on the electoral roll (the Royal Commission (1993) has proposed that better efforts should be made to ensure that the electoral role is as comprehensive as possible);

ii) has been ordinarily resident in the UK for at least five years; and

iii) is not ineligible or disqualified for jury service.

b) A person is disqualified if he:

i) has been sentenced to imprisonment for life or to a term of five years or more, custody for life or youth custody for a term of five years or more; or

ii) has had passed on him a sentence of imprisonment of any duration during the last ten years or any order of community service during the last ten years; or

iii) has been placed on probation during the last five years;

iv) has been granted bail in criminal proceedings.

Note that s321 and Sch 33 of the Criminal Justice Act 2003 abolish the categories of ineligibility and excusal as of right. This increases the pool of potential jurors significantly. It is now the responsibility of the potential juror to show 'good reason' why he or she should not serve as a juror.

c) Deferral: s120 Criminal Justice Act 1988

The court may defer jury service if the person summoned shows a good reason. This power is entirely within the discretion of the court.

The Phillips Royal Commission on Criminal Justice (2003) proposed a scheme whereby alternative dates should be offered to people unable to attend.

Also note that the Secretary of State for Constitutional Affairs is duty-bound to publish guidance concerning how the Jury Central Summoning Bureau will exercise its functions and discretionary deferrals and excusals. This is part of the initiative of the Department for Constitutional Affairs to make the jury service moer open and transparent.

Checking and challenging of jurors

a) The defence may challenge the presence of particular jurors. Jurors may be challenged for cause on three grounds: see s12(4) Juries Act 1974:

i) the juror is in fact not qualified; or

ii) the juror is for some reason biased; or

iii) the juror may reasonably be suspected of bias against the defendant.

It is necessary to establish a 'real danger' of bias. It is not enough to allege general prejudices, eg that an all-white jury may be less sympathetic to a black defendant than a multi-racial jury: *R v Ford* [1989] 3 All ER 445.

In this respect, see the recent case of *Sander v United Kingdom* (2000) The Times 12 May (ECHR), in which the court emphasised the issue of impartiality.

b) The prosecution may also challenge jurors. They do so by means of a stand by. The *Practice Note* [1988] 3 All ER 1086 provides the circumstances in which the prosecution may exercise its stand by rights:

i) where information justifying this right is discovered by a jury check and the Attorney-General authorises the stand by; or

ii) where a particular juror is manifestly unsuitable and the defence agree.

The effect of a stand by is that the particular juror is not selected, but must wait until the end of the jury selection process and then only if there are no other jurors left on the panel will he become a member of the jury.

c) Jury checks by the police are permitted in exceptional cases (see *R v Mason* [1980] 3 All ER 777):

   i) if it appears that a juror may be disqualified;

   ii) if it is believed that a juror was involved in a previous aborted trial where there had been an attempt to interfere with jurors; or

   iii) where the police consider it particularly important that no disqualified person serve on the jury.

d) Jury vetting is the investigation of jurors' backgrounds to ensure that there are no unsuitable jurors. There is much controversy on whether jury vetting should continue as it undermines the idea of random selection. The *Practice Note* issued by the Attorney-General (above) now allows the check of a juror's background:

   i) if it is a case of national security;

   ii) where it is a case involving terrorists, the police can check the criminal records of a juror to ensure that he is not disqualified.

Empanelling the jury

Once 12 jurors have been chosen from the panel summoned, they are sworn in.

Secrecy of the jury room and safety of the jury

The jury conducts its deliberations in secret and its verdict is not accompanied by reasons. Jurors may not be questioned on their deliberations, opinions or arguments: see s8 Contempt of Court Act 1981. Section 8 has been used against newspapers which published detailed accounts from members of particular juries in celebrated cases, eg *Attorney-General* v *Associated Newspapers Ltd* [1994] 1 All ER 556 (HL), in which the *Mail on Sunday* was fined a total of £60,000 for disclosing interviews with the jury in the 'Blue Arrow' fraud trial. The Runciman Commission recommended that s8 should be amended to enable research to be conducted into the way juries reach their decisions.

It is well established that the Court of Appeal will refuse to enquire into jury deliberation in the jury-room when hearing an appeal against a conviction: *R v Thompson* [1962] 1 All ER 65 (CA). However, it will be different if the jury are being accommodated overnight at a hotel and there is evidence of improper discussions between some of them which throws doubt on the safeness of the subsequent conviction: *R v Young (Stephen)* [1995] 2 WLR 430 (CA).

It should be noted that s43 of the Criminal Justice and Public Order Act 1994 permits a Crown Court jury to separate at any time, whether before or after it begins to consider its verdict, if the court thinks fit. Separation during consideration of the verdict will be refused if there is a real danger of individual jurors being subjected to improper pressure, such as bribery or intimidation. Improper approaches to a juror should be drawn to the attention of the judge. Section 51 of the Criminal Justice and Public Order Act 1994 creates specific offences concerning intimidation of and reprisals against jurors (or witnesses).

Retention of the present system

Some of the arguments for retention of the present system can be briefly summarised as follows:

a) the independence of the jury from the judiciary and executive provides a safeguard for the defendant;

b) the lay participation in the form of the jury contributes to the public's confidence in the criminal justice system;

c) the combined judgment of 12 jurors is particularly useful in the evaluation of evidence and in judging the credibility of witnesses.

Conversely, the following are examples of the arguments against the retention of juries in the criminal justice system:

a) there is doubt on the ability of randomly selected jurors to carry out satisfactorily their task of fact-finding in complex criminal cases (this is especially so where there are many defendants);

b) the jury may be too easily swayed by counsel's arguments or by strong minded individuals within their number;

c) the jury may be inappropriate on complex cases, eg serious fraud trials: see the Roskill Report (1986).

Alternatives to the present system

a) Trial by judge alone.

b) Trial by a judge and two lay assessors.

c) Trial by judge with a lay magistrate.

d) The Phillips Royal Commission on Criminal Justice (2003) proposed various amendments to the present system:

   i) That for either way offences the defendant should no longer have a right to insist on trial by jury (see Chapter 14).

   ii) Changes could be made in all areas to improve the quality of jury decisions, eg selection; checking; ethnic representation; training and instruction.

Refer to www.criminal-courts-review.org.uk to find out the recommendations made by Auld LJ in respect of jury trials. Some of the Auld recommendations have been implemented through the Criminal Justice Act 2003 and the Courts Act 2003.

6.3 Key cases and statutes

- *Grobbelaar v News Group Newspapers Ltd* [2002] 1 AC 32
  Court of Appeal overturns a jury award

- *John v MGN Ltd* [1996] 2 All ER 35 (CA)
  Court of Appeal reduced the award by a jury

- *R v Sheffield Crown Court, ex parte Brownlow* [1980] QB 530
  Jury vetting won ruled by the Court of Appeal to be illegal

- *Sander v United Kingdom* (2000) The Times 12 May (ECHR)
  Court emphasised the issue of impartiality

- Courts and Legal Services Act 1990 – allowed the Court of Appeal to slash jury awards

- Criminal Justice Act 2003 – introduces new rules affecting jury composition, empanelling and the right to trial by jury

- Defamation Act 1996 – abolished jury trial in defamation actions of £10,000 or less

- Jury Act 1974 – laid down the general principles relating to juries

- Supreme Court Act 1981 – allowed the use of a jury in some civil matters

6.4 Questions and suggested solutions

QUESTION ONE

'Most defenders of jury trials are seduced by rhetoric and ignorant of its history. In reality there are no rational arguments for its retention.'

Discuss.

University of London LLB Examination
(for External Students) English Legal System June 2001 Q6

General Comment

This question requires a historical appreciation of the practice of jury trials, and whether it represents the very fabric of the English legal system. Should it be retained, abolished or reformed? This should be addressed by students. Political, judicial and academic observations must therefore be made.

The Jury System

Skeleton Solution

The role of the jury – its role within the criminal justice system – support for jury competency – representative or unrepresentative of society? – the value of decision-making by jury – suggested reforms and arguments for and against its retention.

Suggested Solution

In order to do justice to this question, mention must be made of the historical evolution of the 'jury'. Perhaps an apt beginning would be the dicta of Lord Denning MR in *Ward* v *James* [1966] 1 QB 273, wherein he stated:

> 'Let it not be supposed that it has been the bulwark of our liberties for too long for any of us to seek to alter it. Whenever a man is on trial for serious crime, or when in a civil case a man's honour or integrity is at stake, or when one or the other party must be deliberately lying, then trial by jury has no equal.'

These words reflect the passion of the English judiciary in so far as jury trials are concerned. As Darbyshire (Eddey & Darbyshire, *English Legal System* (7th edn, 2001)) rightly observes: 'this ancient institution arouses strong emotions in the hearts of the English and Welsh, as it does with the Americans and many others living in common law systems which are daughters of the English legal system'. Why is this so? Well, simply because for centuries, jury trial has been central to the legal system in the United Kingdom. The use of ordinary folk (men and women) as factfinders in civil and criminal cases was, and still is, perceived by most people to be the only democratic way of deciding the issue of guilt or blame. Rather than leaving it entirely in the hands of lawyers, perhaps allowing a small proportion of the community to make or take a decision on the facts of the case is the main purpose of having a jury. This practice fits in well with one of the Diceyan principles of the Rule of Law which is 'that man should be pronounced guilty of an act or crime by his peers alone'. Whilst this is so, it must be stated that the jury has no part to play in the decision as to sentence. Equally, the jury has no part in decisions which are concerned with law or legal procedure. They are, and have always been, purely factfinders and no more.

Originally, the jury were in fact the 'police' of the community. They made arrests, investigated into those arrests and other suspected offenders, they provided witness statements and in some cases prosecuted as well in front of their visiting judges. They were seen as local law enforcers, a kind of 'accusing jury'. When the police force was created, this responsibility of upholding the peace and law and order was transferred from the community to the police. One argument for this approach is that there can be no better person to judge an individual in the community than the community itself. A small proportion of the people from the local community is/was selected to represent the community. It is these people who appreciate the 'culture and climate' of the community, by deciding the issue of whether an individual is guilty or innocent of the offence that he or she has been charged with.

However, Zander (*Cases and Materials on the English Legal System* (9th edn, 2003)) argues that 'the original concept of the jury was precisely the opposite of what it later became'. This is very true. The original juries were extremely inquisitorial in nature. In fact it was they who decided whether a true bill of indictment actually existed as against a defendant. This was the grand jury consisting of 24 members. As Darbyshire (above) states:

> '... the petty jury, of 12 members, emerged in the thirteenth century to take the place of trial by ordeal, which the ecclesiastical authorities saw fit to condemn. It became increasingly distinct in its functions from the previous grand jury, although it long maintained its composition from local witnesses of fact deciding matters from their local knowledge.'

It was not until the fifteenth century that the jury assumed its modern role in criminal trials as judges of fact alone.

Nowadays, every effort is made to ensure that the jury have no prior knowledge of the case. This seems to be the philosophy behind the Juries Act 1974, which states that every adult, aged 18–70, who is on the annual electoral register and who has lived in the United Kingdom for at least five years is qualified to serve as a juror. The Act also stipulates who is disqualified from jury service. However, s321 and Sch 33 of the Criminal Justice Act 2003 abolishes the categories of ineligibility and excusal as of right. This has increased the pool of potential jurors. This random selection can now be said to provide the basis of the continued retention of juries. In *R v Ford* [1989] 3 WLR 762 the court held that the absence of any particular ethnic minority in the jury does not amount to an injustice or unfairness, but rather compounds the randomness principle.

There are many arguments that challenge the competency of juries. Whilst it is not possible to state them exhaustively, some may be made mention of. Firstly, juries are perceived as a 'bunch of amateurs'. They are unable to deal with technical or complex evidence. Secondly, research conducted by academics, such as Baldwin and McConville (*Jury Trials* (1979)), reveal that juries have frequently reached wrong or questionable verdicts. In some cases, juries have shown favour to extreme methods of deciding, for example, in *R v Young (Stephen)* [1995] 2 WLR 430 it was discovered that the jury had used an 'Ouija board'. One of the problems in making a rational assessment of the competency of juries is the dearth of knowledge about how they reach their verdict. Their deliberations in the jury room are protected by the prohibition on disclosure imposed by s8 Contempt of Court Act 1981. Plus, the verdict itself is given without reasons for why it has been reached. Expert evidence may seem lengthy, confusing and even unmanageable to ordinary people. This, and perhaps other reasons, impressed upon the former Lord Chancellor, Lord Irvine, to effect reforms in relation to jury trials within the criminal justice system. Projects such as the National Mode of Trial Guidelines 1985, the Narey Report 1997, the Government Consultation Paper on Jury Reform 1998 and the Auld Review 2000 have provided the impetus for reforms, some of which have been implemented by the Criminal Justice Act 2003.

Whilst this may be so, there are equally as many arguments for its continued retention. The Human Rights Act 1998 now protects any accused in a sense that he or she is entitled to a fair trial by virtue of art 6 European Convention on Human Rights. Jury supporters also argue that a decision by 12 lay people is fairer than one by a single judge, since it is likely that 12 people will cancel out one another's prejudices. Further, there has been a move towards the simplification of presentation of complex evidence, as well as allowing jurors a more proactive participation at the judge's discretion. Perhaps a reminder of how the jury was, and still is, perceived would reinforce support for its continued retention.

Lord Devlin (*Trial by Jury* (1966)) hailed it as a guardian of democracy; he stated: 'no tyrant could afford to leave a subject's freedom in the hands of his countrymen. So that trial by jury is more than an instrument of justice and one wheel of the constitution: it is the lamp that shows that freedom lives'.

QUESTION TWO

'The Home Secretary's proposals to limit the right to jury trial represents a serious attack on the due process protections for defendants in the criminal justice system.'

Discuss.

University of London LLB Examination
(for External Students) English Legal System June 2000 Q5

General Comment

A question on jury trials with emphasis on the proposed reforms and how those reforms impact on a defendant's rights within the criminal justice system.

Skeleton Solution

The rationale for jury trials – the right to jury trial – Home Secretary's proposals – Criminal Justice (Mode of Trial) Bill – arguments for and against – effects of the Human Rights Act 1998.

Suggested Solution

The English jury system is regarded by many as one of the most essential and central features of the legal process: 'the bulwark of individual liberties'. However, both the jury selection process and the value of decision-making by juries have been frequently criticised, and recent concerns over the length and cost of jury trials for serious fraud or complicated cases have added to the debate as to whether juries should be retained at all.

It is at this juncture that the rationale for jury trials should be made mention of. The purpose of having the jury, it is said, is to enable a decision on the facts to be taken by a small group from the community from which the accused or defendant comes, rather than for it to be left entirely in the hands of the lawyers. As remarked by Lord Devlin (*Trial by Jury* (1966)), the institution of jury is 'the lamp that shows that freedom lives'. The use of ordinary people as factfinders in both civil and criminal cases always was and is perceived by some as the only democratic way of upholding justice in a legal system. In fact, it is this system of the random selection of juries that provides the basis for its continued retention, in that, arguably, there cannot be a fairer means of deciding the issue of innocence or guilt of an accused. The Juries Act 1974 provides that every adult (with certain exemptions and disqualifications) is qualified to serve as a juror provided he or she is aged between 18 and 70 and has lived in this country for at least five years, and whose name appears on the annual electoral register of a constituency.

Be that as it may, there seems to be an ongoing debate between civil libertarians and others about several issues surrounding the jury, all of which are very interconnected, according to P Darbyshire (Eddey & Darbyshire, *English Legal System* (7th edn, 2001) at p314). Firstly, she argues that the debate mainly concerns the pros and cons of retaining the jury and jury equity. Secondly, the debate often relates to randomness, representatives and jury vetting – its desirability and constitutionality, the fairness of prosecution and defence challenges. Debates on jury reform can be traced back to the early 1980s where in the Roskill Report, it was suggested that juries should be replaced by a species of tribunal staffed by judges and professional assessors, especially in complicated criminal trials. Subsequently, the Royal Commission on Criminal Justice in 1993 recommended that the random selection should be slightly altered to ensure that the selection of the jury includes up to three people from minority communities, although it must be stated that in *R v Ford* [1989] 3 WLR 762 the court held that the absence of any particular ethnic minority in the jury does not amount to an injustice or unfairness, but rather compounds the randomness principle.

In 1995 the Home Office published a consultation document, 'Mode of Trial', in which the then Home Secretary, Michael Howard, outlined various options to shift more cases from the Crown Court to the Magistrates' Court. The National Mode of Trial Guidelines 1985, issued by the Director of Public Prosecutions, it must be stated, had already gone to some extent in achieving this. As Darbyshire argues (ibid, at p422), given the sentimental attachment of the English to jury trial in criminal cases, it would be politically inexpedient to remove the defendant's right to opt for jury trial in all triable either way cases. In this respect, s49 Criminal Procedure and Investigations Act 1996 requires magistrates, before determining mode of trial, to ascertain the accused's plea. Hence, if the defendant opts for a summary trial (assuming the plea is one of not guilty) or if he/she intends to plead guilty, then the right to opt for a Crown Court trial is lost. Essentially, the entire reform process seeks to challenge this specific right of the defendant to elect which mode of trial he or she would prefer. This was the sum total of the recommendations of the Narey Report (Narey M, *Review of the Delay in the Criminal Justice System* (1997) Home Office: see www.homeoffice.gov.uk) in 1997.

After New Labour replaced the Conservative Government in 1997, the Home Secretary, Jack Straw, published a new Consultation Paper *Determining Mode of Trial in Either Way Cases* in 1998 (see www.homeoffice.gov.uk), setting out the familiar arguments in abolishing the defendant's right to elect jury trial. This culminated in the Criminal Justice (Mode of Trial) Bill in 1999 going through its motions in the Houses. The Bill attracted much criticism from the Bar, the Law Society and other civil rights groups. With so much opposition, it is perhaps unsurprising that this Bill suffered a heavy defeat in the House of Lords in January 2000. This, however, did not stop, prevent or deter the Home Secretary from introducing the Criminal Justice (Mode of Trial) Bill (No 2), which once again was defeated in the House of Lords in autumn 2000.

Auld LJ was commissioned by the Government in 2000 to commence another wide-ranging review of the entire criminal process, and it is interesting to note that in his review (*Criminal Courts Review* (2001)) Auld LJ reiterated the recommendation that the right to elect jury trial should be removed, adding, however, that the defendant should in serious cases be entitled to opt out of a jury trial by choosing trial by judge alone. Some of the recommendations of Auld LJ's review have been codified through the Criminal Justice Act 2003.

Arguments in support of retaining the jury still revolve around issues relating to fairness, justice and randomness, but the study conducted by Darbyshire, Maughan and Stewart in 2000 (updated in 2001) (Darbyshire, P, Maughan, A and Stewart, A, 'What Can the English Legal System Learn from Jury Research Published up to 2001?' [2001] Crim LR 970) revealed that reforms are necessary and inevitable. Some of their findings disclose the following interesting points.

1. Juries should be made more representative, for example by referring to the Department of Vehicle Licensing Authority, the Department of Social Security, phone and other mailing lists.
2. The inclusion in jury trials of three black or Asian jurors in a racially sensitive case should be made.
3. Multiple charges and multiple defendants confuse jurors.
4. Legal jargon should be replaced with plain, intelligible English.
5. Jurors should be given written instructions on the law and pre-deliberation instructions.
6. Technical phrases such as 'beyond reasonable doubt' create confusion and misunderstanding amongst jurors.
7. Criminal trial juries may be required to give reasons (contrary to the old practice) if the jury trial is to satisfy art 6 (fair trial) European Convention on Human Rights.

In conclusion, it is submitted that the reforms, while seemingly radical, will not by any degree reduce the notion of fairness or deprive the defendant of any fundamental right or civil liberty, as this is now protected by the Human Rights Act 1998, which incorporated the European Convention on Human Rights into English law in autumn 2000.

QUESTION THREE

Assess the value of lay decision-making in the criminal justice system by reference to the role of the jury and Justices of the Peace.

University of London LLB Examination
(for External Students) English Legal System June 1999 Q6

General Comment

This question is a good example of the way in which an examiner can choose to bring together associated topics within one question. Thought needs to be given to this approach when undertaking revision for the examination. Good marks may only be gained by a more or less equal discussion both of juries and lay magistracy, and by directing the discussion to the question asked, ie the *value* of their decision-making in the *criminal* justice system. An answer that is predominantly a rambling discourse on all that is perceived as wrong with juries will not suffice!

Skeleton Solution

Role of the jury and the lay magistracy and their place in the scheme of criminal justice – research and other evidence supporting concerns over the competency of the jury; complex cases, eg serious fraud crimes; defects in the selection process; value of their lay role – concerns over the unrepresentative character of the lay magistracy; local advisory committees – the amateur nature of the lay magistracy; comparison to stipendiary magistracy; training programmes; value of lay representation for local needs and interests.

Suggested Solution

The jury represents a microcosm of society and offers trial by one's equals. The lay magistracy represents a microcosm of the local community and ensures that national law is enforced in a way that reflects local needs and interests. Both are ancient and closely guarded traditions of our legal system. Their independence from the judiciary and executive provides a constitutional safeguard for the citizen that is so unique and strong in character that no satisfactory alternative for either has yet been found. The winds of change, however, have led society away from unfailing confidence in lay representation. Modern society believes in, and strives toward, things like equality, minority representation and a classless society. The ancient institutions of the jury and the lay magistracy still have their place in this scheme of things but have had to adapt to meet new criteria. In particular, there has had to be reform directed at increasing their representative character. Inextricably entwined with this there has been debate about the competency of lay people to deal with some of the complex cases that now come before the courts.

It can be argued that the affairs of man are always complicated and that, relatively speaking, there is no difference in complexity as between our lives and those of former generations. The argument thus runs that if lay representation was a satisfactory process in the past, it is equally as satisfactory now. There are many who do not agree with the simplicity of this argument. They see things like our advances in forensic and medical knowledge and the complexity of events leading to such as serious fraud crimes as resulting in evidence too complex to be comprehensible to anyone other than an expert in the field. Some support for this view can be found in cases indicating difficulties the jury appear to have had in determining innocence or guilt. Examples include the difficulty in determining the fine distinction between murder and manslaughter on the basis of abstruse psychological evidence and difficulties experienced with complex technical evidence presented in serious fraud cases.

One of the problems in making a rational assessment of the competency of juries is the dearth of knowledge about how they reach their verdict. Their deliberations in the jury room are protected by the prohibition on disclosure imposed by s8 of the Contempt of Court Act 1981, and the verdict itself is given without reasons for why it has been reached. Inferences have to be drawn from the decisions they reach, the length of time it takes them to reach a decision, notes they send to the judge during their deliberations and other surrounding information such as the composition of the jury. All of these are unsatisfactory determinants of the adequacy of the jury to deal with complex and technical evidence, but there is strong opposition to any erosion of the jury's right to secret deliberations. The recommendation of the Royal Commission on Criminal Justice (1993) (Cmnd 2263) that there be amendment of s8 to permit genuine academic research was not implemented for this reason.

Research that has been conducted within the confines of the parameters allowed, reveals that juries have frequently reached wrong or questionable verdicts. Statistics compiled by Baldwin and McConville (*Jury Trials* (1979)) concluded that 5 per cent of those convicted by a jury were convicted in doubtful circumstances. The extraordinary revelation that the jury in *R v Young (Stephen)* [1995] 2 WLR 430 had used an ouija board to contact the deceased to find out whether her husband had killed her may be dismissed as exceptional behaviour but it nonetheless raises enquiry about the role the jury perceive they have. It is has been suggested, for example, that questionable acquittals may not only be the result of sympathy for the defendant or antipathy for the victim, but based on the juries' perception of the high burden of proof in criminal cases. Juries confused by conflicting forensic and medical evidence, or other complex and highly technical evidence, may feel bound to give the benefit of the doubt to the accused. It was suggested that this may have been a factor in the acquittal of Ian and Kevin Maxwell in 1996 after their lengthy serious fraud trial at the Old Bailey which involved evidence regarded by many as being comprehensible only to experts in the field. Their acquittal may, of course, have been just and correct but the public surprise with which it was received cannot be entirely ignored. Concern as to whether a jury should be asked to consider such evidence had been expressed in the previous year following the collapse of a fraud trial because the evidence had become unmanageable and too difficult for the jury to understand.

Cases such as these renew calls for the replacement of the jury by a judge and panel of expert assessors along the lines proposed in the Roskill Report (1986). The proposal was not implemented because of the strong opposition to any form of abolition of the jury. In 1993 the Report of the Royal Commission on Criminal Justice (see above) instead recommended that steps be taken to simplify the presentation of complex evidence and to allow jurors a more pro-active participation, for example, by asking questions on points on which they are confused. The fact that pro-active participation would do little in a case where the evidence has admittedly become too complex for the jury to understand goes a long way toward rebutting the claim that this is a solution to the problem, at least for cases like serious fraud crimes. It has also been pointed out that, in the absence of proper compensation for loss of work, cancelled holidays and so on, the Department of Constitutional Affairs can do little other than be lenient in its selection of jurors for lengthy trials. However, s321 and Sch 33 of the Criminal Justice Act 2003 abolish the categories of ineligibility and excusal as of right for jury service. This will increase the pool of potential jurors, and it is now the responsibility of a potential juror to show 'good reason' why he or she should not serve as a juror. In a letter to *The Times* in 1966, Lord Donaldson, a former Master of the Rolls, commented on the inevitably of a jury selected to hear a serious fraud case by this process being made up of those 'who would not otherwise be more gainfully occupied' and as such 'wholly unrepresentative'. Implicit in such criticism is the view that such a jury may lack sufficient intellect to understand the evidence, as well as possibly lack responsibility to deliver an objective and carefully considered verdict.

Whilst there does appear to be strong evidence of the difficulties experienced by a group of 12 lay people to get at the truth of a complex issue presented to them on an adversarial basis, there is also evidence that this is mainly confined to cases of exceptional complexity. The majority of criminal cases turn upon the credibility of simpler evidence and the general view is that a typical jury probably is capable of reaching a fair result in such cases. Given that juries are now used only in a small part of the administration of criminal justice, there will have to be very good cause for them to be abolished altogether, and what is known about their operation would not yet seem to have provided such cause.

Trial by jury is in fact only used in about 2 per cent of criminal trials. The majority take place summarily in the magistrates' courts and a large proportion of these are heard by the lay bench, the adequacy of which has also been challenged in recent years. Concerns were expressed both over the wholly amateur nature of the lay magistracy and its unrepresentative character. In an attempt to redress the imbalance between the number of male and female JPs, and the lack of representation from ethnic minorities, Lord Mackay, the former Lord Chancellor, set up local advisory committees to advise him on appointments. A few years ago ethnic minorities comprised less than 2 per cent of the lay magistracy, but efforts to improve on this have resulted in an increase to between 6 per cent and 7 per cent of new appointments. Despite these small improvements, the lay magistracy is predominantly white, male, middle class and employed in professional or white-collar jobs. Only about 15 per cent have a manual labour background and research findings indicate that the majority of the lay magistracy support the Conservative Party. In 1997, in a letter to *The Times*, Lord Irvine, the former Lord Chancellor, expressed his desire for greater political and social balance among the lay magistracy and in 1998, as part of the revision of the procedures for appointing lay magistrates, he urged the local advisory committees to give greater consideration to this when putting forward suitable candidates. A practical problem facing these committees is the lack of ability of suitable candidates to apply for appointment because of the amount of time they require off work to perform their duties. A scheme aimed at persuading local employers to give paid time off to employees who serve as JPs was introduced by Lord Mackay, but more is needed to address this problem if a true balance of social and political backgrounds is to be achieved.

It is nonetheless a somewhat astonishing fact that such a large proportion of criminal trials are heard entirely by what may be described as 'a bunch of amateurs'. Some redress of the concerns expressed over this came with the expansion of the role of the Judicial Studies Board in 1985 to include the training of lay and stipendiary magistrates. Newly appointed magistrates complete two stages of training. The first stage comprises instruction in the duties of a justice of the peace, practice and procedure in the courts, and methods of punishment and treatment. Trainees also attend court as observers. The second stage consists of further instruction and visits to penal institutions. There are voluntary refresher courses for all serving JPs and compulsory refresher courses every five years for chairmen-magistrates. Both of these contain assessments by judges, justices' clerks and fellow lay magistrates.

Training is seen as being a better solution than the outright abolition of the lay magistracy. The alternative would be their replacement by a professional, salaried stipendiary system and it is argued by some that this would be a much more efficient method of ensuring consistent handling of cases. It is also claimed that stipendiary magistrates deal with cases quicker and are less reluctant to challenge delaying tactics of defence counsel. The argument against the abolition of the lay element rests on the valuable benefits that are gained by having a non-permanent body of citizens to offset the permanence and rigidity of the rest of summary jurisdiction and act as a counter-balance to the case-hardened professionalism of lawyers and law enforcement agencies such as the police. Whilst their sentencing discretion is open to criticism for inconsistent treatment of similar cases, it too has a valuable role to play in ensuring justice to suit the locality rather than the imposition of penalties to suit a national average. Particular kinds of crime are more prevalent in some areas than others and a harsher local law enforcement is needed as a deterrent. Such local enforcement no more detracts from the interests of society as a whole than bye-laws for particular parking restrictions or the holding of markets.

QUESTION FOUR

'Juries are ill-equipped to deal with complex cases. Some alternative needs to be found.'

Discuss.

University of London LLB Examination
(for External Students) English Legal System June 1998 Q6

General Comment

The answer to this question must be confined to a discussion of the use of the jury in complex cases, which are principally serious fraud cases, but there are other examples. The thrust of the question lies with *alternatives* to the use of the jury rather than with the fact that they are 'ill-equipped', so discussion of evidence of their inadequacy needs to be given as the reference point for an alternative under discussion and not as a general discussion of perceived inability to hear complex cases.

Skeleton Solution

Introduction to the problems caused by complex and technical evidence – effect of s8 of the Contempt of Court Act 1981; sovereignty of jury verdict; deliberations outside of the jury room; USA openness and why not favoured here – selection methods and composition of the jury; alternative selection methods; compensation scheme – Roskill Report (1986) recommendation for a panel of judges and professional assessors – Royal Commission on Criminal Justice (1993) recommendations for more proactive jury and regulatory penalties for serious fraud cases – other alternatives: trial by a judge sitting alone; trial by a bench of three to five judges – conclusion: whether answer lies more with reform of the adversarial process than with abolition of the jury.

Suggested Solution

Concern over the adequacy of a jury to hear complex cases mainly centres on their competence to understand evidence presented in serious fraud trials. The acquittal of Ian and Kevin Maxwell in 1996 after a lengthy serious fraud trial at the Old Bailey highlighted a number of the reasons for this concern. They may, of course, have been correct verdicts but there was considerable public surprise at them and open debate about whether the unmanageable quantity of complex and technical evidence presented during the trial was comprehensible only to experts. It was felt by some that the jury had become so confused by the evidence that they felt bound to give the benefit of the doubt to the accused. The case was yet another example in a growing list of such cases provoking demands for radical reform. In the previous year for example, a fraud trial costing an estimated £2 million heard at Newport Crown Court collapsed after six months when the trial judge, Crowther J, ruled that the evidence had become unmanageable and too difficult for the jury to understand.

One of the difficulties in making a rational assessment of the competency of juries is the prohibition on disclosure of their deliberations imposed by s8 of the Contempt of Court Act 1981. This includes indirectly obtained disclosures (*Attorney-General* v *Associated Newspapers Limited* [1994] 2 WLR 277) so effectively prevents any form of research into the operation of the jury system. The Royal Commission on Criminal Justice (1993) (Cmnd 2263) recommended that s8 should be amended to permit genuine academic research but this was opposed by some senior judges who feared that exposing the jury to open scrutiny would focus attention onto their weaknesses at the expense of reinforcing their strengths, with the result that there would be calls for its abolition and the consequent loss of a constitutional safeguard for the citizen.

The right to a jury trial is a deeply entrenched constitutional fundamental. It is generally accepted that the jury system should be reformed or replaced only for very good cause and there is as much support for the benefits obtained by its retention as there is for its abolition. Since most cases turn upon the credibility of evidence, the typical jury is probably capable of reaching a fair result. It is cases of exceptional complexity that give rise to doubts, but in the absence of empirical research there can only be speculation about the difficulty that a typical jury may have in deciding guilt or innocence. Even where there is evidence of irrational deliberations, the general principle remains that the jury's verdict is sovereign and unchallengeable on appeal and the Court of Appeal has shown great reluctance to investigate allegations of impropriety in jury proceedings. However, the rule applies only to deliberations made in the jury room (*R* v *Miah; R* v *Akhbar* (1996) The Times 18 December) and not to discussions that take place elsewhere, such as in the extraordinary case of *R* v *Young (Stephen)* [1995] 2 WLR 430 where the Court of Appeal did take the unusual step of investigating the deliberations of a jury who had been sent to an hotel overnight and decided to contact the deceased by means of an ouija board to find out whether her husband had killed her!

Part of the sovereignty of the jury is that they do not give reasons for their verdict and the introduction of this information would assist not only the decision as to what types of trial they should be used for but also public confidence in their role. In the USA jurors are frequently interviewed by the media as to their reasons for reaching particular decisions but there is considerable reluctance to introduce such an open inquiry here out of fear of the undesirable influence that media interest in one case would have on the future deliberations of another jury in a similar case. However, until some form of research into their operation is permitted, it remains impossible to assess with certainty the ability of a passive group of 12 lay people to get at the truth of a complex issue presented to them on an adversarial basis. Conclusions may only be inferred from the decisions they reach and other surrounding evidence. The latter includes notes that can be sent to the judge by a jury during their deliberations which, if it relates to the defendant, necessitates the reconvening of the court without the jury to invite submissions on the matter, and then recall of the jury so as to give any necessary directions: *R* v *Green* [1992] Crim LR 292.

The method by which juries are selected for lengthy trials raises questions about whether most do meet the notion of being the valuable cross-section of society they are supposed to represent. When it comes to complex trials that may last six months or more, requests from individuals who wish to be excused from service by reason of employment, booked holidays and so on, are more favourably looked on and the outcome is a jury chosen because they are available rather than from a general cross-section of society. However, s321 and Sch 33 of the Criminal Justice Act 2003 abolish the categories of ineligibility and excusal as of right for jury service. This will increase the pool of potential jurors, and it is now the responsibility of a potential juror to show 'good reason' why he or she should not serve as a juror. Lord Donaldson, a former Master of the Rolls, commented in a letter to *The Times* in 1996 on the inevitably of a jury selected to hear a serious fraud case by this process being made up of those 'who would not otherwise be more gainfully occupied' and as such 'wholly unrepresentative'. Implicit in such criticism is the view that such a jury may lack sufficient intellect to understand the evidence, as well as possibly lack responsibility to deliver an objective and carefully considered verdict. One solution that has been suggested to preserve the proper random selection of a jury for complicated cases is the introduction of a compensation scheme whereby employers and employees who suffer disruption as a result of long jury service and others who have to suffer inconvenience, for example, the cancellation of a booked holiday, would be paid some compensation by the state. Attention could then be switched to giving a traditional jury considerable guidance in the complex aspects of evidence without undue concern over the extent to which this lengthened the trial. Since trials already cost amounts running into hundreds of thousands of pounds, this is not a desirable solution as regards the litigants. Given the present pressure on funding that already exists in the provision of the whole system of justice, it is unlikely that such a scheme, or at least one of any effectiveness in terms of compensation paid, will be introduced.

The inferences that can be drawn from what is known of the operation of the jury do indicate causes for concern not just for serious fraud trials but also for other cases. The distinction between murder and manslaughter, for example, can turn on abstruse psychological material, and advances in forensic investigation and medical knowledge have led to the presentation of complex and conflicting evidence. It is felt by many that expert assessors rather than lay people selected at random are the proper panel to assess complicated evidence, ask relevant and searching questions, and generally perform the inquisitorial function that is required for an adversarial trial. In 1986 the Roskill Report recommended that the jury should be replaced by a panel of judges and professional assessors. Serious fraud cases, for example, would be decided by the trial judge with the help of a panel of expert assessors such as accountants and auditors, but the Government decided against this approach and chose instead to reform the nature of fraud trials: Criminal Justice Act 1987. In this regard, the Criminal Justice Act 2003, introduces changes in the allocation procedure in the magistrates' court, which, in turn, affects the right to trial by jury in criminal cases.

The right of the accused to be tried by his equals is a safeguard for the accused that cannot easily be replaced and the 'overwhelming evidence' for the retention of the jury was recognised in the Report of the Royal Commission on Criminal Justice (see above) which advised against the abolition of the traditional jury but recommended steps to encourage proactive participation from jurors. These included: dispensing with lengthy speeches from counsel and a minimal use of jargon and technicality to simplify the issues; allowing questions from jurors to clarify points on which they are confused; and increased use of audio-visual aids to assist communication. It has since been suggested that the computerisation of evidence should be introduced with provision of laptop computers for jurors for use during the trial, but the obvious need to select for computer literacy again raises issues about the need to preserve a randomly selected jury. In respect of serious fraud cases, however, the Commission recognised the particular complexity of evidence and recommended a change of approach away from criminal penalties and over to a system of regulatory penalties similar to that used in some states in USA where the Securities and Exchange Commission administers the process of discipline as an alternative to the adversarial system of trial.

Other alternatives are trial by a judge sitting alone who would assess questions of law and fact, and trial by a bench of three to five judges and no jury. Judges are less likely to be distracted from the main issues but there is a danger that they will become case-hardened and perhaps pro-prosecution minded in criminal trials. The jury acts as a counter-balance to 'the establishment' and, if randomly selected, brings a diversity of knowledge of everyday occurrences and social norms and expectations that a judge sitting alone cannot replicate and a bench of judges is unlikely to represent. The Roskill Report proposal for trial by a composite tribunal of lawyers and lay people goes considerably further toward meeting this goal, so can be viewed as being a better alternative to total judicial control.

There are so many factors working against the abolition of the jury that the solution for ensuring a fair and objective trial for complex cases would seem to lie more in reform of the adversarial system of law so as to permit more proactive involvement of the jury. Jury participation would reveal the point at which a case takes on such exceptional complexity as to be beyond the comprehension of the lay person and alternatives could be considered to deal with these isolated cases without the clutter of the other issues involved in retaining the jury system as a whole. There could, for example, be a process by which evidence that the jury indicate they cannot understand, despite attempts to simplify and explain it, are referred to a panel of experts appointed independently for the purpose (for example, by the Department for Constitutional Affairs) and whose advice is taken into account by the jury in their deliberations.

QUESTION FIVE

What criticisms can be made of the social and ethnic composition of the magistracy? Are these criticisms important and how could selection procedures be changed to make the magistracy more representative of the wider community?

University of London LLB Examination
(for External Students) English Legal System June 1997 Q6

General Comment

A rather difficult question since it assumes knowledge of the detailed statistical composition of the magistracy in terms of race and social background. It also puts the emphasis on selection procedures, thereby excluding discussion of training as a method of tackling race or social bias on the bench. Examination candidates need to keep up to date with the proposals constantly emanating from the Department for Constitutional Affairs on this issue, as well as advancing their own views as to how the problems of racial and social imbalance might be tackled.

Skeleton Solution

Role of local advisory committees – why racial/social imbalance on the bench is an important problem – nature of the racial imbalance and possible reasons for it – possible solutions to the problem of racial imbalance – nature of the social imbalance and possible reasons for it – possible solutions to the problem of social imbalance – why party political balance is a significant part of the problem of social balance.

Suggested Solution

Advisory committees on the appointment of lay magistrates have to recommend suitable candidates who will help create benches broadly reflecting the communities they serve in terms of gender, ethnic origin, occupation, geographical location and political persuasion. Broadly speaking gender balance is good throughout the country, but concern has been expressed about social balance and the representation of ethnic minorities. It may well be that existing lay magistrates are people of integrity who hold no social or racial bias, but such criticisms of their unrepresentative character remain important because of the old adage that 'justice must not only be done but must be *seen* to be done'. A general public perception that the lay magistracy is unrepresentative in terms of social and racial balance can lead to a damaging loss of confidence in an institution which deals with 95 per cent of all criminal prosecutions.

In regard to ethnic representation matters have improved statistically. A few years ago ethnic minorities comprised less than 2 per cent of the lay magistracy, but recent efforts to improve recruitment from such minorities have resulted in an increase to 6 to 7 per cent of new appointments. Although this may reflect the national ethnic minority population there is concern about under-representation in areas heavily populated by ethnic minorities, since 6 to 7 per cent would not accurately reflect the local community mix in inner city areas such as Southall and Brixton. Many a convicted defendant from an ethnic minority may feel that he or she did not have a fair hearing purely and simply because all the lay magistrates were white. It may not be true, but that doesn't stop him or her from thinking it.

There is no easy answer as to why ethnic minorities are under-represented. It may be that many are in manual labour jobs and cannot take time off work. Perhaps black people feel that they will be out of place in an institution that is dominated by white people? Perhaps they fear rejection by their local black community? Similar problems account for the difficulty of recruiting black and Asian police officers, yet here, as with the lay magistracy, efforts need to continue to resolve the problem since otherwise important institutions in the administration of justice will not command the trust and confidence of significant sections of the population.

A former Lord Chancellor, Lord Mackay, rejected positive discrimination as a method to boost the number of lay magistrates from ethnic minorities, but he did favour the active encouragement of applications from ethnic minorities, notably through the placing of advertisements for vacancies on local benches in the local ethnic minority newspapers and by encouraging the advisory committees to be more positive in recruiting suitable candidates from under-represented sections of their local community. It is difficult to see what more could be done, except perhaps to provide greater information about the work of the magistracy so as to 'demystify' the institution and reassure potential applicants that they need not have legal knowledge or legal skills.

In terms of social balance it is probably correct to say that the average person conceives a lay magistrate as a middle-aged and middle-class person. There is much truth in this perception because for years advisory committees have been dominated by well-educated, relatively wealthy individuals who can afford the time off to do such work, and who probably have a predisposition towards choosing candidates of similar background and outlook. It is especially troubling that so many magistrates are over the age of 40, because whatever social background they may have they may find it difficult to command the trust and confidence of those of a younger generation (most defendants are under the age of 40). Since it is possible to apply to become a magistrate at the age of 21 it may be desirable to advertise this fact more widely, as well as the fact that a candidate may nominate himself/herself. However, the greatest deterrent to becoming a magistrate is the requirement of sitting at least 26 times a year, plus attending a number of training courses. This deters all of those who need to work for a living, including many young people anxious to obtain promotion. Employers do not take kindly to someone who wants to take off more than two days a month. Civic responsibility does not contribute to company profits. Lord Mackay made several appeals to large organisations to set an example by giving paid time off to employees who wish to serve as lay magistrates, but the response has been lacklustre and, from a commercial viewpoint, unlikely to be followed by smaller firms.

The former Labour Lord Chancellor, Lord Irvine, stated his personal determination to tackle the problem of social balance, though he provoked controversy by emphasising the political character of the current imbalance. Statistics show that the Conservative Party in 1995 had twice as many supporters on the bench as the Labour Party, and that even in Labour strongholds, such as Wales and the big English metropolitan districts, Conservative-supporting magistrates outnumbered those who supported Labour. For example, in Northumberland there were 83 Conservative Party supporters on the bench compared with only 12 Labour Party supporters. Whilst Lord Irvine stressed that personal political beliefs are irrelevant in deciding a candidate's suitability for appointment, there needed in his view to be a proper balance on benches between the main political parties if such benches were to be microcosms of their communities. To achieve this aim Lord Irvine suggested raising the upper age limit to 65 to provide a larger pool of suitable candidates, particularly of those who have taken early retirement. The White Paper, *Justice for All* (2001), and the Criminal Justice Act 2003 have now put measures in place which have significantly increased the pool of eligible jurors. The Act is also intended to 'fine tune' the jury process and make it more open and transparent.

QUESTION SIX

'The jury is a fundamental part of the English criminal justice process and is necessary to ensure that justice is actually done to individuals, especially in complicated cases.'

Discuss.

University of London LLB Examination
(for External Students) English Legal System June 1996 Q4

General Comment

A traditional question on the jury system, though it should be noted that emphasis is put on the role of the jury in 'complicated' cases. Obviously serious fraud cases will feature prominently in the discussion, but it should not be overlooked that there may be other types of case which are regarded as 'complicated' and unsuitable for jury trial. Issues such as the random selection of juries and guidance for juries need to be examined because they relate to the question of the jury's competence. Useful research material on these points can be found in Zander's *Cases and Materials on the English Legal System* (9th edn, 2003), especially those sections dealing with serious fraud trials and alternatives to jury trial. A useful article on complicated cases and the use of the jury in them is by Bonnington ('The Jury: a Suitable Case for Treatment?' [1995] NLJ 847).

Skeleton Solution

Difficulty of assessing the competence of a jury because of the statutory ban on research – definition of 'complicated' cases and the suitability of the jury for such cases – recommendations of Roskill Report (1986) on serious fraud trials – methods of selecting juries in serious fraud trials – guidance for the jury in complicated cases – reform proposals: the alternatives to jury trial.

Suggested Solution

In the absence of research, which is currently prohibited by s8 of the Contempt of Court Act 1981, it is impossible to assess whether the traditional English jury has difficulty in deciding guilt or innocence in complicated cases. The right to jury trial has become so well established that it is generally accepted that it should be reformed or replaced only for very good cause. Since most cases turn upon the credibility of evidence the typical jury is probably capable of reaching a fair result. However, concern has been expressed that juries may become confused by complicated evidence and that, therefore, either more should be done to assist them in understanding such evidence, or an alternative method of deciding such cases should be substituted for the jury.

It should not be assumed that complicated evidence is the preserve of serious fraud trials alone, although these are, of course, the best example. Arcane medical and forensic evidence is often given in rape cases, for example, and the distinction between murder and manslaughter can turn on abstruse psychological material.

The Roskill Report (1986) recommended that juries should not hear complicated fraud trials which instead should be entrusted to a species of tribunal staffed by judges and professional assessors. The Report remained unimplemented despite continuing concern. In early 1995 a fraud trial costing an estimated £2 million collapsed after six months at Newport Crown Court because the trial judge (Judge Crowther) ruled that the evidence was too difficult for the jury to understand. In early 1996 Ian and Kevin Maxwell were acquitted after a lengthy serious fraud trial at the Old Bailey. These may, of course, have been correct verdicts but there was considerable public surprise at them and concern was expressed in the newspapers and by some politicians to the effect that the jury may have become so confused by the evidence that they felt bound to give the benefit of the doubt to the accused.

The Maxwell trial is also interesting because it illustrates the different method of selection now used in such cases. In theory jury service is a possibility for anyone between the ages of 18 and 70 who has lived in this country for a minimum of five years. However, the new Criminal Justice Act 2003 has since abolished the categories of ineligibility and excusal as of right. It is now the responsibility of the potential juror to show 'good reason' why he or she should not serve. This means that the pool of eligible jurors has increased significantly . However, when it comes to complex trials which may last six months or more the officials in the Department of Constitutional Affairs, which sends out the summonses for jury service, are more accommodating and sympathetic in hearing requests from individuals who wish to be excused because of their jobs, booked holidays, etc. The outcome may be a jury which is chosen from those who are available rather than from a general cross-section of society. In a letter to *The Times* (23 January 1996) Lord Donaldson, a former Master of the Rolls, made the following comment on serious fraud trials:

> 'They are not tried by traditional juries but by a new variety of the species, consisting of men and women specially selected for their ability to devote so much time to jury service. Inevitably they are those who would not otherwise be more gainfully occupied and who have no pressing commitments in the period of the trial. As such they are wholly unrepresentative.'

Implicit in such criticism also is the view that such a jury may lack sufficient intellect to understand the evidence, as well as possibly lack responsibility to deliver an objective and carefully considered verdict.

It has therefore been argued that, instead of changing traditional random selection methods for complicated cases, compensation should be paid by the state to employers and employees who suffer disruption as a result of long jury service, and that compensation should also be paid to those who have to cancel holidays or who suffer similar inconvenience. Attention could then be switched to giving the typical jury better guidance during a complicated case of any description. Such guidance could necessitate changes in the way the evidence is presented, eg, dispensing with lengthy speeches from counsel, minimising the use of jargon and technicality, and making more use of audio-visual aids to assist communication. Perhaps even the computerisation of evidence could be considered, with each juror being provided with his/her own laptop computer for use during the trial. The latter reform depends for its success on the computer literacy of the jury and would justify modification of the random selection principle: but at least this would be likely to produce a more suitable juror than the more negative methods used in the Maxwell trial and similar cases.

In the end it may be that the institution of the jury has become unadaptable to try the complicated trials that now bedevil the criminal justice system. Apart from the Roskill suggestion of a panel of judge and assessors, other alternatives to jury trial are trial by judge sitting alone, or trial by a composite tribunal of lawyers and lay people. For serious fraud cases it may even be necessary to consider alternative ways of regulating such anti-social behaviour, eg, by regulatory penalties rather than criminal penalties. This is the system used in some American states where the Securities and Exchange Commission administers the process of discipline as an alternative to the adversary system of trial. Such an approach was supported by the Royal Commission on Criminal Justice (1993) and by Auld LJ in his subsequent review (see below).

The jury system, therefore, needs to be subject to proper research and for this purpose it is essential that the ban imposed by s8 of the Contempt of Court Act 1981 is lifted. The Government in 2001 appointed Sir Robin Auld to review the criminal justice and the jury systems. The Auld review in relation to juries recommends the following: abolishing the use of juries completely in fraud trials; replacing juries with a specifically trained single judge; retaining jury trial, albeit with some restrictions, or replacing the randomly selected jury with a specially selected jury based on skill, qualifications and knowledge. The Criminal Justice Act 2003 has implemented some of the Auld recommendations: see, for example, ss41 and 321 of the 2003 Act.

Chapter 7

The Legal Profession

7.1   Introduction

7.2   Key points

7.3   Key cases and statutes

7.4   Question and suggested solution

7.1 Introduction

The legal profession in England and Wales is a divided profession with both barristers and solicitors. There has been much debate as to whether the system should be retained in its present form or be fused. This chapter will consider in outline the functions of each branch profession and finally will consider the reforms to the system, including the system of payment for legal services. Minor changes were introduced by the Courts and Legal Services Act 1990 and the Access to Justice Act 1999 brought about further changes.

7.2 Key points

Solicitors

The Law Society is the controlling body of solicitors. It is the Law Society that has the power to make rules regulating professional practice and the conduct and discipline of solicitors. The nature of solicitors' work may require the enforcement of regulations. The Solicitors' Disciplinary Tribunal was set up by the Solicitors Act 1974. A new complaints body, the Office for the Supervision of Solicitors (Ofsol) also began work in September 1996.

Qualifying as a solicitor

Where a graduate has a law degree, he must follow this by completing the Legal Practice Course (formerly Law Society Finals). Once this has been passed the graduate must complete two years of a training contract (formerly articles).

A non-law graduate is required to take the Common Professional Examination, otherwise known as the Graduate Diploma in Law, which is a one-year full-time course (two years part-time), in which the student is expected to pass the seven core subjects essential for a QLD (Qualifying Law Degree) in addition to a research module. Having passed the GDLP (Graduate Diploma in Law Programme), the student must pass the Legal Practice Course and complete the training contract.

It is only after this process that the entrant will be admitted and his name put on the roll.

Rights of audience

Solicitors have automatic rights of audience in the following:

a) magistrates' court;

b) county courts;

c) certain tribunals;

d) Crown Court – where the proceedings are on appeal from the magistrates' court to the Crown Court or the case has been referred to the Crown Court for sentencing: see *Practice Direction* [1972] 1 All ER 608 and s12 Courts Act 1971;

e) The European Court.

The Courts and Legal Services Act 1990 contains provisions that will affect the rights of audience. The former Lord Chancellor's Department created the Advisory Committee on Legal Education and Conduct (ACLEC) which has now been abolished by the Access to Justice Act 1999, which in turn has established the Legal Services Consultative Panel (LSCP) whose main function is to assist in the maintenance and development of standards in education, training and conduct of all persons offering legal services.

Consequently, the Law Society has established training courses in advocacy skills for solicitors in private practice who wished to obtain an advocacy certificate. The Law Society announced that it would grant such certificates to solicitors who passed the tests on these courses and who can show three years' regular practice of advocacy in the magistrates' and county courts. The certificates grant the right to appear as an advocate in all proceedings in the higher courts, eg Crown Courts and the High Court. The first solicitor-advocates began to appear in High Court proceedings in the spring of 1994. It is clear that the Access to Justice Act 1999 has brought about a simpler and cheaper system of qualification for solicitors. The Higher Rights Qualification Regulations 2000 provided three routes to qualification, namely: exemption, accreditation and development. By April 2003, a total of 1,768 solicitors had qualified for rights of audience in the higher courts. See also the Law Society website: www.lawsociety.org.uk for more details

Liability of a solicitor

a) A solicitor can be sued in tort or contract by third parties (in contract the action will be governed by the rules of agency).

The Legal Profession

b) The solicitor owes contractual and tortious duties of care to his client.

c) There is limited immunity from an action in damages where the solicitor is carrying out litigation work: see *Saif Ali v Sydney Mitchell & Co* [1978] 3 All ER 1033.

This may now be interpreted restrictively in the light of the House of Lords' decision: *Arthur J S Hall v Simons* [2000] 3 WLR 543.

Barristers

The General Council of the Bar consists of representatives of all sections of the Bar and is responsible for the implementation of the Code of Conduct. Unlike solicitors, the Bar is not regulated by any statutory instruments.

Qualifying as a barrister:

a) As with solicitors, a non-law graduate must take a conversion course (CPE).

b) The next stage is termed the vocational stage and graduates are required to become members of one of the four Inns of Court. All graduates wishing to practise in the UK must complete the Bar Vocational Course. They can then be 'called' to the Bar.

c) The final stage is the practical stage whereby the entrant must undertake a year of pupillage. This is also known as 'work shadowing' a barrister.

Rules of conduct

a) The cab-rank rule is one of the most important rules governing barristers. The rule requires a barrister to accept any brief within his professional competence, regardless of how his client is being funded, the nature of the case or any other factor.

b) A barrister must draw the court's attention to all relevant authorities even if they may be harmful to his case.

c) A barrister is not permitted to conceal facts from the court, especially if his client has made an admission of guilt to him.

Barrister's liability

a) It used to be the case that barristers enjoyed immunity from being sued for negligent work in court: *Rondel v Worsley* [1969] 1 AC 191 (HL). However, the House of Lords in the case of *Arthur J S Hall v Simons* (see above) abolished this protection, thereby making all barristers potentially liable for negligence per se.

b) A barrister may not sue for his fee even though his relationship with his client is based upon contract, but the instructing solicitor is liable for the barrister's fees.

c) A barrister may potentially be sued by his instructing solicitor for negligent advice under the rule in *Hedley Byrne & Co v Heller & Partners Ltd* [1964] AC 465.

Reforms of the legal profession

The profession has undergone considerable change instituted by both governing bodies and legislation and reports, eg the Royal Commission on Legal Services (1979) (the Benson Commission) and the Marre Committee Report (1988) and the Courts and Legal Services Act 1990, and more recently the Access to Justice Act 1999. See also the former Lord Chancellor's White Paper: *Modernising Justice* (www.dca.gov.uk).

Barristers

The reforms instituted by the Bar's governing body improve conditions for the practising Bar and in particular for younger barristers. For example:

a) a system of funded pupillages;

b) lifting restrictions on setting up chambers;

c) removal of the need for a barrister's clerk;

d) an improved complaints machinery covering 'shoddy work';

e) lifting restrictions on the advertising of the Bar's specialist skills.

Solicitors

The reforms instituted by the Law Society appear to be less wide ranging:

a) firms of solicitors are required to operate a formal system to handle client complaints;

b) solicitors are now permitted to publicise specialisation or expertise in particular areas of the law.

c) the establishment of a complaints body to receive complaints from the public body (Office for the Supervision of Solicitors (OSS)).

In July 2003 the Legal Services Ombudsman delivered her Annual Report for 2002–2003 which disclosed a disappointing complaints handling procedure, particularly the workings of the OSS. The Legal Services Ombudsman investigates any allegation which relates to the manner in which a complaint to a professional body has been dealt with. The Legal Services Ombudsman has the power to have the complaint reconsidered by the professional body in question or to require that compensation be paid.

Other suggestions for reforms

The main thrust of the reforms is aimed at abolishing the conventional monopolies held by the respective professions, for example solicitors' conveyancing monopoly, abolition of the probate and litigation monopolies, and abolition of the Bar's monopoly over rights of audience. Arguably this closes the gap between the professions and encourages fusion.

The Legal Profession

The Access to Justice 1999 also set up the Legal Services Consultative Panel which monitors and advises the profession on whether or not they should retain their right to be self-regulating.

In March 2000 the Office of Fair Trading issued a report on widening the access to justice and the delimitation of consumer choice.

In July 2003 the Department for Constitutional Affairs published a Consultation Paper which questioned Queen's Counsel status. The Department also set up an independent review of the regulatory framework for legal services aimed at promoting competition and innovation, and improving services for the customer. For full details see the Department for Constitutional Affairs website: www.dca.gov.uk/legalservices.

7.3 Key cases and statutes

- *Arthur J S Hall* v *Simons* [2000] 3 WLR 543
  Barristers no longer enjoy any form of immunity

- *White* v *Jones* [1995] 2 AC 207
  Solicitors and barristers are both liable in negligence

- Access to Justice Act 1999 – introduced changes to both professions, increased solicitors' rights of audience, created multi-disciplinary partnerships – promoted 'conditional fee' arrangements

- Courts and Legal Services Act 1990 – attempted fusion of the professions and introduced some internal changes

7.4 Question and suggested solution

Note: There have been no specific questions set on this topic since 1999.

'The introduction of conditional fees under the Courts and Legal Services Act 1990 and, now, under the Access to Justice Act 1999, will solve the problems of paying for legal services experienced by litigants on low incomes.'

How far do you agree with the above statement?

Adapted from University of London LLB Examination
(for External Students) English Legal System June 1994 Q4

General Comment

For students hoping for a straightforward question on legal services this question must be a big disappointment. It invites detailed critical analysis of the relatively new concept of conditional fees and only those students who have made the effort to research the topic in specialist articles would be entitled to feel confident of tackling it. The question illustrates the challenge that can be presented to a London LLB external student, particularly as it is worded in such a way as to invite an immediate challenge on the ground that it is based on a fallacy.

Skeleton Solution

Exposing the fallacy of the assertion in question – explaining the scope of s58 Courts and Legal Services Act 1990 – the implications for a winning client's compensation – views of Department for Constitutional Affairs – the risk of damaging lawyers' integrity by creating a conflict of interests – the costs problem and comparison with the American system of contingency fees – Law Society proposals for insurance cover against costs in conditional fees cases – assess the changes introduced by the Access to Justice Act 1999.

Suggested Solution

It is debatable whether the conditional fee system contained in Courts and Legal Services Act (CLSA) 1990, s58 was aimed at 'low income' litigants because the latter will normally be covered by legal funding managed by the Legal Services Commission (LSC). The system was probably intended as a supplement to the reduced legal funding service and therefore aimed more at those in the 'middle-income' trap, ie those rich enough to be ineligible for legal funding but poor enough to worry about the costs of losing a case. Even if this group are regarded as 'low income litigants' for the purpose of the question under discussion it must be considered doubtful whether, by itself, the system can solve the problem.

Section 58(2) of the CLSA 1990 defines a conditional fee agreement (CFA) as 'an agreement with a person providing advocacy or litigation services which provides for his fee and expenses, or any part of them, to be payable only in specified circumstances.' That simply means, if the lawyer wins the case, then he gets the 'agreed' fees, but if he loses, then he gets nothing.

However, for CFAs to be binding, certain prescribed conditions must be followed. For instance, the agreements must be in writing, they must satisfy the requirements as specified by the Secretary of State for Constitutional Affairs and must conform to regulations. CFAs are prohibited in relation to criminal matters and virtually all family cases.

Interestingly, s29 provides that insurance premiums for policies insuring against the risk of losing the case may be recovered in costs awarded by the court. This is because the rule that the losing party must pay the winners' costs remains unchanged.

Under the CLSA 1990, CFAs only applied to personal injury, insolvency and human rights cases, but with the advent of the Access to Justice Act 1999 the Secretary of State for Constitutional Affairs has extended CFAs to all other areas of civil law, except family law and criminal law. This means that CFAs are set to become a fundamental method of funding legal cases, since the Act removes state funding.

Advantages and disadvantages of CFAs will now be considered. In terms of advantages CFAs cost the state absolutely nothing, thereby allowing resources to be applied to the more 'needy' cases. Additionally, CFAs offer wider access to justice (the only requirement being insuring against losing a case). CFAs also increase competition, thus producing more efficient and competent professionals, and cover all areas except civil family law and criminal law. CFAs are more readily accepted by the public – for example, research by the Lord Chancellor's Department reveals that by 1999 25,000 CFAs were signed and in operation.

The disadvantages are that CFAs will only encourage solicitors to take on cases which have a high chance of success, leaving the 50/50 cases out. This might perhaps explain why clinical negligence cases have been maintained within the state-funded system. Insuring against losing a case may prove to be a costly affair. If the idea is to receive funds to assist in the litigation, then to spend money on an insurance policy prior to the case going to trial does not make sense or appear logical. Further, the Bar has criticised the idea of allowing lawyers a financial interest in the outcome of a case on the basis that it might lead to compromising standards and conflicts of interest. There may also be pressure from the insurance companies to settle the case for fear of paying out in the event the insured loses a case. Clearly, the interest of the insurance company is competing with the interests of the litigant in this respect.

The Department of Constitutional Affairs has strongly advocated the use of CFAs as part of a move to modernise and revolutionise the entire civil and criminal justice systems, as well as making the legal profession more accessible. The Government is currently considering introducing collective CFAs. These are designed for bulk users of legal services – for example, insurers and trade unions.

Chapter 8

Tribunals and Alternative Dispute Resolution

8.1 Introduction

8.2 Key points

8.3 Key case and statutes

8.4 Question and suggested solution

8.1 Introduction

Tribunals developed in the late 1940s and are now an established and useful part of the English legal system dealing with more cases than the county courts. Alternative dispute resolution is a newer but growing area. The former Lord Chancellor, Lord Irvine, showed a keen interest in this American import. See also, in this respect, the changes introduced by Auld LJ in *Criminal Courts Review and Criminal Justice: The Way Ahead* (2001): www.dca.gov.uk; www.criminal-courts-review.org.uk.

8.2 Key points

Tribunals

Organisation and role

a) This is supervised by the Council on Tribunals under the Tribunals and Inquiries Act 1992.

b) Tribunals specialise in dealing with specific subject matter such as the Employment Tribunals or Social Security Appeal Tribunals.

c) The internal organisation varies from tribunal to tribunal. Some general points are common:

   i) They are not part of the main court hierarchy.

   ii) However, if a case is within the tribunal's jurisdiction it must be commenced there.

   iii) Tribunals often use the Court of Appeal as a higher appellate body.

iv) To hear cases they will use a chairman with legal knowledge assisted by two lay-wingmen (not lawyers) from the relevant specialist background.

d) Other examples of administrative tribunals are the National Insurance Tribunal, the Rent Review Tribunal, the Inland Revenue Tribunal and the Immigration Appeals Tribunal.

Characteristics

They were essentially introduced to provide cheap, quick and informal processes for decision-making. The Franks Report (1957) Cmnd 218 identified three key features: 'openness, fairness and impartiality'.

a) To encourage informality, procedures are not governed by strict rules.

b) The chairman may choose whatever approach best suits that aim of informality.

c) Litigants in person are encouraged.

d) Legal funding is, therefore, not available, in order to discourage the use of legal representatives. This has led to discussion and criticism.

e) In recent years, tribunals have been criticised for becoming inflexible in their approach and procedures and for excessive 'legalism'.

Reforms

In 2000/2001 tribunals were the subject of a major review undertaken by Sir Andrew Legatt (a retired Lord Justice of Appeal) at the request of the then Lord Chancellor. The report of the review, *Tribunals for Users: One System, One Service*, was published in 2001 and can be consulted at www.tribunals-review.org.uk. The website of the Council on Tribunals is: www.council-on-tribunals.gov.uk. The main concern of the review was the conformity of the tribunal system with the Human Rights Act 1998.

Alternative dispute resolution

The phrase 'alternative dispute resolution' (ADR) encompasses several possibilities, all designed to find ways of resolving disputes without using the court system. The aim is to reduce time and costs and sometimes acrimony so as to allow for an ongoing relationship between the parties. It is formally encouraged in the Commercial Court: *Practice Note* [1996] 3 All ER 383 (QBD).

Settlement

This is the most commonly known form of ADR, and is used in many civil cases. Whilst it is quicker and cheaper than a full trial, questions have arisen as to the equality of bargaining power between the parties and undue pressure on the claimant.

Ombudsmen

A recent trend, often found in the financial services sector. The Courts and Legal Services Act 1990 created the office of the Legal Ombudsman to deal with allegations of misconduct or negligent services in the legal profession.

Arbitration

An informal system of trial operates for small claims in the county court and often by agreement between the parties in commercial matters. The parties will often agree in advance of a dispute to use an arbitrator and be bound by his decision. The system has the advantages of speed, privacy and in some cases specialist knowledge. Arbitrations are presided over by arbitrators who are commonly barristers.

Conciliation

Here the conciliator plays a more active and interventionist role. He brings both parties together and suggests solutions to help achieve a settlement.

Mediation

A mediator is more of an evaluater. He assesses the strengths and weaknesses of the case before him, assists the parties in defining the issues and helps them come to an agreement. Once an agreement is reached a contract can be drawn up.

Reforms

A research was carried out by Professor Hazel Genn in 1998 on the use of the mediation scheme at the Central London County Court, and is available for consultation on the Department for Constitutional Affairs website at www.dca.gov.uk/research/1998/598 esfr.htm.

A consultation paper, entitled *Alternative Dispute Resolution – A Discussion Paper* (1999), is also available at www.open.gov.uk/dca/consult/civ-just/adr/section1.htm.

8.3 Key case and statutes

- *Peach Grey & Co* v *Somners* [1995] 2 All ER 513
  Distinguishes tribunals from ordinary courts
- Arbitration Act 1996 – aimed to promote commercial arbitration by providing a clear framework for its use
- Tribunals and Inquiries Act 1992 – provided for appeals to the High Court from some important tribunals

Tribunals and Alternative Dispute Resolution

8.4 Question and suggested solution

Consider the alternative means available to resolve a legal dispute other than by way of a court hearing. Your answer should specify any advantages that such means may have over a court hearing.

University of Wolverhampton LLB (Hons) by Distance Learning
English Legal System Examination September 1993 Q3

General Comment

This is a straightforward question provided the candidate has a thorough knowledge of all the alternatives and puts some thought into their suitability.

Skeleton Solution

Introduction: adversarial process; expense; delay; complexity – need for alternatives – tribunals: origins; features; success – alternative dispute resolution: settlement; arbitration; Ombudsmen; conciliation; mini-trials; the features and success of ADR – conclusion.

Suggested Solution

The English legal system is said by many to be the envy of the world. However, it is not without criticism especially when it comes to the finer points of procedure and processes. Based on an adversarial system, the court hearing is intended to elicit the facts through a 'contest' between the two sides with the judge acting as umpire. This process can be daunting for the uninitiated. Furthermore, the complex rules that surround it mean that expensive legal representation is required and the litigant is often left bemused, out of pocket and far from feeling that he has had a fair hearing. This expense and complexity, along with the delay caused by an increasingly overburdened civil system have led to the growth of alternatives, often intended to provide a more efficient and less hostile solution to the dispute. It should be noted that these alternatives are only appropriate to civil proceedings. Broadly speaking, they can be divided into the headings of tribunals and alternative dispute resolution (ADR).

The origins of the tribunal system can be found in the late 1940s and early 1950s. Despite their legal 'youth' tribunals are now an established part of the legal system, dealing with more cases each year than the county courts, and regulated by legislation: Tribunal and Inquiries Act 1992. They operate alongside the main court hierarchy, with compulsory jurisdiction over their subject matter and often an ultimate right of appeal to the Court of Appeal. They were introduced to provide a quick, cheap and informal forum for decision making. The Franks Report of 1957 was the first thorough examination of their use and identified three valuable characteristics of 'openness, fairness and impartiality'. These were reaffirmed by Sir Andrew Legatt in his review of tribunals in 2001.

These characteristics are advantages of the system and to a large extent still exist today.

The internal organisation of tribunals is generally intended to be quite unlike that of the traditional adversarial court hearing. Specific tribunals now deal with specific areas of law eg Employment Tribunals, Employment Appeal Tribunals, Social Security Appeal Tribunals. Cases are heard by a legally qualified chairman assisted by two specialist lay advisers from the appropriate field of expertise (known as wing members), which allows for a more balanced final decision. The litigant in person is encouraged and no strict rules of evidence and procedure apply, in order to try and foster the feeling of informality and accessibility. The lack of legal representation should ensure costs are minimal and opponents 'equal'.

Whilst they are acknowledged to have avoided many of the problems of the main court system, there are criticisms to be made of tribunals. Legal funding is not available (in order to discourage legal representation) but this does not prevent the wealthy party (eg an employer) from using his lawyer to represent him, nor does it allow for the expertise of a Government social security administrator who may appear before a tribunal on a regular basis. Increasingly, tribunals are criticised for becoming inflexible in the approach with excessive legalisation of their procedures. This is especially true where lawyers are often used or where decisions are reported, as in the case of Employment Tribunals, creating a system of precedent. The Social Security Appeal Tribunals have been criticised for arbitrary decisions and procedures, particularly with the growth of more complex rules of administration and narrower rights of appeal. They are also often not without delay and confusion!

Despite these criticisms tribunals still remain a valuable and indeed essential part of the legal process which is much more accessible to the individual than the courts.

Alternative dispute resolution, or ADR as it is known, is an area of growing importance in the modern legal system. Its popularity is due to the general features of speed, economy and, in particular, privacy and comparative lack of hostility. The phrase covers several different approaches which are usually used at the choice of the parties, unlike tribunals with their compulsory jurisdiction.

Perhaps the commonest form of ADR is the traditional concept of 'settlement', ie where two parties have commenced proceedings but through negotiation reach an out of court settlement, bringing an end to the matter. This is undoubtedly quicker than going to full trial (although it often takes place 'at the doors of the court') and removes the uncertainties of judicial decision-making. However, there have been criticisms regarding undue pressure on the claimant, especially against an experienced and powerful defendant, to settle at an unreasonably low level of damages. But it is a part of the civil process which is now essential: without many cases being settled, the civil system would be subject to even more delay and possibly even collapse.

Arbitration is another well known form of ADR, now partially regulated by legislation (Arbitration Act 1996) and an everyday part of commercial life. This involves the parties agreeing (sometimes at contract stage) to use a specialist arbitrator to decide any dispute. This is not a process of negotiation as the arbitrator will make a decision which is legally binding (though the jurisdiction of the courts cannot be ousted). It is favoured because of its speed, the specialist knowledge of the arbitrator, privacy and, in commercial matters, the ability to maintain an on going business relationship. It is sometimes regarded as a cheaper means of dispute resolution, although this is not always the case. One example of arbitration is the small claims procedure in the county court (now known as the small claims track) where all claims for less than £5,000 are automatically referred to the district judge who will hold an informal, sometimes inquisitorial hearing to decide the issues. Survey statistics suggest that even the losing party feels the small claims track is fair.

A newer development is that of the Ombudsman, often seen in the financial services sector and now a part of the general legal system since the Courts and Legal Services Act 1990. Such a person is intended to investigate and whenever possible resolve allegations of misconduct without the need for any form of hearing. Whilst this clearly removes the anxiety and expense of normal legal proceedings, some Ombudsmen have been criticised for lacking any real disciplinary powers.

The newest form of ADR is that of conciliation, not to be confused with reconciliation or arbitration. This involves negotiation under the guidance of a specialist third party whose expertise lies not in the legal issues but in the skills of mediation. The conciliator assists the parties in finding a compromise, without imposing a decision. This process is very popular in the United States where many major corporations regard it as an essential part of any potential proceedings, saving them billions of dollars. In the United Kingdom it is in its infancy, although it has great potential in family and commercial matters due to the privacy, speed, low costs and amicable nature of the process. Pilot schemes have been greeted with praise but the system has not yet received Government backing, although a voluntary scheme – the Centre for Alternative Dispute Resolution – is achieving growing success.

There has also been minor use in the UK of 'mini-trials' where both parties agree to conduct a trial before a chosen expert (eg a QC) who will give a legally based decision. An obvious advantage here is again speed, but the parties also feel that they have had a chance to properly present and argue their case before a legal authority. To date, the American west coast concept of 'Rent a Judge' where retired judges can be hired to hear legal arguments has not spread to the English legal system!

In conclusion, there are nowadays many alternatives to the traditional adversarial process. Whilst these enjoy varying degrees of success, it is submitted that anything that helps to reduce the problems of a constantly criticised civil system is worthwhile. In this respect, the recent changes introduced in both the civil and criminal justice systems lends support to the argument that we are heading in the right direction.

Chapter 9

Legal Services and Funding

9.1 Introduction

9.2 Key points

9.3 Key statutes

9.4 Questions and suggested solutions

9.1 Introduction

In April 2000 civil legal aid was largely replaced by the new legal services scheme provided for in the Access to Justice Act (AJA) 1999. The Act created the Criminal Defence Service (CDS) (replacing criminal legal aid) and the Community Legal Service (replacing civil legal aid).

This effectively made redundant the previous framework for the provision of legal aid established by the Legal Aid Act 1988.

9.2 Key points

The Legal Services Commission

a) The Commission was established by s1 AJA 1999. It replaced the Legal Aid Board and now acts as the administrative body.

b) It consists of seven to 12 members, appointed by the Secretary of State for Constitutional Affairs according to their knowledge of social conditions, work of the courts, consumer affairs and management.

c) Section 2 provides for the creation of two bodies, one civil and one criminal.

d) Section 3 empowers the Commission to make contracts, loans, investments, undertake enquiries and advise the Secretary of State for Constitutional Affairs.

The Community Legal Service (CLS)

a) Section 4 states that the CLS is to provide funding for the following civil law matters: legal advice and assistance, representation, enforcement of judgments and the provision of information on law and legal services.

b) The source of financing comes from the Community Legal Fund which has a ceiling.

c) The following matters are excluded from funding:

   i) personal injury claims, death and damage to property;

   ii) defamation;

   iii) claims involving sums less than £5,000;

   iv) most tribunal hearings, except immigration and mental health.

d) The criteria for funding:

   i) under s8 the CLS prepares a funding code, supervised by the Secretary of State for Constitutional Affairs, which sets out the criteria;

   ii) s10 states the instances where recipients would be asked to pay a fixed fee or make contributions as appropriate;

   iii) s11 provides for costs against a funded litigant (this should be a reasonable amount, taking into consideration his resources and making allowances for personal effects and tools of trade).

e) One of the more radical initiatives introduced by the CLS is the provision of funding to appointed firms of solicitors through a franchise programme. Firms go through a tight audit before qualifying as a franchisee.

Conditional fees agreements (CFAs)

Section 58 CLSA 1990 permitted the Secretary of State for Constitutional Affairs to make delegated legislation to allow lawyers to operate a 'conditional fee' system under which a lawyer may agree to accept a case on the basis that if he loses it he will not be paid a fee. It would allow a lawyer who wins a case under a conditional fee to be paid up to double his normal fee, with the uplift coming out of the general costs paid by the losing party or, if no such costs are available, out of the winning claimant's damages. A losing party who engaged a lawyer on a conditional fee will have no fee to pay but will still face a costs bill. Conditional fees are different from the USA system of 'contingency fees' under which each side pays their own costs and the lawyer may bargain for a percentage of his client's compensation if he wins the case for that client. The UK system became operational in September 1995 and is at present limited to personal injury, insolvency and human rights cases.

The Access to Justice Act 1999 also gives discretion to the courts to make order for costs as appropriate. The Conditional Fee Agreements (Miscellaneous Amendments) Regulations 2003 discuss the enforceability of these agreements and the liability of solicitors to clients under them.

It remains to be seen whether this 'no win, no fee' scheme sustains the interest it currently holds. There have been serval cases in this area, including *Halloran* v *Delaney* [2003] 1 WLR 28; *Re Claims Direct Test Cases* [2003] 4 All ER 508; and *Hollins* v *Russell* [2003] 4 All ER 590.

For further information and details, see: www.legalservices.gov.uk; www.justask.org.uk and www.hmso.gov.uk.

The Criminal Defence Service (CDS)

a) Section 12 establishes a CDS for the purpose of securing that individuals involved in criminal investigations or criminal proceedings have access to 'such advice, assistance and representation as the interests of justice require'.

b) The Criminal Defence Service (Advice and Assistance) Act 2001 expanded the scope of s13 AJA 1999, so that it is now extended to cover schemes like the duty solicitor and ABWOR (assistance by way of representation).

c) Section 15 states that the entitled recipient is allowed to choose his own legal representation subject to satisfying the requirements of the Commission.

d) Section 16 obliges the Commission to prepare a Code of Conduct for its employees and funded providers which, inter alia, includes a duty of non-discrimination and other duties to the court.

e) Section 17 empowers the court to order the recipient to pay for some or all of their representation.

f) As far as budgeting is concerned, there is no fixed budget for the funding of criminal cases. It is purely demand-based. Alternative sources of funding will be considered should the demand exceed the supply (for example, the transfer of funds from the CLS to the CDS).

Alternative legal services

When discussing sources of legal advice it is important to consider those sources outside of the main legal profession.

a) Law centres – provide a less formal environment for advice, usually based in a town's high street with a 'shop frontage' to make them more approachable.

   i) They are not centrally administered or funded and so exist on a haphazard and voluntary basis.

   ii) They provide a valuable and informal first source of advice for many people.

   iii) They have been criticised for bias in the way in which they tackle local community issues, sometimes bringing actions against local authorities.

b) Citizens Advice Bureaux – are centrally organised by the National Association of Citizens Advice Bureaux (NACAB) though not centrally funded.

   i) Their provision is more uniform with one in almost every town.

   ii) They assist with all kinds of advice, not just legal issues.

Legal Services and Funding

  iii) They are well recognised as a valuable agency but are beginning to suffer from lack of funding.

c) Other advice agencies

  i) These may take various forms and their existence will be dependent upon localised needs and financing.

  ii) Examples would be Legal Advice Centres, Neighbourhood Advice Centres, Housing Advice Centres and so on.

d) Free Representation Unit (FRU)

  This is run largely on a voluntary basis by trainee barristers and solicitors.

  i) It receives some funding from the Law Society and Bar Council.

  ii) It provides representation (free) in matters involving unfair dismissal, social security claims, sex or race discrimination and immigration cases.

  iii) It only exists in London.

  iv) In the summer of 1996 the Bar established a Pro Bono Unit, run on a charitable basis, under which a register of barristers is kept. Those on the register are prepared to offer up to three days of their time to deserving cases in any field of law in cases where the applicant would otherwise be unable to afford legal advice or representation, provided the case does not require the assistance of a solicitor (unless the referring solicitor, or another solicitor, volunteers to assist).

e) Media, motoring organisations, trade associations, unions and professional bodies all provide valuable sources of legal advice ranging from a 'legal problem page' to specialist advice and representation.

f) An alternative method of funding legal representation can be found in the form of legal expenses insurance.

9.3 Key statutes

- Access to Justice Act 1999 – set up a new regime to govern the granting of civil and criminal legal funding – set up the Community Legal Services (CLS) to provide funding for civil matters – set up the Criminal Defence Service (CDS) to provide funding for criminal matters – extended the rights of audience for solicitors

- Conditional Fee Agreements (Miscellaneous Amendments) Regulations 2003 – provides a simplified definition of a conditional fee agreement

- Courts and Legal Services Act 1990 – introduced the conditional fee system (no win, no fee) (the AJA 1999 promotes conditional fees strenuously)

9.4 Questions and suggested solutions

QUESTION ONE

Evaluate the advantages and disadvantages of the recent reforms to the legal aid system in England and Wales.

> University of London LLB Examination
> (for External Students) English Legal System June 2001 Q4

General Comment

Whilst this seems to be a straightforward question, it requires a critical appreciation of the developments affecting legal aid in recent times. Students should be conversant with all the changes and developments in this area and thus be able to evaluate advantages and disadvantages.

Skeleton Solution

Purpose of the legal aid scheme – the need for reforms – the actual reforms – the nature of the changes and how they affect accessibility – is it reflective of a fair system? – is it a fundamental right or a privilege or luxury? – advantages and disadvantages.

Suggested Solution

The Access to Justice Act (AJA) 1999 has replaced the framework for legal aid as established by its predecessor, the Legal Aid Act 1988. Briefly, the 1999 Act brought into operation a new regime to govern civil legal aid in April 2000, and a new framework to regulate criminal legal aid was introduced in April 2001.

One of the main reasons for the 'dire need for reforms' was the costs issue, which was 'spiralling out of control'. The previous Government was spending billions but yet was not successful in realising the aims and objectives of the legal aid system. This 'unmet legal need' was still an issue for the new Government. In 2000, research conducted by the Lord Chancellor's Department (now the Department for Constitutional Affairs) revealed that the unmet legal need was caused by several factors, such as: the high cost of legal fees; fear of lawyers; fear of cost; lawyers' lack of training and unwillingness to serve poor clients' needs for advice in welfare law; the inaccessibility of lawyers' offices for poor or rural clients; the creation of new legal rights without the funding to enforce them; peoples ignorance that the law could solve their problem; and the fact that the legal aid scheme omitted certain services, such as representation at tribunals (Eddey & Darbyshire, *English Legal System* (7th edn, 2001)).

Section 1 Access to Justice Act 1999 established the Legal Services Commission (LSC), the new governing and regulatory body responsible for the administration of legal funding. It is a body appointed by the Lord Chancellor consisting of seven to 12 members. Section 2 AJA 1999 provided for the creation of the Community Legal Service (CLS) and the Criminal Defence Service (CDS), and s3 AJA 1999 provided the

LSC with sufficient jurisdiction to undertake inquiries, to make contracts, loans and investments, and accordingly advise the Lord Chancellor.

The reason for creating a new CLS to regulate civil legal funding is reflected in s4 AJA 1999, which states:

> '... for the purpose of promoting the availability to individuals of services of the descriptions specified ... and, in particular, for securing (within the resources available) ... that individuals have access to services that effectively meet their needs.'

The new civil regime introduced a new funding criteria, which is given to successful firms of solicitors on a 'franchise basis'. The money for this comes from the Community Legal Fund. The CLS also introduced conditional fee arrangements, which basically echo the 'no win, no fee' practice.

The CDS was established under s12 AJA 1999 for the purpose of securing that individuals who are involved in criminal investigations or criminal proceedings have access to 'such advice, assistance and representation as the interests of justice require'. It is funded in a similar way to the CLS, by the issue of 'franchise contracts', grants or loans, or through the establishing and maintenance of advice and assistance bodies. It includes assistance by way of representation (ABWOR) and the duty solicitor scheme. Unlike its predecessor, these services have now been extended to many magistrates' courts. The CDS also introduced the concept of Public Defenders, or salaried defenders, working for the CDS. The main advantages of the reforms may be summarised as follows:

1. to give the taxpayer, and, indeed all prospective litigants better value for money;
2. to ensure a 'level playing field' between those who qualify for legal funding and those who don't;
3. to end the 'milking' of legal aid by unscrupulous practitioners;
4. to place the burden on solicitors who have the 'franchise' to justify the funding of individual cases;
5. to require annual accounts to justify expenditure;
6. to provide free on-line advice to the public;
7. to encourage a litigant to pursue his claim as a result of the conditional fee arrangement (no win, no fee);
8. to allow the Law Society and the Bar Council to provide pro bono or charitable services.

The main disadvantages, on the other hand, are arguably:

1. it ignores the poor and the rural areas, and deters some prospective litigants from enforcing or defending their rights;

2. it restricts choice and does nothing to increase eligibility (the whole idea is to make legal aid more accessible) for help with funding cases;
3. it does not extend to the tribunals and alternative dispute resolution mechanisms;
4. it creates costly bureaucracy, and has a tendency to direct resources away from the needy to the bureaucrats;
5. the conditional fee arrangement is problematic and may not last long (contingency fees would be more beneficial and practical);
6. there is no fixed budget for criminal cases and the funding of such cases is demand led;
7. impecunious claimants and/or defendants may still be required to pay costs, which raises issues of fairness and accessibility;
8. the criteria for deciding eligibility for both civil and criminal funding still remains questionable;
9. the following categories are excluded by the CLS: all personal injury/negligence cases, defamation and cases involving a claim of less than £5,000;
10. even if a claimant wins the case, the statutory clawback (charging system) may mean that the claimant has little left at the end;
11. it encourages solicitors to become 'case choosy' and they may turn away cases which are 'triable' or 'test cases';
12. there is a lack of commitment and poor communication or response from practitioners;
13. the community centres and local law centres are still proving to be more effective in giving help to the public, and this raises the question of how the CLS has extended the element of accessibility.

It is perhaps too early to criticise the system, as it is only in its early stages. Perhaps time will be the best judge to evaluate the success of the reforms.

QUESTION TWO

What, in your view, are the advantages and disadvantages of the Lord Chancellor's package of reforms to the legal aid system?

University of London LLB Examination
(for External Students) English Legal System June 2000 Q3

General Comment

A straightforward question requiring an examination of the civil justice reforms affecting the legal aid system.

Skeleton Solution

A brief history of the legal aid system – recent reforms – advantages and disadvantages – conditional fees – Access to Justice Act 1999.

Suggested Solution

It is perhaps undeniable that under the doctrine of the Rule of Law, every person should be treated equally before the law, and that this means that everyone should have equal access to the law and to justice. Whether the old legal aid system achieved this has been the subject of endless debates and has indeed provided the basis and impetus for the Lord Chancellor (now the Secretary of State for Constitutional Affairs), who is responsible for legal services, to come up with a White Paper entitled *Modernising Justice*, which led to the passing of the Access to Justice Act (AJA) 1999. This Act replaced the framework for legal aid established by its predecessor, the Legal Aid Act 1988.

As a result of the coming into force of the AJA 1999, civil legal aid was largely replaced in April 2000. Similarly, criminal legal aid was also replaced in April 2001. Essentially, unlike the old system, the AJA 1999 provided for two new schemes. There is the Community Legal Service (CLS) which is responsible for civil matters, and the Criminal Defence Service (CDS) which is responsible for criminal matters. The Legal Services Commission (LSC) has supervisory jurisdiction over both the CLS and the CDS. These will now be examined in turn.

Section 1 AJA 1999 established the Legal Services Commission, which is the body that replaced the Legal Aid Board, and is now the administering body. It is made up of seven to 12 members appointed by the Lord Chancellor. Section 2 AJA 1999 allowed the CLS and the CDS to be created to replace the old civil and criminal schemes. Section 3 AJA 1999 provides the LSC with sufficient jurisdiction to undertake inquiries, to make contracts, loans and investments, and accordingly advise the Lord Chancellor.

The CLS was established by s4 AJA 1999, 'for the purpose of promoting the availability to individuals of services described as available under the civil justice system, and that individuals have access to services that effectively meet their needs'. To this end, s5 AJA 1999 provides the budget for the LSC to maintain a CLS fund. The LSC funds these services by entering into contracts with solicitors by way of a franchise, which basically means that solicitors who have successfully secured the franchise must manage the fund given to them and justify their expenditure on the basis of each case handled by them. This transfers the burden to the solicitors to show that their case or cases should be funded. The aim of the LSC in introducing the franchise scheme was to secure value for money. Hence, if solicitors feel that the chance of success in a case is unlikely to materialise, they are deterred from expending money given to them by the LSC. This leads to effective fund management on the part of the solicitors.

The apparent disadvantages of the CLS scheme were identified by the Consumers' Association in 2000 (Eddey & Darbyshire, *English Legal System* (7th edn, 2001) at p362).

The Association published research on people's experiences with obtaining help, especially those in vulnerable groups, and it showed:

1. concern about lack of commitment and poor communication from the lawyers;

2. community centres and law centres were more effective in giving help;

3. a lack of advisers in areas like social security, housing, disability discrimination, employment and immigration;

4. under the new scheme, only about 5,000 firms of solicitors have funding contracts (this is half the number who previously did legal aid work); this means that there is a distinct problem of 'access to justice' in certain areas where there are no solicitors doing publicly-funded work;

5. even those solicitors who do publicly-funded work cut back on the number of cases they take on board owing to low rates of pay;

6. the statutory charge (clawback system) may mean that a claimant may have nothing much left even though he/she has won the case;

7. the following categories are not funded by the CLS: all personal injury/negligence cases, defamation, almost all tribunal hearings (except immigration and mental heath) and cases where the quantum does not exceed £5,000.

It is interesting and intriguing to observe that in a review article by Yarrow in 2001 ((2001) 151 NLJ 998) no horns were sounded echoing the success of the CLS. So, those who are ineligible for public funding have to pay privately for legal services, and this can be expensive, particularly in London. This therefore discourages people from pursuing their rights. For this reason, the Lord Chancellor has developed the conditional fee arrangement (CFA). It was introduced by the Courts and Legal Services Act 1990 and extended recently by the AJA 1999. It echoes the much debated and publicised 'no win, no fee' arrangements between solicitors and clients. Under the AJA 1999, not only can the court order a losing party to pay the costs and success fee to the winning party, but it is also possible, by virtue of s29 AJA 1999, to insure against losing a case, which if won, the court may order the losing party to pay the cost of the insurance premiums. P Darbyshire, in her book (Eddey & Darbyshire, *English Legal System* (7th edn, 2001) at p356), argues that CFAs are complex and problematic and predicts that they will be abandoned eventually in favour of contingency fees.

The Criminal Defence Service (CDS) was established under s12 AJA 1999 for the purpose of securing that individuals who are involved in criminal investigations or criminal proceedings have access to 'such advice, assistance and representation as the interests of justice require'. It is funded in a similar way as the CLS, by the issue of franchise contracts, grants or loans or through the establishing and maintaining of advice and assistance bodies. Further, the Criminal Defence Service (Advice and Assistance) Act 2001 ensured that the scope of s13 covered the existing schemes, such as ABWOR (assistance by way of representation). A duty solicitor scheme, which is free, is available to those people who are arrested and held in custody at a police station. This service has also been extended to many magistrates' courts for people to receive free advice on their cases. The following observations can be made of the new CDS. The LSC decides which defendant, is in the interests of justice, entitled to state funding and there is not a fixed criteria for deciding this issue. Although there are salaried defenders (known as Public Defenders) working for the CDS, a defendant may choose an independent lawyer, but only from those firms which have secured a contract with the LSC. At the end of the case, a defendant may still be required to pay costs to the state. There is no fixed budget as the funding of criminal cases is demand led.

Perhaps it is a little early for judgments to be passed on the success or efficacy of the CDS. One should let time take its course to see whether the Lord Chancellor's efforts bear fruit.

QUESTION THREE

'The extension of conditional fees will significantly increase access to justice.'

Discuss this assertion in the context of proposed changes to the legal aid system of England and Wales.

University of London LLB Examination
(for External Students) English Legal System June 1999 Q4

General Comment

This is a question that should not be attempted unless one has a good knowledge of the nature and effect of conditional fee agreements – the controversial no win, no fee arrangement. The answer should explore the justification for the introduction of this arrangement and the extension of it, as well as the arguments that have been raised against it. There should also be comment on the duties of the Criminal Defence Service and the role of the Community Legal Service.

Skeleton Solution

Courts and Legal Services Act 1990, s58; Secretary of State for Constitutional Affairs' power to make orders specifying the proceedings; specifically excluded proceedings – nature and effect of conditional fee agreements; no win, no fee; lawyers and clients to share the risk of litigation; expenses paid by clients – justifications for introduction of conditional fees; counter arguments – extension of proceedings (1995); maximum amount of success fee – Legal Services Commission under Access to Justice Act 1999 – Criminal Defence Service.

Suggested Solution

Conditional fees were introduced into English law by s58 of the Courts and Legal

Services Act 1990. The Act allowed the Secretary of State for Constitutional Affairs to make orders specifying the proceedings in which agreements to charge on that basis could lawfully be made. The Act specifically excluded criminal and family proceedings from the newly authorised regime. Conditional fee agreements are also known as no win, no fee agreements, and the way they operate is to allow a lawyer to agree to take a case on the understanding that, if the case is lost, she will not charge her client for the work she has done. If, however, the case is won, she is entitled to charge a 'success fee', calculated as a percentage of her normal costs, to recompense her for the risk she runs of not being paid. The conditional fee is further defined in the Conditional Fee Agreements (Miscellaneous Amendments) Regulations 2003.

Were that the full story, it is perhaps likely that lawyers as a whole would have decided that the game would not be worth the candle, and the risks of losing might be too great to justify them funding what could be many abortive actions. In order to avoid this clients are often expected to pay the disbursements incurred in the litigation, such as medical or other expert reports, court or enquiry agent's fees. In some cases the lawyer may agree to fund such disbursements.

The effect, therefore, is that conditional fees allow lawyers and clients to share the risk of litigation, with the success fee being set according to the risk the lawyer is taking. The principle under the Act was that higher the chance of winning, the lower the success fee should be set, and vice versa.

There were several justifications given by the Government for this step. It was said that it helps to ensure that the risks are managed by the lawyers who are better placed than clients to know what those risks are. It was also argued that lawyers working under conditional fee agreements are likely to be more keen to win. This may be a slight on many reputable solicitors, but there have been reports over the years of what sound like unjustifiable legally aided cases for rich and/or foreign clients who turned out to have substantial hidden assets and whose chances of success in litigation were eventually revealed with hindsight to be pretty slim. The Legal Aid Board had to share the responsibility for bad judgements on this.

A counter argument to the 'keener to win' point of view might be that some lawyers tempted to try too hard could go beyond the bounds of acceptable professional behaviour. Nevertheless, the introduction of conditional fees was a significant step towards removing the barrier of high costs that deterred many potential litigants from starting legal proceedings even when they had a strong case, and clients can always take out an insurance policy to mitigate the risks and expenses of losing.

Progress was made in 1995 when the then Lord Chancellor allowed conditional fee agreements for proceedings involving personal injury, insolvency and cases before the European Commission and the European Court of Human Rights. The maximum amount of success fee a lawyer was entitled to charge was then set at 100 per cent of the lawyer's normal fees for the work undertaken. Regulations were made under s58 to specify the information a conditional fee agreement had to contain, and this was followed by the Law Society producing guidance for solicitors about the use of conditional fees and a model agreement. It advised solicitors to apply a voluntary limit on the proportion of damages that could be taken by the success fee, suggesting it should not be more than 25 per cent. By the end of 1997 some 34,000 policies had been issued with premiums ranging from about £90 to £150. Conditional fees are now as enforceable as any other, as exemplified by recent cases such as *Hollins* v *Russell* [2003] 4 All ER 590 and *Re Claims Direct Test Cases* [2003] 4 All ER 508.

It can therefore be seen that the idea of conditional fees would appeal to many potential litigants and perhaps to more commercially minded members of the legal profession. The Access to Justice Act 1999 established a new executive, non-departmental public body called the Legal Services Commission whose duty it is to develop and administer two schemes in England and Wales. The first is the Community Legal Service which replaces the old civil scheme of legal aid, bringing together networks of funders (eg local authorities) and suppliers into partnerships to provide the widest possible access to information and advice.

The second is the Criminal Defence Service which from April 2001 replaced the old system of criminal legal aid and provide criminal services to people accused of crimes. It is hoped that these steps, combined with further development of no win, no fee arrangements, will ensure that access to justice by persons who could not otherwise afford to pay for legal representation will continue and expand.

Chapter 10

Civil Justice System

10.1 **Introduction**

10.2 **Key points**

10.3 **Key cases and statutes**

10.4 **Questions and suggested solutions**

10.1 Introduction

Prior to the Woolf reforms, civil justice was always perceived as being too expensive and too complex, with long delays. The fact that the civil court was divided into two distinct courts (county and High), with two separate regimes governing them, was of no help to a litigant or prospective litigant.

It was with this in mind that the Woolf reforms were introduced in 1999 and, as a result, a breath of fresh air was given to the English civil justice system.

10.2 Key points

a) As a result of Lord Woolf's report, *Access to Justice*, the Civil Procedure Act 1997 was passed, and soon afterwards the Civil Procedure Rules 1998 came into force. It was intended that one simplified set of rules for both the High Court and the county courts, drafted in plain English and introducing judicial case management, would greatly revolutionise the civil justice system. Also see the Civil Procedure (Amendment No 4) Rules 2003, which came into force in October 2003 and deal with legal costs.

b) The new court structure:

   i) All cases are now allocated to one of three tracks:

   - multi-track cases (complex cases involving £15,000 or more);
   - fast-track cases (cases involving between £5–15,000);
   - small-claims track (minor cases of up to £5,000).

   ii) Essentially the two courts, ie the county court and the High Court, have been retained as first instance courts.

Civil Justice System

- The county court hears all small claims and fast-track cases. Certain county courts are also designated as civil trial centres and these courts deal with multi-track cases of up to £15,000 value.

  Cases involving more than £50,000 are rarely tried in the county courts.

- The three divisions within the High Court is still maintained – Queen's Bench Division, Chancery Division and Family Division.

- For certain types of cases, pre-action protocols have been issued – for example in personal injury litigation, clinical disputes, professional negligence and defamation. For other case parties are encouraged to state or disclose the facts of their case prior to commencing any court action.

iii) Outline of the procedure:

- The claimant issues a claim form stating the particulars of his/her claim.
- There must also be a statement of truth as to the facts in the particulars of claim.
- The court then serves these forms (claims and particulars) on the defendant.
- The defendant or respondent then has 14 days to respond.
- The respondent may admit or partly admit the claim, pay the claim or contest the claim. If he does so, he must file a defence within 14 days of receipt of the documents from the court.
- Once defence is filed, the court sends out an allocation questionnaire to all the parties. This is meant to help the judge determine which track the case should go to.
- For all claims of more than £1,000, an allocation fee is payable at this stage.
- Parties can apply for re-allocation if dissatisfied.

iv) Specific procedure:

- Small-claims track:
  - heard in open court by a district judge in an informal and interventionist way;
  - parties are encouraged to 'self-represent' as costs are not awarded to cover legal representation.
- Multi-track cases:
  - judge uses pre-trial reviews and case management conferences as there is no standard procedure for pre-trial directions;
  - all issues are identified into agreed and non-agreed – this encourages early settlement and only the contested issues go to trial;

- if expert evidence is necessary, the court will appoint someone to provide it independently;
- strict time limits (set by the judge) apply. Penalties are imposed for non-compliance.

- Fast-track cases:
  - the intention is for the court to maintain proportionality, ie ensuring a fair balance between the parties;
  - this track helps parties obtain justice speedily by means of increasing access to justice by way of removing uncertainty;
  - standard directions apply, and the court directs the timetable – trial fixed at no more than 30 weeks ahead;
  - if expert evidence is needed, the court will appoint a qualified person in the event parties cannot agree – expert will give written evidence;
  - there are fixed costs for legal representation;
  - judicial case management is most prominent in the fast track.

c) A brief analysis of the post-Woolf civil reforms

The Lord Chancellor's Department (now known as the Department for Constitutional Affairs) issued a report, available on the internet, with what it called the 'emerging findings' following the Woolf reforms.

The overall assessment is that the Woolf reforms are having, to a large extent, their intended effect, in that:

i) there is evidence that litigation is being resorted to less often;

ii) litigants are cooperating more, eg there appears to be more settlements earlier on during litigation;

iii) litigation is less complex, eg case management conferences are helping to clarify the issue(s) between the parties; and

iv) litigation is taking less time: evidence shows that fast track and multi-track cases are taking less time to reach trial.

However, there are reasons to exercise caution:

i) the evidence of the costs of litigation is mixed, and certainly there is some indication that some costs have gone up;

ii) there is little evidence that the litigation process is any fairer to those appearing in person; and

iii) the evidence provided for the Report is of variable quality, including views from law firms and various questionnaires and surveys. An in-depth qualitative analysis has yet to be undertaken.

The report can be found at: www.dca.gov.uk; search under 'Emerging Findings'.

10.3 Key cases and statutes

- *Swain* v *Hillman* [2001] 1 All ER 91
  Court laid down guidelines on appeals

- *Tanfern Ltd* v *Cameron-Macdonald* [2000] 1 WLR 1311
  The new procedure is likely to reduce appeals

- *Vinos* v *Marks and Spencer plc* [2001] 3 All ER 784
  Procedural rules applied very strictly, particularly time-limits

- Civil Procedure Act 1997 – passed to implement the Woolf reforms

- Civil Procedure Rules 1998 – introduced one unified procedural code for both the county court and the High Court

10.4 Questions and suggested solutions

QUESTION ONE

To what extent is it possible to construct a statement of the objectives of the civil litigation system as a whole? Will Lord Woolf's reforms achieve those objectives?

University of London LLB Examination
(for External Students) English Legal System June 2001 Q3

General Comment

The question calls for a general discussion of the changes in the civil justice system affected by the Woolf reforms, and an analysis of their main aims and objectives. Accordingly, the student is required to assess whether these objectives have been met since the introduction of these reforms. This topic seems to be an 'annual feature' in the examination.

Skeleton Solution

Aims and objectives of the Woolf reforms – the main principles – concept of case management – the new track system – the use of information technology – the promotion of alternative dispute resolution methods – conclusion as to whether objectives have been achieved.

Suggested Solution

In analysing the contents of Lord Woolf's reform of the civil justice system, one can perhaps appreciate the reason(s) why Lord Woolf regards them as amounting to a revolution in civil justice. Statistics carried out post-reforms disclose that this claim is probably undisputed, though there have been some criticisms levelled at it. What is in dispute is whether the reforms, or 'the revolution', will achieve the objectives of securing access to justice for all classes of the community through methods acceptable to users of the new services.

The access to justice reforms were implemented on 26 April 1999 by the new Head of Civil Justice, Sir Richard Scott. The result is a new Act, called the Civil Procedure Act 1997, as well as the Civil Procedure Rules 1998 supplemented by a variety of *Practice Directions*.

The impact of the changes introduced cannot be overstated; it represents a complete overhaul of the system. Let us first attempt to set out the main aims and objectives of these reforms (as perceived and intended by Lord Woolf).

1. By the creation of a new framework for the High Court and county courts, involving the creation of three or four new 'civil trial centres' in the regions, with each centre headed by a senior civil judge, the aim is to create and achieve a better working environment between the judiciary and court administrators. There will also be new specialist courts at the High Court and in the regions reserved for medical negligence cases. Housing cases should be handled by specialist judges in the local county courts.

2. The High Court and county court jurisdiction was to be fused to create one simple jurisdiction with one set of simplified procedural rules to replace those in the existing (now the former) White and Green Books. The aim is, of course, to create 'open door entry' for litigants; ie prospective litigants will be able to start a case in any court and a procedural judge at that court will then take responsibility for allocating the case to the appropriate part of the system. The new system will consist of three tracks, and cases will be allocated to a track according to their value and complexity.

    a) A 'fast track' for non-complex or non-contentious claims between £3,000 and £10,000 (currently £5,000 and £15,000 respectively) in which the hearing will be held in county courts within 30 weeks of the issue of proceedings (compared to an average of 80 at present). The hearing will be a fixed three-hour hearing, subject to an absolute maximum of one day, if necessary. Much of the preliminary work will be done on paper as opposed to by oral submissions. No oral evidence from expert witnesses will be allowed. No interrogatories will be allowed. Legal aid will be available for fast track claims.

    b) A 'small claims track' for non-complex claims up to £3,000 (currently £5,000) (other than claims for possession of land and for personal injury, which will be dealt with on the fast track system). The small claims track will involve county court use of alternative dispute resolution methods, such as arbitration, by the district judges without legal aid.

c) A 'multi-track system' for claims over £10,000 (including complex claims of less than £10,000) (currently £15,000), with claims being allocated according to their individual complexity. Estimates of costs in each case will be either published by the court or agreed by the litigants and approved by the court. Teams of judges will be involved in making allocation decisions on the multi-track, whereas a single judge (a district 'procedural' judge) will allocate cases on the fast track or small claims track. For the more complex cases on the multi-track, there should be a case management conference before a single procedural judge, followed by a pre-trial review before the High Court or trial judge. Interrogatories will require the leave of the procedural judge. The trial judge will be a High Court judge for complex cases, regardless of the amount claimed. Non-complex cases will be heard by circuit or district judges under a special streamlined 'no frills' procedure with fixed budgets.

3. Judges to be formerly trained as case and trial managers so that they can become properly involved in the administration of the courts and provide 'hands on' management of cases by dictating the pace of hearings, enforcing strict time limits, and taking responsibility for the calling of witnesses (especially expert witnesses) so as to ensure equality for litigants.

4. Judges should also become familiar (training will, of course, be provided) with information technology facilities, such as laptop computers and video conference facilities.

5. Judges are to have a greater power to strike out unworthy actions, or to settle cases or parts of them summarily. There will also be greater powers to impose sanctions (for example, striking out the whole or part of the claim, or ordering costs to be paid immediately, or imposing a higher rate of interest for costs) in cases where lawyers fail to meet required deadlines. There would be a new discretionary power to allocate the burden of costs at the end of a case by reference to the conduct of parties.

6. The establishment of a Civil Justice Council as a general supervisory body to oversee the implementation and reforms effected by the Access to Justice Report.

The message of the Report is crystal. It is an agenda which puts the client first by ensuring that litigation is less complex, less expensive, is processed according to a set timetable, and that costs are predictable. Simplification of litigation is achieved by a single set of rules for all civil courts and new trial centres. Proceedings have been made 'user-friendly' and 'non-technical'.

Lord Woolf described his reforms as providing a new landscape for civil justice in the new millennium. He summarised the advantages of his proposed reforms as follows:

1. they would end the present system of 'trial by combat', which had encouraged unreasonable behaviour by litigants;

2. they would create a simpler, more accessible and flexible system;

3. cases would be handled in a manner proportionate to their value and complexity;

4. there would be greater certainty over costs and duration of proceedings; and

5. the new 'reformed system' would ensure a 'level playing field' for litigants, thereby preventing wealthier litigants (for example, insurance companies) from playing with the system to their advantage.

According to the Lord Chancellor's Department (now the Department for Constitutional Affairs) (*Emerging Findings: An Early Evaluation of the Civil Justice Reforms* (2001)), the reforms and the new rules are working well and the aims and objectives of the reforms are being broadly realised. Less claims and less trials would certainly support this contention. Robert Turner, a senior Master in the High Court, welcomed the new rules, stating that the old system has now been replaced by a new efficient and cooperative system ((2000) 150 NLJ 149).

QUESTION TWO

'The adversarial system lies at the root of all the problems of the English civil justice system. Real reform can only be achieved by abandoning the adversarial system.'

Discuss this statement in the context of the Woolf reforms of civil procedure.

University of London LLB Examination
(for External Students) English Legal System June 2000 Q4

General Comment

This question calls for an examination of the changes effected by the Woolf reforms affecting civil procedure. Contextual analysis of the adversarial system is also necessary.

Skeleton Solution

A brief history of civil procedure – changes introduced by Woolf – aims and objectives of reforms – significance of adversarial system – need for reform.

Suggested Solution

One of the hallmarks of the English legal system, and almost all common law systems, is the adversarial system as opposed to the inquisitorial system practised by most civil law jurisdictions in Europe. Whilst adversarial procedure allows the parties complete freedom in the trial and management of their cases without any help, assistance or aid from the court, the inquisitorial procedure, on the other hand, allows court officials to be involved in the fact-finding process, which basically means that judges can examine, cross-examine and re-examine with a view to establishing certain facts in a case. It is debatable that the English legal system has not always been adversarial. In fact, inquisitorial elements seem to be appearing at many points in the system.

Whether the recent civil justice reforms reinstate the adversarial process, or whether they lend support to the contention that inquisitorial elements do exist within our system, will now be examined within the canvass of the Woolf reforms affecting civil procedure.

The debate on reforms to the civil justice system started as early as the late 1980s and early 1990s culminating in the Woolf reforms in the Access to Justice Report in 1996. This in turn led to the passing of the Civil Procedure Act (CPA) 1997 and the Civil Procedure Rules 1998 in addition to many *Practice Directions*.

Section 1 CPA 1997 provided for one set of practice rules for the Court of Appeal, High Court and county courts, 'with a view to securing that the civil justice system is accessible, fair and efficient'. Section 6 CPA 1997 further established a Civil Justice Council comprising the Master of the Rolls, judges, lawyers and other consumer/lay advice and litigant representatives, to keep the civil justice system under review.

The new regime as exemplified by the Civil Procedure Rules 1998 was devised to enable the court to deal with a case justly, so as to: ensure that parties are on an equal footing; save expenses; deal with a case in a proportionate manner; and deal with a case expeditiously and fairly whilst allotting to it an appropriate share of the court's resources. This is submitted to be in line with the requirements of art 6 of the European Convention on Human Rights which deals with a litigant's right to a fair trial, as illustrated by the Court of Appeal in *Daniels* v *Walker* [2000] 1 WLR 1382.

Essentially, the reforms introduced a new track system into the court structure. This means that all civil cases which are tried or defended will be allocated to one of three tracks, namely, the small claims track, the fast track and the multi-track.

The small claims track deals with the majority of cases where the amount claimed does not exceed £5,000. The fast track deals with cases where the claims are between £5,000 and £15,000, although it is not unusual for these cases to be allocated to the multi-track if they involve complex points of law. The multi-track attracts all claims in excess of £15,000 or complex cases. Whilst the county court manages all small claims and fast track cases, the High Court deals with multi-track matters. Certain county courts which are designated as Civil Trial Centres by the Lord Chancellor have jurisdiction to deal with cases above £15,000. This is, of course, subject to a maximum limit of £50,000, which if exceeded, must be tried in the High Court unless the parties expressly agree for the case to be heard in the county court.

Perhaps it would be wise at this juncture to note the aims of the pre-action protocols which form part of the reforms. These protocols are known as statements of best practice in negotiation, encouraging exchange of information and putting the parties into a position to settle fairly. According to Professor M Zander (*The State of Justice* (2000) Chapter 2), it is important to see that negotiations are conducted fairly at the pre-trial stage, because only a small fraction of cases, under 20 per cent of civil disputes, are ever brought to court.

The question of whether the reforms inadvertently introduced a form of inquisitorial procedure within the existing adversarial nature of the English civil justice system could perhaps best be analysed from the creation of the concept of the judicial management of cases. Although the court's duty to manage cases had already been introduced from 1994 in *Practice Directions*, under the Woolf reforms the duty for judges to 'case manage' now includes: encouraging parties to cooperate; identifying issues at an early stage; deciding promptly which issues can be disposed of summarily; deciding the order of the issues; encouraging alternative dispute resolution; helping parties settle; fixing timetables; considering cost issues; dealing with a case in abstention; and directing the trial process quickly and efficiently.

Judges now have more say in a case, even before it is set down for trial. Whilst this is intended to encourage settlement and discourage litigation, it is arguable that the practice is more inquisitorial as opposed to being adversarial. This is evident from the sanctions imposed for failure to comply with case management, which includes striking out, costs and debarring part of a case or evidence. Postponements of trials are frowned upon by judges and only granted as a last resort. According to the Lord Chancellor's Department (now the Department for Constitutional Affairs) Minister, David Lock (*Emerging Findings: An Early Evaluation of the Civil Justice Reforms* (2001)), the reforms and new rules are working well and the objectives of the reforms are being broadly realised. Less claims and less trials seem to compound his view. Robert Turner, a Senior Master in the High Court ((2000) 150 NLJ 149), welcomed the new rules, stating that the pervading adversarial approach has gone and has been replaced by a degree of cooperation. Master of the High Court John Leslie (Counsel 2000, vol 12, p41) also commented on 'a new spirit of cooperation'.

Be that as it may, cries of the shortcomings of the new regime must not be ignored. Nigel Foster, a law lecturer ((2000) 150 NLJ 318), gave a condemnatory personal account of the apparent weaknesses of the new rules. Similarly, Sarah Rowlands ((1998) The Times 17 March) tells a hideous tale of the palaver she went through in realising her claim through the small claims court. Richard Harrison ((2000) 150 NLJ 541) stated that processing cases brusquely, efficiently and driving litigants away from the system did not mean that they were enjoying 'access to justice'.

Whether the reforms are a resounding success, or whether they are an expected failure, is a subjective issue, which only time can tell. There seems to be a distinct division of opinions on this issue between Government bodies and non-Governmental bodies. Statistics seem to support both views.

In any case, it can safely be concluded that whilst the reforms have clearly introduced new measures within the civil justice system, which in a way reflects an inquisitorial nature, it must be borne in mind that this is purely at the pre-trial stage. The adversarial procedure is still very much intact as far as trials are concerned.

QUESTION THREE

'The existing justice system is not as effective as it should be ... A large part of the community feels unable to turn to the law for assistance and remedies. Part of the problem is that the services and remedies sought from the justice system are often disproportionate to the issue at stake.' (White Paper *Modernising Justice* 1998).

Discuss this statement and evaluate the extent to which the changes proposed to civil procedure in the Government's White Paper are likely to overcome the problems referred to.

University of London LLB Examination
(for External Students) English Legal System June 1999 Q5

General Comment

The question requires discussion of the reforms to civil procedure implemented as a result of the Woolf Report, *Access to Justice*. It requires evaluation of the extent to which the new regime is likely to improve matters for those seeking to enforce or defend rights through the civil justice system.

Skeleton Solution

Reasons for services and remedies not being available to all; persons who are affected the most – the main objectives stated in the Government White Paper; evaluation of these – comment on whether the White Paper promise to provide a more efficient and effective user-friendly service is achieved – the improvement in access to information; role of the Community Legal Service – enhancement of alternative legal services.

Suggested Solution

This (edited) statement relates to services and remedies that ought to be available to all via the justice system but which often have not been in the past partly because of lack of affordability. Litigation costs are, and are likely to remain, not only high but also unpredictable, and this has tended to mean that only the rich with plenty of money, or the poor who have been funded by legal funding, have been able to litigate without having to worry too much about the consequences either of losing or of being able to carry on beyond a certain point if the case did not appear to be going well. The 'large part of the community [who] feels unable to turn to the law for assistance and remedies' are those reasonably well off working and middle classes who earn sufficient to enjoy a decent living but who have concomitantly high expenditure levels and who therefore cannot afford to risk getting deep into debt by the unpredictability of litigation.

It is not only the litigant who has been disadvantaged. In the White Paper the Government bemoaned the cost to those who have to fund legal aid and the courts, probably largely those who were not able to benefit by being entitled to it. The mantra of wanting the highest possible quality at the best possible price was to the fore. In this regard, the Government said that it had two main objectives, namely bringing about a significant increase in access to justice and obtaining the best value for the taxpayer's money spent on legal services and the courts. The measure of success would be the publication of targets so that the public could judge for themselves.

The White Paper emphasised that access and affordability began with fundamental first principles that citizens should be able to understand and enforce their rights through the courts and that they should be entitled to protection from crime. A peaceful, socially and economically fair society depended on such basics, which 'underpinned' order and the rule of law. People would only respect this if they could see that it was fair, and that they would not be excluded by absence or shortage of means from exerting basic rights.

Access to justice does not simply depend on money, of course; it requires efficiency, speed, and fair and effective solutions that are not disproportionate to that which is at stake. If, for example, the expense of recovering a debt is greater than the amount owed, and the legal system then leaves the successful litigant with the responsibility of incurring further expenditure by having to enforce the payment of the judgment herself, the court system is failing the client. Civil litigation should be action of last resort, and other methods should be available to settle relatively minor disputes, as it is in no one's interests to live in a trigger-happy litigious society. If one is charged with a criminal offence, however, it is not pertinent to talk about alternative methods of dispute resolution, because the accused must be afforded access to proper legal advice and representation. In this context, some of the Government's other proposals do not entirely ring true and inspire confidence where, for example, it can be seen that they are trying to reduce access to the right of the accused to choose jury trial on grounds of cost.

The Government says that they will achieve their aims in a number of ways, including provision of better access to information, substantive law reform, promotion of the provision of affordable legal services of 'appropriate quality', and by developing alternative ways of resolving disputes. They hope to combine these measures with improvement of the management of the court system, streamlining and simplifying procedures and jurisdiction, and in the White Paper they promise to provide a more efficient and effective user-friendly service. Citizens who in the past have attended county court offices will doubtless applaud this.

The improvement in access to information is to be achieved through the Community Legal Service whose role is to co-ordinate the way in which the services of advice agencies are planned and funded, assisted by information technology. It is to be hoped that they are more successful in this latter objective than the Home Office has been with its attempts to computerise immigration procedures and services. Clients of the court system will know in the great majority of cases from the day they initiate proceedings how long it is likely to take to resolve their case. To facilitate these objectives further, the Government hopes that more widespread use of conditional fees, fixed trial costs in 'fast-track' cases and fixed-price legal funding contracts will all help – on the one hand in reducing costs and on the other by increasing certainty.

Although not a change to civil procedure as such, the Government also places considerable faith in substantive law reform, stating their intention to keep the law up to date, relevant and usable. More vaguely they also talk about getting rid of fragmentation, obsolete and redundant law, and say that they recognise the importance of consolidation and revision of statute law. If this is so, no doubt they will also take steps to enhance the status and work of the Law Commission, and take more note of their recommendations. A recent example of this initiative is the Land Registration Act 2002.

The availability of affordable, and where appropriate alternative, legal services is to be enhanced, with more use made of voluntary agencies and mediation at the lower end of the scale and better legally funded representation by a solicitor or barrister in court in more serious cases. To help to achieve these aims it is the Government's intention to remove unjustified restrictive practices and to encourage more competition, of which the 'no win, no fee' scheme is one example. The same will be done for some types of family case, and yet another promise has been made to remove the restrictive practices that prevent solicitors and employed lawyers from appearing in the higher courts. This has been resisted by the senior legal establishment for so long that it will be believed by most non-barristers only when it has been achieved. The reform of the system of awarding legal funding contracts is set to continue, with the contradictory objectives of higher quality and cheaper services. Considerable faith is also manifested in alternative dispute resolution (ADR), as they think the existing system is 'top heavy'. This alternative would be less formal, less adversarial, quicker and cheaper. It is to be hoped it will also be rather more effective in, for example, small debt collecting. An ADR order will be no better than a court order if it cannot be enforced.

Finally, notice now has to be taken of the human rights implications on all these reforms. These rights can now be enforced in domestic courts and, combined with the changes in the civil court procedures, the Government is confident that unnecessary cost, delay and complexity will be 'rooted out' of the system. How justified they are in this belief remains to be seen. The jury is out. At least, the jury is out for the moment. If further reforms go ahead, there will not be many juries left to go out in a few years time, and this will no doubt save a lot of money. Whether it improves the quality of justice, as opposed to the conviction rate, is also one of the things to be looked at in the brave new world.

Chapter 11

Civil and Criminal Appeals

11.1 Introduction

11.2 Key points

11.3 Key cases and statutes

11.4 Questions and suggested solutions

11.1 Introduction

In 1998 the Government issued a White Paper entitled *Modernising Justice* which culminated in the passing of the Civil Procedure Rules 1998, the Access to Justice Act 1999, the amended Rules of the Supreme Court and various Practice Directions. Part 52 of the Civil Procedure Rules 1998 (which deals with appeals) came into force in May 2000 and introduced new changes to the appeal structure. Research was commissioned by the then Lord Chancellor's Department to consider the impact of the reforms to the Court of Appeal (Civil Division) and to assess the achievements of the Access to Justice Act 1999 with respect to appeals. See *Research on Impact of Reforms to Court of Appeal (Civil Division)* (2003): www.dca.gov.uk.

11.2 Key points

Civil appeals

Appeals from multi-track cases

a) From the county court to the Court of Appeal.

b) From the High Court to the Court of Appeal, unless leapfrogging applies (then straight to the House of Lords).

c) From High Court to the Court of Appeal, then further appeal to the House of Lords.

Appeals from small claims and fast track

a) Decisions of a district judge are appealable to a circuit judge: Part 52 CPR.

b) For fast-track cases, appeals from a district judge go to a circuit judge, and appeals from a circuit judge go to a High Court judge.

c) The Court of Appeal is empowered to hear a second appeal if the appeal raises an important point of practice, procedure or principle; or, alternatively, if there is some other compelling reason for the Court of Appeal to hear it: s55(1) Access to Justice Act 1999.

d) See also the relevance of the recent case of *Tanfern Ltd* v *Cameron-Macdonald* [2000] 2 All ER 801.

The guiding principles on appeals generally

a) Permission to appeal will only be given where the court considers that an appeal would have a real chance of success: *Swain* v *Hillman* [2001] 1 All ER 91.

b) Under normal circumstances more than one appeal cannot be justified.

c) There should be no automatic right to appeal. Leave (now called permission) is to be required in all appeals to the Court of Appeal (not required if it involves the issue of the liberty of an individual).

d) Changes to the composition, procedures, working methods and management of the Court of Appeal (Civil Division) have generally been designed to help it operate more efficiently. See, in this regard, the Department of Constitutional Affairs, *Emerging Findings: An Early Evaluation of the Civil Justice Reforms* (2001): www.dca.gov.uk.

Criminal appeals

Appeals from the magistrates' court

a) Appeals to the Crown Court

The defendant may appeal as of right, if he pleaded guilty, against his sentence and if he pleaded not guilty, against his conviction. The prosecution may not appeal against an acquittal.

The procedure:

i) notice of appeal must be given within 21 days of decision or sentence;

ii) the notice must contain the grounds of appeal;

iii) an appeal is treated as a re-hearing.

The powers of the Crown Court – it may:

i) confirm, reverse or vary the decision;

ii) remit the case with an opinion to the magistrates' court;

iii) make any order it thinks just.

b) Appeals to the High Court

These may be made by way of case stated to the Queen's Bench Division by any party to the proceedings or any aggrieved party. The appeal may be made on the grounds that the decision was wrong in law or made in excess of jurisdiction.

The procedure:

i) application is made to the justices' clerk to state a case for the opinion of the High Court;

ii) the application must be made within 21 days and once made, any rights of appeal to the Crown Court are lost;

iii) the justices' clerk can refuse to state a case where it is frivolous;

iv) a draft is sent to all parties and it must state the question of law or jurisdiction on which guidance is sought.

The powers of the High Court – on appeal it may:

i) reverse, affirm or amend the decision;

ii) remit to the magistrates' court for reconsideration in the light of the court's opinion;

iii) make such order as it thinks fit, eg, order a re-hearing by the same or a different bench: *Griffith v Jenkins* [1992] 1 All ER 65.

c) Appeals from the High Court to the House of Lords

The defence or prosecution may appeal to the House of Lords on a point of law or an issue of general importance. Leave must be obtained from either court. The House of Lords can make whatever order it thinks fit, including remitting the case to the High Court.

Appeals from the Crown Court

The prosecution has no right of appeal against an acquittal by a jury, however perverse the verdict. The defendant tried on indictment may appeal to the Court of Appeal. The appeal may be made against the conviction and/or sentence.

a) Appeals against conviction

All appeals require leave to appeal: s1(1) of Criminal Appeal Act 1995. The following procedure must be followed:

i) notice of appeal must be given within 28 days of conviction to the registrar of criminal appeals;

ii) the notice must contain the grounds of appeal;

iii) the registrar may refer the appeal for summary determination if he finds there are no substantial grounds for appeal;

iv) a court may dismiss an appeal if it considers it to be frivolous or vexatious.

The powers of the Court of Appeal are provided for by s2 of the Criminal Appeal Act 1995. The court can allow the appeal if it thinks that the verdict of the jury is unsafe.

In considering an appeal the Court of Appeal may receive fresh evidence which it regards as 'capable of belief': s23 of the Criminal Appeal Act 1968, as amended by s4 of the 1995 Act. It has a power to order a retrial if the interest of justice require it: Criminal Justice Act 1988, s43.

b) Appeals against sentence

A person convicted may appeal against sentence (other than a sentence fixed by law) provided that leave is obtained from the Court of Appeal or from the judge who passed the sentence: see ss9 and 11 Criminal Appeal Act 1968. The Court of Appeal will only alter a sentence if it is wrong in principle, or manifestly excessive.

Section 36 of the Criminal Justice Act 1988 allows the prosecution to ask the Attorney-General to refer an 'unduly lenient sentence' to the Court of Appeal. On review the Court of Appeal may:

i) quash any sentence; and

ii) pass an appropriate sentence within the power of the Crown Court.

Appeals from the Court of Appeal to the House of Lords

a) Both the defence and prosecution may appeal to the House of Lords provided the Court of Appeal certifies a point of law of general public importance. Leave must be obtained from the Court of Appeal or House of Lords.

b) The following procedure must be followed:

i) the application for leave to appeal must be made 14 days after the Court of Appeal's decision;

ii) if the certificate is refused, the matter cannot be taken further;

iii) if the leave is granted the petition of appeal is generally made within three months;

iv) the House of Lords may exercise the powers of the Court of Appeal or remit the case to the Court of Appeal: *R v Mandair* [1994] 2 All ER 715 (HL).

The Criminal Cases Review Commission

This body, set up by ss8–14 of the 1995 Act, started work at the end of March 1997 and deals with approximately 800 petitions annually. Its task is to refer to the Court of Appeal cases where it believes that there is a real possibility that there was a wrongful conviction and a miscarriage of justice. Its independent membership and inquisitorial methods are designed to reassure the public that the risk of miscarriages of justice such as the Birmingham Six will be avoided or minimised in future trials. The Court of Appeal retains the ultimate power to allow or dismiss an appeal but, particularly in fresh evidence cases, tends to take a more sympathetic approach to references from the Commission compared to the way it handled cases such as the Birmingham Six (1991), the Guildford Four (1989), the Winchester Three (1990), the Maguires (1990).

11.3 Key cases and statutes

- *Caballero* v *United Kingdom* (2000) 30 EHRR 643
  Domestic law was reformed so as to be compatible with the European Convention on Human Rights

- *Keenan* v *United Kingdom* (2001) The Times 18 April
  Illustrates the operation of art 3 of the European Convention on Human Rights

- *Kingsley* v *United Kingdom* (2001) The Times 9 January
  Allegation that a fair trial was not given formed the basis of an appeal

- *R* v *Mandair* [1994] 2 All ER 715 (HL)
  House of Lords may exercise (if it so wishes) powers of the Court of Appeal

- *Swain* v *Hillman* [2001] 1 All ER 91
  Further guidelines were laid down in respect of appeals

- *Tanfern Ltd* v *Cameron-Macdonald* [2001] 1 WLR 1311
  New procedural rules are likely to reduce appeals

- Access to Justice Act 1999 – introduced, inter alia, new rights of audience

- Civil Procedure Rules 1998 – introduced new changes to the appeal structure

- Criminal Appeal Act 1995 – governs criminal appeals and set up the Criminal Cases Review Commission

11.4 Questions and suggested solutions

QUESTION ONE

'Recent miscarriages of justice can be understood as drawing attention to a conflict of fundamental values within criminal justice.'

Discuss.

University of London LLB Examination
(for External Students) English Legal System June 2001 Q7(a)

General Comment

This question calls for a discussion of recent cases where miscarriages of justice have evidently materialised. A fair amount of judicial and academic opinions on this area should be examined, and the effect of such miscarriages on the criminal justice system must be analysed.

Skeleton Solution

Recent cases of miscarriages: Guildford Four, Birmingham Six, Tottenham Three, Maguire Seven – reasons why the Court of Appeal quashed their convictions – Royal Commission on Criminal Justice – Runciman Commission – Criminal Cases Review Commission – 'justice served' or 'justice denied'?

Suggested Solution

Whilst the law and its legal rules are intended as the primary means of preventing errors, it is undeniable that errors, whether deliberate or accidental, do occur. Within the criminal process, errors, such as the innocent being found guilty owing to a variety of factors such as the withholding of information, or material non-disclosure, or irregularities in the trial procedure, have resulted in calls for reforms. The judicial and academic lobbying culminated in the passing of the Criminal Appeal Act (CAA) 1995, which amends its predecessor, the Criminal Appeal Act 1968. Section 2(1)(a) CAA 1995 now sets out a new and simplified ground upon which the Court of Appeal may allow a criminal appeal. It states that the Court of Appeal 'shall allow an appeal against conviction if they think that the conviction is unsafe'. Section 4 CAA 1995 also allows the Court of Appeal to 'receive any evidence which was not adduced in the proceedings from which the appeal lies'.

The CAA 1995 arguably increased the powers of the Court of Appeal in correcting miscarriages of justice. This is achieved by allowing the Court of Appeal to look at the conviction on a wide perspective, ie from a 'safe' or 'unsafe' point of view. Miscarriages of justice may occur in many ways, but the problems of miscarriages of justice have come into focus with three leading cases that involved the IRA, namely the Guildford Four, the Maguire Seven and the Birmingham Six. In all three cases, the defendants were all convicted in the first instance, and on appeal all convictions were quashed by the Court of Appeal as being 'unsafe' and 'unsatisfactory'. These cases will now be examined in more detail.

Firstly, the Guildford Four. Four defendants were found guilty in 1976 of murder by causing an explosion in a public house in Guildford. Initially, their appeal against conviction under the Criminal Appeal Act 1968 was turned down, but in 1989, the Home Secretary (who then, under s17 CAA 1968, had powers to refer cases to the Court of Appeal) referred the case to the Court of Appeal. The primary ground identified in this case was the dubious nature of the prosecution evidence. Tests on police documents undermined the evidence of police officers that the crucial interviews were recorded contemporaneously. The Director of Public Prosecutions therefore stated that he no longer sought to support the convictions, and the Court of Appeal accordingly quashed them.

Similarly, in the case of the Birmingham Six the defendants were convicted in 1975 of murder by causing explosions in a public house in Birmingham. Like the Guildford Four, the Birmingham Six had their appeal against conviction dismissed. The Home Secretary exercised his powers to refer the case back to the Court of Appeal on the grounds that: fresh scientific evidence had become available; and the defendants had been beaten after their arrest, and this resulted in the confessions which were subsequently used to convict them. This appeal was dismissed in 1987. In 1990, the Home Secretary once again referred the case to the Court of Appeal as a result of further fresh evidence being available. It was discovered that there were irregularities surrounding the police interviews and that there was a material non-disclosure by the prosecution to the defence (certain findings from the Forensic Science Services had not been disclosed). Interestingly, while the Crown Prosecution Service decided that there was sufficient evidence to prosecute three police officers involved in the case for perjury and conspiracy to pervert the course of justice, the judge stayed the prosecution on the grounds of the publicity surrounding the Birmingham Six case, which would make a 'fair trial' impossible. The convictions of the Birmingham Six were, however, quashed.

Likewise, in the case of the Maguire Seven the seven defendants, most of whom were members of the Maguire family, had been convicted in 1976 of the offence of possessing explosive substances that were linked, by the prosecution, to bombings in London and Guildford. Leave to appeal was refused in 1977. In 1992, the case was once again referred to the Court of Appeal. This time the Court of Appeal quashed the conviction on the grounds of material irregularity during trial, and that forensic scientific evidence raised other issues which the defence had no opportunity to address by virtue of their non-disclosure. The sad thing is that by this time, the defendants had spent some 13 years in prison, and one of them had died there.

There are other cases, such as *R v Ward (Judith)* [1993] 2 All ER 577, where the defendant was released after serving 18 years' imprisonment when it was discovered that relevant medical evidence had been withheld from the defence by the prosecution at her trial. This case provided the impetus for the Government to pass the Criminal Procedure and Investigations Act 1996, which introduced better judicial management of the trial process and new rules requiring pre-trial disclosure.

In the case of the Tottenham Three, the defendants were initially found guilty in 1986 but the Court of Appeal quashed their convictions on appeal in 1991 on the grounds of irregularity surrounding the interviews and confessions. Similarly, the Cardiff Three had their convictions overturned in 1990, when the Court of Appeal found that the convictions had been obtained oppressively.

On a closer analysis, the following 'trend' or 'grounds' emerge as the reasons behind miscarriages of justice. Firstly, the allegations of the concoction of forensic scientific evidence by police officers. Secondly, the non-disclosure of forensic scientific evidence. Thirdly, the non-disclosure of material evidence by prosecution to defence. Fourthly, as has sometimes been proven, the conduct of police officers during interrogation and

Civil and Criminal Appeals

interview: it is in some cases oppressive and, in some cases, violent and it is this conduct that produces unreliable confessions. Fifthly, the appeals post-conviction are subject to slow and cumbersome procedures, apart from other hurdles that the appellant must surmount before his/her/their appeal is heard. These issues play a vital role, in a sense that their values are of unquestionable importance. They form the very fabric of justice that is represented by the criminal justice system.

In conclusion, therefore, whilst it can be submitted that the cases discussed above do raise a presumption of the conflict of fundamental values within the criminal justice system, the presumption is now rebuttable in the light of the extended powers of the Court of Appeal, the creation of the Criminal Cases Review Commission, and recent legislation which is designed to control and/or prevent miscarriages of justice, such as the Criminal Procedure and Investigations Act 1996, and more recently the Human Rights Act 1998.

QUESTION TWO

Discuss the reasons for the establishment of the Criminal Cases Review Commission and evaluate its success to date.

University of London LLB Examination
(for External Students) English Legal System June 1999 Q7

General Comment

This question illustrates the importance of keeping abreast of developments in the law. It cannot properly be answered without reference to such as its lack of resources in the context of a large caseload and the extent to which criticism of the composition and powers of the Criminal Cases Review Commission (CCRC) have been justified. The opening discussion of the reasons for the establishment of the CCRC should be put in the context of the evaluation of its success and not be allowed to stray into a disproportionately long account of causes of miscarriages of justice.

Skeleton Solution

The need for an independent review body to replace the powers formerly held by the Home Secretary – the composition and powers of the Criminal Cases Review Commission (CCRC) – the role of the CCRC in the context of other reforms brought in by the Criminal Appeal Act 1995 – the conditions limiting referrals to exceptional cases with strong fresh evidence – the anticipated caseload and actual caseload of the CCRC – the extent to which criticism of the likely effectiveness of the work of the CCRC has been justified.

Suggested Solution

During the latter part of the twentieth century the reputation of the criminal justice system was damaged by a number of miscarriage of justice cases in which the Court of Appeal (Criminal Division) had dismissed appeals or rejected references from the Home Office, sometimes several times, and then eventually found grounds for allowing them, usually after long public campaigns. In 1991, after several referrals, the Court of Appeal was persuaded to quash the convictions in the 'Birmingham Six' case and the publicity this case attracted led to the setting up of the Royal Commission on Criminal Justice which conducted a comprehensive review of the criminal appeal system. The Report of the Commission, the Runciman Report, recommended that the role of the Home Secretary in post-referral appeals be abolished and that an independent authority be established with powers analogous to those of the Police Complaints Authority. The implementation of this proposal was the establishing of the Criminal Cases Review Commission (CCRC) by the Criminal Appeal Act 1995: ss8–14 and Sch 1. It has the power to review and investigate cases of suspected wrongful conviction, and/or sentence in England, Wales and Northern Ireland, and to refer cases to the appropriate court of appeal whenever it considers that there is a real possibility that the conviction, verdict, finding or sentence would not be upheld. It may also refer cases to the Secretary of State with a view to his recommending to the Queen the exercise of the royal prerogative of mercy.

The establishing of a review body that has constitutional independence both from the executive and the judiciary was welcomed by the Bar, the Law Society, by civil liberties groups and by senior members of the judiciary, such as the Lord Chief Justice. The quasi-judicial involvement that the Home Secretary had in the appeal process was constitutionally unsound and was suggested by some to be a reason for the traditional reluctance of the courts to interfere with convictions referred to them. The 1995 Act seeks to develop an independent, but close, relationship between the Commission and the Court of Appeal with the Commission referring matters to the Court for advice and the Court requiring the Commission to undertake investigations and report back. The impartiality of the Commission is also important to public perception of the way in which miscarriage of justice cases are dealt with. The Home Secretary was open to the conflicting accusations of making a reference out of political motivation and failing to make a reference out of reluctance to interfere with the judicial process. These and other similar concerns are addressed by the establishing of a body that 'shall not be regarded as the servant or agent of the Crown' (s4(2) Criminal Appeal Act 1995) and by laying down a composition for the Commission that requires a two-thirds lay majority made up of people who have some experience of the criminal justice and complaints system. It may consider on broad grounds any allegation of a miscarriage of justice resulting from either a conviction or a sentence in either the Crown Court or the magistrates' courts, either upon referral with leave of the Court of Appeal (which may wish to have the matter investigated in an inquisitorial manner) or after dismissal of an appeal. For the first time it will also be possible to make referrals in summary cases. Complaints may be received direct from members of the public and the Commission has the power to interview all applicants, including prisoners.

At the time the Commission was set up there were three main areas of doubt about the likely effectiveness of its work: the procedure for investigation of cases, the lack of provision of legal aid to applicants in prison and the lack of representation in its membership of persons experienced in criminal defence work. There is no specific evidence that any of these have detracted from the proper operation of the Commission. The failure to provide legal aid to convicted persons who have lost their appeal for the costs of advice and assistance in making representations to the Commission was contrary to the proposals of the Runciman Report, which had envisaged that that it would be available but would end once the Commission decided to investigate unless the Commission required further information or assistance from the applicant's solicitor. It is feared that this will prove to seriously restrict the work of the Commission who will have to be mindful of costs during their investigations and may find it difficult to instigate the investigation they require for some cases, but it remains to be seen whether this is a concern that is justified. The lack of ability for the Commission to rely on its own investigators to carry out an investigation is probably the most controversial of the issues. For cases originally investigated by the police the basic duty of investigation lies with the chief constable who may appoint an investigating officer either from his own force or from another. The Commission is intended to be analogous to the Police Complaints Authority which instructs the police to carry out investigations, and the Runciman Report concluded that there was no suitable alternative to this method of investigation. Since some of the most notorious of the miscarriages of justice have been caused and covered up by police misconduct, this continuing reliance on police investigations is seen as undermining the apparent independence of the Commission from the police. The Labour Party in opposition and lawyers groups such as the Legal Action Group argued that the police become judges and jury in their own cause. Chris Mullin, the Labour MP who campaigned successfully on behalf of the 'Birmingham Six', described it as 'an absolutely fatal flaw' in the new system, but others might regard this as an overreaction – it is insulting and false to suggest that no policeman can be trusted to carry out such work. Indeed, the wrongdoings of the West Midlands police force in the 'Birmingham Six' case were uncovered and exposed by the officers of the Devon and Cornwall police force.

The main complaint is about the long delays in dealing with the cases. This has detracted from the perceived success of the Commission but cannot be remedied without Government action in the form of funding to increase the provision of staff and facilities. The Commission inherited some 280 Home Office and Northern Ireland cases when it took office in 1997 and received over a 1,000 new applications in its first year. This is double the caseload that was anticipated and the Commission has been unable to cope with it on its present level of funding and resources. It may be that there was a surge of applications because there was a new Commission and that applications will level out. Nonetheless, it will take the Commission years rather than months to reduce the backlog and another surge, for example, as a result of the implementation of the European Convention on Human Rights, would quickly bring them back to having the same, or a worse, backlog of cases. By the end of its first year the Commission had referred 12 cases to the relevant courts of appeal and two appeals had been heard and had been successful. The Commission reported in its first Annual Report and Accounts: 'These are creditable statistics for the Commission's first year of caseworking, with potential for improvement as casework experience grows'. Their referral rate has since increased and a high percentage of these cases have been successful.

Any evaluation of the success of the Commission has to be made in the context of the other reforms introduced by the 1995 Act. Two changes are of particular importance: the substitution of a conviction that 'is unsafe' as the single ground for appeal to replace the three overlapping grounds under the 1968 Act, and the lowering of the threshold for the admission of fresh evidence. These changes are intended to keep cases of merit within the appeal system and so reduce the number of applications for post-appeal referral. The conditions placed on the power of the Commission to make a referral clearly intend to limit referrals to cases with strong fresh evidence which have exhausted their appeal remedies: there must be 'a real possibility' that the conviction will be quashed; an appeal must have been heard or leave to appeal refused; and the reference must be because of an argument or evidence not raised at trial or on appeal. Provision for post-appeal referral is thus seen as being confined to exceptional cases of particular merit. A Government discussion paper published in 1994 reflected this sentiment: 'A "last resort" procedure should be precisely that: a vehicle for remedying miscarriages of justice not an extra stage in the ordinary criminal justice process to be used routinely'. It is difficult to assess whether this balancing act has worked. There is a drop in the number of referrals being made to the Commission but sceptics believe that this may be in part attributable to the deterrent effect of the considerable delays caused by the backlog of work. The Commission is dedicated to reducing its backlog and states this to be its area of primary concern. Early investigations indicate that it is doing a good job.

QUESTION THREE

'Given that the whole structure of the English criminal process is weighted against the accused it is little wonder that miscarriages of jusstice have often occurred.'

Discuss.

University of London LLB Examination
(for External Students) English Legal System June 1998 Q7

General Comment

This is a very wide debate and care has to be taken to structure the answer so as to provide a broad discussion without losing too much detail. Discussion of the Police and Criminal Evidence Act 1984, the impact of the Criminal Justice and Public Order Act 1994 and the changes to the appeal system under the Criminal Appeal Act 1995 and work of the Criminal Cases Review Commission has to be included in the answer.

Skeleton Solution

Identification of the several causes of miscarriage of justice – purpose and success of PACE; impact of the CJPOA 1994; impact of European Convention on Human Rights – reasons for passing of the Criminal Appeal Act 1995 – changes to the appeal system – role of the Criminal Cases Review Commission.

Suggested Solution

Allegations of a miscarriage of justice arise from a number of causes. Cases alleging police misconduct receive the most media attention and this has the effect of focusing public reaction and calls for reform onto this one part of the criminal justice process. Legal representation, court procedure, rules of evidence, directions to the jury, grounds for appeal and rules for matters, such as the admissibility of fresh evidence, are all equally as important to the proper functioning of the criminal justice system and an allegation of a miscarriage of justice can arise from any one of them. There is a considerable amount of legislation in place controlling each of these parts of the system, some of which has been passed specifically to address defects and remedy problems that may result in a miscarriage of justice. The Police and Criminal Evidence Act (PACE) 1984, the Criminal Justice and Public Order Act (CJPOA) 1994, and the Criminal Appeal Act (CAA) 1995 are examples of the latter. They add to, and form part of, the myriad of legislative provision that attempts to create a criminal justice system which detects, investigates and prosecutes offences in a way that balances the interests of the public against the rights and liberties of suspects. The fact that the system is still the subject of highly contentious political debate suggests that this purpose has not yet been achieved and a proper balance has yet to be struck.

PACE was passed as a result of recommendations from the 1981 Royal Commission on Criminal Procedure. It deals principally with police powers relating to: stop and search; entry, search and seizure on premises; arrest; and interrogations and confessions. Codes of Practice are also issued by Home Secretary in respect of these powers and are used as a guide to the conduct of criminal investigations by the police. The purpose behind PACE was to strengthen police powers to combat crime whilst at the same time to preserve and strengthen the safeguards against abuse of such powers by clarifying on a statutory basis the exact extent of those powers and the rights of detainees. The extent to which the provision of the Act achieves a balance between these competing interests is a matter of heated debate. It cannot be denounced as being wholly ineffective if only for the reason that it significantly tidied up a morass of varying general and local powers and provides a centrepoint for the protection of a suspect's rights. There are, however, examples of the interpretation of its provision by the courts that lend weight to the contention under discussion that the structure of the criminal process is weighted against the accused. For example, in *R v Samuel* [1988] 2 WLR 920 evidence obtained after unreasonable denial to consult privately with a solicitor was excluded from the trial under s78 but, in that same year, *R v Alladice* [1988] Crim LR 608 decided that this rule of exclusion did not apply if the police had adequately informed the suspect of his rights and in *R v Dunford* (1990) 91 Cr App R 150 this erosion of the rule was further extended by the finding that it should also not apply if the suspect was a 'hardened criminal' well aware of his rights. It is difficult to see how this decision does anything other than make a mockery of the safeguard intended by the Act.

There has been amendment of the provisions in PACE by the CJPOA 1994. The Act also introduces new provisions, some of which sit alongside provisions in PACE, for example, the new powers of stop and search introduced by s60. Among the more controversial of the provisions of the CJPOA 1994 are the inferences that may be drawn from a suspect's silence and the taking of intimate samples from persons not in police detention. The incorporation of the European Convention on Human Rights into our law is likely to have a major impact on these and on a considerable amount of the other provisions in the CJPOA and the provisions in PACE. By virtue of s6 of the Human Rights Act 1998, which became effective in October 2000, it is now unlawful to act in a manner incompatible with the Convention rights. Further, the courts will have to interpret the provisions of all statute law so as to ensure consistency with the requirements of the Convention.

The unacceptably high proportion of allegations of miscarriage of justice also served to focus attention onto our system for appeals. The substantial referral of cases back to the courts can be seen as a mark of failure in the system of criminal justice. As was noted in a Government Discussion Paper published in 1994: 'A "last resort" procedure should be precisely that: a vehicle for remedying miscarriages of justice not an extra stage in the ordinary criminal justice process to be used routinely.' The late 1900s was marked by a number of cases in which the Court of Appeal (Criminal Division) had dismissed appeals or rejected references from the Home Office, sometimes several times, and then eventually been persuaded to find grounds for allowing them, usually after long public campaigns. The release of the 'Birmingham Six' after years of wrongful imprisonment in 1991 acted as the spur to the setting up of the Royal Commission on Criminal Justice which conducted a comprehensive review of the criminal appeal system. It reported in 1993 (the Runciman Report) and the proposals were enacted, with slight modifications, by the CAA 1995. Much of the criticism of the inadequacy of the referral system centred on the role of the Home Secretary as the authority responsible for investigating and referring cases back to the Court of Appeal. It was claimed that the judiciary resented the quasi-judicial involvement of the Secretary of State in criminal appeals and looked unfavourably on referral cases. Whether this suspicion was true or not, there can be no doubt that the Court of Appeal was reluctant to interfere with convictions. Critics of the Home Secretary's role also pointed to the dilemma that he faced as a result of the conflicting accusations of making a reference out of political motivation and failing to make a reference out of reluctance to interfere with the judicial process. The C3 Division of the Home Office responsible for reviewing cases and making referrals was criticised for its low referral rate which many attributed to a reluctance to interfere in the judicial process. A more practical criticism was the small size of the Unit and its obvious inability to deal with the caseload. With the intention of overcoming all of these concerns, the Criminal Cases Review Commission was established by the 1995 Act as part of the implementation of the proposals in the Runciman Report. It provides the sort of independent body that is required, but it also has insufficient resources to deal with the caseload actually received. The Criminal Cases Review Commission deals with approximately 800 petitions annually.

Two changes introduced by the CAA 1995 are important to the legislature's attempt to rectify problems under the old appeal system: the new single ground for an appeal and the new test for the admissibility of fresh evidence. The new single ground for an appeal is that a conviction 'is unsafe'. This replaces the former three overlapping grounds for an appeal under the 1968 Act which caused much confusion and were so narrowly interpreted by the Court of Appeal that they came to be criticised as acting as a 'straightjacket' fettering the exercise of discretion by appeal judges. The new single ground has been welcomed by some as creating a broader ground of appeal but it has also been criticised for not following the wording of 'is or may be unsafe' proposed by the Runciman Report. It is thought that this would have ensured the sort of interpretation required and brought within the appeal process cases that are still in danger of being excluded. The Law Lords rejected this view during the passage of the Bill thinking the additional words to be unnecessary for the reason that they were already implicit in the word 'unsafe'. Professor J C Smith ([1995] NLJ 533 and 572) suggested that the omission of them was an indication that the appeal judges need no longer apply the 'lurking doubt' principle and his view has since been confirmed by the Court of Appeal in *R v Farrow* (1998) The Times 20 October when it was said that the new test of 'unsafeness' under the amended s2(1) of the 1968 Act has the advantages of brevity and simplicity and that it would not be appropriate to place a gloss on that test in the form of the 'lurking doubt' principle.

The second change has been the lowering of the threshold for the admission of fresh evidence. By s4 of the 1995 Act the old test of 'likely to be credible' for fresh evidence which the Court of Appeal is allowed to receive has been replaced by the more generous phrase of 'capable of belief'. The Runciman Committee saw the role of the Criminal Cases Review Commission as being a broad one and decided against specifying criteria by which the new body should select cases for further investigation. Instead they expressed the view that, in practice, justification for investigating a case would rest on 'a conclusion on the part of its members that there is, or may be on investigation, something to justify referring it back to the Court of Appeal'. This is no doubt intended to allow the Criminal Cases Review Commission to adopt a different approach to investigating and referring back cases than that adopted by the Home Office which would not investigate unless there was fresh evidence. The Commission may investigate cases which involve the finding of fresh evidence where there is lurking doubt that such evidence will serve to persuade the Court to quash the conviction. A criticism of the former system was that investigation relied on there being fresh evidence but fresh evidence could not be discovered unless there was an investigation. A criticism of the new system is that it is for the Commission to decide whether to allocate resources to investigations where there is only a 'lurking doubt' and, given the financial constraints that the Commission finds itself in for its more important workload, this would seem to be an unlikely hope.

Miscarriages of justice that receive the most publicity are those concerned with 'wrongful convictions' resulting from police malpractice (such as in the 'Birmingham Six' case) or from faulty forensic evidence (such as in the case of the Maguires) or from failure to disclose relevant material as in the case of Judith Ward, or from other evidence of prosecution bias on the part of the trial judge. There is a second category that should not be ignored, that is, 'mistaken convictions' resulting from an honest misunderstanding of the issues or from reluctance to believe a defence which seems to lack credibility. It can be argued that the Runciman Report rather neglected this category and that there is a risk that insufficient attention will be paid to matters like uncorroborated accomplice evidence and the care which ought to be taken with eye-witness testimony. Greer ((1994) 57 HLR 58 at 73) has pointed out that less than one page of the 261 pages of the Runciman Report is devoted to identification evidence, even though there are grounds for suspecting that misidentification could be the most potent of all the sources of routine mistaken conviction. Out of the 49 cases referred to the Court of Appeal by the Commission in the period up to 31 October 2000, only one was concerned with identification evidence and the conviction was quashed.

It is to be hoped that, in time, the new appeal process and the work of the Criminal Cases Review Commission will bring about changes that will go some way to rebutting the contention made in the statement under discussion. The drop in referral of applications alleging a miscarriage of justice made to the Criminal Cases Review Commission set up by the 1995 Act is an encouraging factor in this respect.

QUESTION FOUR

Are the measures that have been taken in recent years sufficient to avoid future miscarriages of justice in criminal cases in England?

University of London LLB Examination
(for External Students) English Legal System June 1997 Q7

General Comment

A challenging question since it requires an examination of the various causes of a miscarriage of justice and an analysis of recent statutory reforms designed to deal with those causes. Whilst the reforms introduced by the Criminal Appeal Act 1995 probably deserve the most emphasis, other significant reforms should not be overlooked, notably those to the pre-trial process introduced by the Criminal Procedure and Investigations Act 1996.

Civil and Criminal Appeals

Skeleton Solution

Distinction between mistaken and wrongful convictions – the setting up of the Criminal Cases Review Commission – abolition of the Home Secretary's role in the appeal process – composition and operation of the new Commission – the legal aid problem – the new ground of appeal, based on the safeness of the conviction – the new approach to fresh evidence – new inquisitional procedures and disclosure rules introduced by the Criminal Procedure and Investigations Act 1996 – setting aside acquittals obtained by intimidation, etc.

Suggested Solution

No system of justice operated by humans can ever ensure that there are no miscarriages of justice, since a mistaken conviction (or acquittal) can arise from an honest misunderstanding of the issues or from honest reluctance to believe a line of argument which seems to lack credibility. If, however, the state is prepared to accept responsibility for wrongful convictions/acquittals, in the sense of those brought about by deliberate malpractice or negligence, it can be argued that recent reforms have gone some way to minimising, if not eliminating, the risks of this kind of miscarriage of justice.

Undoubtedly the centrepiece of reform has been establishment of the Criminal Cases Review Commission (CCRC), which started work on 1 April 1997. The Commission was set up by the Criminal Appeal Act 1995, which abolished the Home Secretary's referral powers previously used to ensure a reconsideration of a case by the Court of Appeal. These powers were unsatisfactory, not merely because of the limited research resources available to the Home Office but also because it was constitutionally unhealthy for the Home Secretary to exercise this quasi-judicial function. Successive Home Secretaries of different political parties were always exposed to the accusation that their decisions concerning certain sensitive applications (eg by convicted terrorists) were politically motivated. The criminal justice system ought to benefit from the transfer of the Home Secretary's referral powers to a body that is publicly acknowledged to be independent.

Indeed, this has proven to be true because since its formation in March 1997 the CCRC received a total of 4,830 cases and had completed 4,128 by March 2002. The CCRC handles up to 800 petitions annually. Amongst many of its successful appeals are cases like the Guildford Four (1989), the Winchester Three (1990), the Maguire Seven (1990), the Birmingham Six (1991), the Tottenham Three (1993) and the Bridgwater Four (1979).

Moreover, the passing of the Human Rights Act 1998, which gained force on 2 October 2000, now imposes the duty of compatibility with the European Court of Human Rights jurisprudence. For example, in *Caballero* v *United Kingdom* (2000) 30 EHRR 643, the UK Government accepted that the law on bail breached art 5 of the European Convention on Human Rights and, as a result, the English domestic law had to be reformed.

Apart from the new Commission, the Criminal Appeal Act 1995 also introduced reforms to the appeal process itself, notably the broadening of the ground of appeal into one based purely on the 'unsafeness' of a conviction, thereby giving the Court of Appeal potentially greater flexibility in considering arguments for appeal, such as those based on the negligence of defence counsel. The 1995 Act also introduced a new test for the reception of fresh evidence by the Court of Appeal, ostensibly to encourage the Court to take a broader, more sympathetic approach to the credibility of such evidence. However, whether the Court of Appeal will utilise this new potential remains to be seen; critics point out that appeal judges remain 'pillars of the establishment' who may be instinctively reluctant to concede that other organs of the establishment, such as the police or forensic service, have colluded in improprieties so as to secure a conviction (as stated by P Duff [2000] Crim LR 341).

Aside from the appeal process reforms have been made to some aspects of the criminal justice system designed to emphasise a more inquisitorial approach so as to help discover the truth behind a particular case. As Professor Zander has pointed out, the adversarial system is designed not to arrive at a 'correct' or 'truthful' decision but rather a finding of guilt or innocence upon a formal legal construction after due process of law. It may be that a switch to a more inquisitional approach is a precondition to the sort of reforms introduced by the Criminal Appeal Act 1995.

For example, the Criminal Procedure and Investigations Act 1996 proposes the introduction of plea and directions hearings for all trials on indictment (other than serious fraud), and of preparatory hearings for complex or potentially lengthy trials on indictment, similar to those held for serious fraud cases under the Criminal Justice Act 1987. The purpose of these proposals is to ensure better judicial management of the trial process and to assist the jury in the comprehension of issues. New rules requiring pre-trial disclosure of evidence are also introduced by the 1996 Act, designed to deal with the particular kind of miscarriage of justice that occurred in the case of Judith Ward, who was released after serving 18 years' imprisonment when it was discovered that relevant medical evidence had been withheld from the defence by the prosecution at her trial: *R v Ward (Judith)* [1993] 2 All ER 577.

Finally s54 of the 1996 Act recognises that a wrongful acquittal is as much a miscarriage of justice as a wrongful conviction by providing that the High Court may set aside an acquittal and order a retrial if the acquittal was obtained as a result of interference with, or intimidation of, witnesses or jurors in the case in question.

It is submitted that, if all else fails, the Human Rights Act 1998 will to some extent prevent miscarriages of justice within the criminal justice system.

Chapter 12

Arrest, Search and Seizure; Interrogations and Confessions

12.1 Introduction

12.2 Key points

12.3 Key cases and statutes

12.4 Questions and suggested solutions

12.1 Introduction

The Police and Criminal Evidence Act (PACE) 1984 was passed as a result of recommendations from the Royal Commission on Criminal Procedure (1981) Cmnd 8092. The provisions of PACE deal principally with police powers. PACE empowered the Home Secretary to issue Codes of Practice for the exercise of police powers within PACE. These are seen as a guide to the conduct of criminal investigations by the police. This chapter will consider the provisions of PACE and the relevant codes of practice connected with these powers. New police powers created by the Criminal Justice and Public Order Act (CJPOA) 1994 will also be considered. A further Act, the Criminal Justice Act 2003, also introduces several changes to the powers of the police.

12.2 Key points

Stop and search powers

Section 1 Criminal Justice Act 2003 extends stop and search powers under s1 PACE in respect of criminal damage.

Section 2 Criminal Justice Act 2003 allows persons accompanying the police under a warrant to actively assist in searching premises.

Police powers to stop and search under PACE:

Section 1 makes provision for the general power of the police to search a person or vehicle. This power can only be exercised if certain conditions are satisfied.

a) Section 1(3) – allows the power to be exercised if the police constable has reasonable grounds for suspecting that he will find stolen or prohibited articles.

b) Section 1(1) – this type of stop and search may only be carried out if the person or vehicle is in a public place.

c) Section 1(4) and (5) – with regard to persons or vehicles that are on land adjacent to dwellings, these may only be searched if the constable has reasonable grounds for believing that:

   i) the person does not reside in that dwelling; or

   ii) the person or the vehicle is not there with the permission of the owners of that dwelling.

The purpose of the search

The police may only stop and search if they have reasonable grounds to suspect that stolen or prohibited articles will be discovered.

a) Stolen goods

   Stolen goods are those goods acquired contrary to Theft Act 1968 and goods obtained by criminal deception, and handling.

b) Prohibited articles – s1(7) and s1(8)

   Section 1(7) stipulates that prohibited articles include the following:

   i) Offensive weapons – s1(7)(a)

   - any article made or adapted to cause injury; or
   - intended for such use by him.

   ii) Prohibited articles – s1(7)(b)

   - articles made or adapted for use in the course of an offence (see s1(8) for the relevant offences);
   - intended by the person for such use by him;
   - the offences concerned here include burglary and theft.

c) If the search results in the discovery of stolen or prohibited articles, s1(6) allows them to be seized.

Reasonable grounds for suspicion

The Codes of Practice give guidance as to the meaning of reasonable grounds for suspicion. The new Codes of Practice A–F were published in July 2004, so ensure that you reference the most up-to-date version. Some factors to be considered are:

a) nature of the article;

b) the time and place the person is seen;

c) behaviour of the person.

Reasonable suspicion cannot be based on personal factors – age, colour, etc.

Conduct of searches

Once s1 conditions are satisfied and the police have reasonable grounds, the search can continue within the procedure laid out in s2. The police constable must give:

a) his name and the name of the station to which he is attached;

b) the object of the search;

c) the grounds for conducting the search.

Duration of detention

To avoid delay persons or vehicles to be searched may only be detained for a reasonable time. What is reasonable is a question of fact. This detention is different from the detention that occurs after an arrest is effected.

Effect of Criminal Justice and Public Order Act 1994

Section 60 provides new powers of stop and search. It provides that where a police officer of the rank of superintendent or above reasonably believes that:

a) incidents involving serious violence may take place in any locality in his area; and

b) it is expedient to grant an authorisation to prevent their occurrence,

he may make such an authorisation in writing permitting the exercise of stop and search powers within a specified locality for a specified time not exceeding 24 hours. Such an authorisation may also be granted by a chief inspector or inspector where that officer reasonably believes that incidents involving serious violence are imminent and no superintendent or senior officer is available to make the written authorisation.

The period authorised may be extended for a further period of six hours if it appears expedient to do so, having regard to the offences which have or are reasonably expected to have been committed in connection with any incident falling within the authorisation.

Where an authorisation has been made, a constable in uniform may:

a) stop any pedestrian and search him or anything carried by him for offensive weapons or dangerous instruments;

b) stop any vehicle and search it, its driver and any passenger for offensive weapons or dangerous instruments.

There is no requirement that the constable should have reasonable suspicion in order to exercise these powers, in contrast to the exercise of the stop and search powers under

PACE (the latter continue to exist, unaffected by the new provisions of the CJPOA 1994).

Offensive weapons include any article made or adapted for use for causing injury to persons or which is intended by the person having it with him for such use by him or by some other person. Dangerous instruments are ones which have a blade or are sharply pointed. Such articles may be seized by the officer conducting the search, but there is no power to seize more general evidence of crime; an officer would have to arrest and use the powers of seizure consequent upon arrest to seize such evidence.

Code A Code of Practice states that all stop and search powers should be used 'responsibly'. Code A continues to regulate the manner in which stop and searches are conducted.

Note the safeguards stated by the courts in relation to the powers of stop and search in *Osman* v *DPP* [1999] 1 FLR 193.

Powers of entry, search and seizure on premises under PACE

Exercise of power with warrant issued by a magistrate

The warrant is generally issued where there are reasonable grounds for believing that:

a) a serious arrestable offence has been committed (s116; Sch 5); and

b) the material in the premises is likely to be of substantial value to investigations; and

c) the material is likely to be relevant evidence.

In addition one of the conditions within s8(3) must be satisfied:

a) it is not practicable to communicate with any person entitled to grant entry to the premises or access to the evidence; or

b) entry to the premises will not be granted without a warrant; or

c) the purpose of the search could be frustrated unless a constable can secure immediate entry to the premises.

The procedure for the application and execution of warrants is governed by ss15 and 16. A warrant remains valid only for one month, after which time it lapses and must be returned to the court. The search must take place at a reasonable hour and if anything is found, it may be seized. The premises to be searched must be specified in the warrant, eg the number of a particular flat in a block of flats: *R* v *South Western Magistrates' Court, ex parte Cofie* (1996) *The Times* 15 August (QBD).

Exercise of power without warrant

Section 17 allows a constable to enter and search premises if he has reasonable ground for believing the person he is seeking is on the premises and for one of the following purposes:

a) to execute a warrant of arrest;

b) to arrest a person for an arrestable offence; (note that s32 PACE states that the police can enter and search premises at the time of arrest or immediately before.)

c) to recapture a person who is unlawfully at large; or

d) to save life, limb or serious damage to property.

There is also a common law power, preserved by s17, to enter premises to prevent a breach of the peace but it has been said that this power must be exercised with great caution and only where really necessary, eg genuine domestic violence, not a mere quarrel: *McLeod* v *Commissioner of Police of the Metropolis* [1994] 4 All ER 553 (CA).

Under s18 PACE police can enter and search an arrested person's premises.

Powers of seizure

Section 19 confers a general power of seizure of property where the police are lawfully on any premises. A police officer may seize anything he has reasonable grounds for believing:

a) is obtained in consequence of the commission of an offence; and

b) is evidence in relation to an offence under investigation or any other offence; and

c) it is necessary to seize to avoid concealment, loss or alteration.

Once seized these articles may be retained so long as is necessary in all the circumstances.

(Note that at all times the police must inform the suspect of their actions or intended actions.)

Powers of arrest

Arrest without warrant: s24

The power of arrest here lies with both private citizens and the police. The power exists for offences where sentence is fixed by law and for offences for which there is a minimum five year sentence. The danger for a private citizen in making such an arrest is the possibility of an action in false imprisonment for a wrongful arrest: *R* v *Self* [1992] 1 WLR 476.

The exercise of the arrest power must be based on reasonable suspicion, ie would a reasonable person be of the same opinion as the arresting officer having regard to the information which was in the mind of the arresting officer? See *O'Hara* v *Chief Constable of the Royal Ulster Constabulary* [1997] 1 All ER 129 (HL) (based on the equivalent terms of s12 of the Prevention of Terrorism Act 1984).

Section 3 Criminal Justice Act (CJA) 2003 adds a power of arrest for possessing cannabis and for fraudulently obtaining a passport and driving licence.

Arrest for non-arrestable offences

Only the police have this power and it can be exercised if it appears that a service of summons is inappropriate and any of the general arrest conditions in s25(3) is satisfied, ie:

a) the name of the suspect is unknown or cannot be discovered; or

b) there are reasonable grounds for doubting that the name the suspect gives is his real name; or

c) the address the suspect gives is improper; or

d) the constable has reasonable grounds for believing arrest is necessary to prevent the suspect from:

   i) causing physical injury to himself or some other person; or

   ii) suffering physical injury; or

   iii) causing loss or damage to property; or

   iv) committing a public decency offence; or

   v) causing unlawful obstruction of the highway.

The procedure following arrest

The police are empowered to use such force as is reasonable under the circumstances to effect an arrest: s117 PACE.

By virtue of s28 PACE a caution must be administered immediately before or at the time of arrest or, if not possible, immediately after the arrest or when it becomes practicable to do so. Once arrested the suspect must be taken to a police station as soon as is practicable: s30. Once at the station the suspect is under the supervision of the custody officer.

a) If there is sufficient evidence the suspect must be charged. Once charged he ought to be released with or without bail unless:

   i) his name or address cannot be ascertained or are suspected to be false; or

   ii) he would abscond or interfere with the investigation; or

   iii) in the case of non-imprisonable offences there are reasonable grounds for believing that he ought to be detained for protection of himself or any other person or damage to property; or

iv) in the case of imprisonable offences there are reasonable grounds for believing that detention is necessary to prevent the person from committing an offence (this ground for refusal was created by CJPOA 1994, s28).

There is an absolute prohibition on the grant of bail to a person previously convicted of either murder, attempted murder, manslaughter, rape or attempted rape and who has now been charged with one or more of those offences: CJPOA 1994, s25.

The age at which a juvenile may be refused bail by the police has been lowered from 15 to 12 by CJPOA 1994, s24.

Under the Bail Act 1976 the police had no power to grant conditional bail, but this restriction has been removed by CJPOA 1994, s27 (although the new power does not include a power to stipulate conditions requiring the accused to reside at a bail hostel or to receive a medical examination). The custody officer is obliged to keep a bail record stating the conditions (if any) imposed and the reasons for them. The suspect is entitled to a copy of this record upon request. The suspect has the right to apply to a magistrates' court for unconditional bail or for a variation of conditional bail granted by the custody officer. The court has discretion to impose more onerous conditions if it thinks fit.

After the advent of the Human Rights Act 1998, art 6 of the ECHR which gives everyone a right to a fair trial, the issue of bail is rarely contested.

b) There is provision within s40(1) of PACE for a suspect's continued detention if the above provisions apply. However reviews of the situation must take place to determine if continued detention is justified.

c) Once arrested, if the suspect is not charged, s41 of PACE allows him to be held for 24 hours. After this time he must be released unless his detention is authorised by a police officer of at least the rank of superintendent or by the authority of a magistrate's warrant. Section 44 PACE allows a maximum detention of up to 96 hours. Note that under the Criminal Justice Act 2003 the superintendants' powers have extended from 24 to 36 hours (for any arrestable offence).

d) After charge and detention the suspect must be brought before a magistrates' court as soon as practicable. The CJA 2003 states that the police should leave the decision to charge or otherwise to the Crown Prosecution Service.

Interrogations and confessions

a) Section 56 allows an arrested person to have someone, eg a friend or relative, informed of his arrest. Delay is only permitted if the suspect is being detained for a serious arrestable offence and there is authority for the delay from a superintendent. This authorisation will generally be given where there is a possibility that allowing contact will lead to interference with evidence or personal injury to others or will alert other suspected persons or hinder the recovery of property.

English Legal System

Where the suspect is under 17 years of age, a parent or guardian should be notified of the detention: s34(2) Children and Young Persons Act 1933.

b) The right to consult a solicitor – suspects are often at a disadvantage because of a lack of knowledge of their rights or the powers of the police. The cautioning of suspects of their right of silence is not sufficient protection. Section 58(1) of PACE redresses the balance and allows a person arrested to consult a solicitor at any time. Delays may be authorised for the reasons given in (a) above. An added protection for the detainee is that he can request a copy of the Codes of Practice.

c) Section 76(2) provides for a confession to be excluded from evidence if it is obtained:

  i) by oppression (s76(2)(a)); or

  ii) in consequence of anything said or done which was likely in the circumstances to render any confession unreliable (s76(2)(b));

unless

  i) the prosecution can prove beyond reasonable doubt that it was not so obtained.

  ii) Oppression is defined by s76(8) as being torture, inhuman treatment, and degrading treatment, and includes the use or threat of violence.

A confession can be defined as an adverse admission in relation to the issue of guilt: see s82 PACE for a statutory definition.

d) Under s78 the trial judge has a discretionary power to exclude evidence if its admission would have such an adverse effect on the proceedings that it would be unfair to admit it. An example of such evidence might include a voluntary confession admissible under s76 but which was obtained by police trickery or deception. Much will depend on the nature of the trickery used by the police. All 'undercover' operations by the police will involve some kind of lie to trap the suspect, but there is no general defence of entrapment in English law and no general rule that evidence so obtained must be automatically excluded (contrast USA law).

The use of the caution and the right of silence

Sections 34–37 of the Criminal Justice and Public Order Act 1994 permit the trial court to draw inferences from a suspect's silence in certain circumstances and accordingly a new caution must be given to a person whenever that person is suspected of an offence (eg whether or not he is under arrest or detained at a police station) and where that person is being questioned about an offence. The new caution must always be given upon an arrest and also at the police station at the start of a formal recorded interview. It should be given again (or the suspect reminded that he is under caution) after any lengthy break in questioning.

The wording of the new caution is as follows:

'You do not have to say anything. But it may harm your defence if you do not mention when questioned something which you later rely on in court. Anything you do say may be given in evidence' (para 10, Code C).

Guidance on the judicial direction to juries for drawing inferences from silence was given in *R v Cowan* [1995] 4 All ER 939 (CA).

12.3 Key cases and statutes

- *Attorney-General's Reference (No 3 of 1999)* [2001] 2 AC 91
  The court retains discretion in admitting evidence obtained as a result of a prohibited investigation

- *O'Loughlin v Chief Constable of Essex* [1998] 1 WLR 374 (CA)
  Illustrates the use of 'reasonable force' in entering private premises

- *R v Aspinall* [1999] 2 Cr App R 115 (CA)
  Illustrates when a police interview should be excluded from evidence

- *R v Khan (Sultan)* [1996] 3 All ER 289 (HL)
  Evidence obtained by unlawful bugging of private property admissible

- *R v Latif; R v Shahzad* [1996] 1 All ER 353 (HL)
  Evidence obtained by undercover operation using dubious practices admissible

- Criminal Justice Act 2003 – introduces several changes to police powers

- Criminal Justice and Public Order Act 1994 – extended and created new police powers and criminal offences

- Police and Criminal Evidence Act 1984 – outlines police powers and the conduct of criminal investigations

12.4 Questions and suggested solutions

QUESTION ONE

The police are called to the Ministry of Defence to investigate a series of computer viruses that have resulted in the deletion of many important files and the corruption of software programmes. They are told that a computer consultancy firm had recently installed a new programme. They go to that firm's offices where they are told that the person who headed that particular contract, Mr Allison, has been off work with stress related sick leave since returning from that assignment.

PCs Eddison and Fisher (who are both in uniform) immediately go to the home address supplied. As they approach the house they observe a man hurriedly leaving and getting into a car. PC Eddison calls out: 'Stop! We need to talk to you'. But the man succeeds in driving off at speed. PC Fisher gives details of the car by radio to station headquarters and other police cars are alerted to try and intercept the man.

English Legal System

PC Eddison proceeds to the door of the house and finds it unlocked. He calls out: 'Is anyone inside? We are police officers, can we come in?'. Upon getting no reply the officers go inside and search the house. They find a quantity of magazines and newsletters devoted to protest movements and anarchism. They take them away along with a laptop computer.

Meanwhile, other police officers have succeeded in stopping the car and have arrested Mr Allison. He is taken to a local police station where he is held for several hours. Mr Allison asks to see a particular solicitor, but Superintendent Sullivan refuses access to a solicitor 'in case any organisation is involved, and the solicitor inadvertently alerts others'.

After six hours Mr Allison is interviewed with a tape recorder running. During that interview he denies any wrongdoing and says he simply panicked when he saw the police. That interview is terminated after two hours. An hour later he is interviewed again. Now he is confronted with the magazines and told that analysis of the laptop computer showed he is involved with international groups devoted to computer hacking (a statement the police know to be a conjecture, as the laptop computer had not yet been analysed). After three hours of interviewing Mr Allison breaks down in tears saying: 'I wish I had not done it, but the whole of western society is corrupt and I was only trying to defend the poor against exploitation'. He is charged with criminal damage.

Assess the police procedures and whether Mr Allison's confession could be used in court.

University of London LLB Examination
(for External Students) English Legal System June 2001 Q8

General Comment

This standard question on the Police and Criminal Evidence Act 1984 makes yet another appearance. It requires the student to assess the common law and statutory powers of the police in relation to powers of stop, entry, search, arrest, interrogation, confessions and the rules surrounding the admissibility of evidence.

Skeleton Solution

General powers of stop and search – powers of entry without warrant and the seizure of property (in the absence of the suspect) – powers of arrest – entitlement to a solicitor – detention, interrogation, confession and admissibility of confessions.

Suggested Solution

Police powers have grown in a piecemeal fashion over the years. They consist of a mixture of common law and statutory provisions. The Police and Criminal Evidence Act (PACE) 1984 deals principally with police powers. This Act empowered the Home Secretary to issue Codes of Practice for the exercise of police powers within PACE

1984. Whilst PACE 1984 itself is binding, the Codes are merely seen as a guide to the conduct of criminal investigations by the police.

The question raises the following issues, which I will then deal with in turn:

1. power of stop in order to question;
2. powers of entry into a private dwelling;
3. powers of search and seizure, post-entry;
4. powers of arrest;
5. rights of a suspect post-arrest;
6. interrogation and admissibility of confession evidence.

First, police powers of stop under PACE 1984. Section 1 PACE 1984 makes provision for the general power of the police to stop and search, but this power must be justified by the police on the basis that they (the police) have reasonable grounds to suspect stolen or prohibited articles will be discovered. This power may also be exercised when the police are investigating a crime or are following up on a complaint. Therefore, in this question, it is clear that the police are following a legitimate line of inquiry, and any stop and search effected by the police against Mr Allison, the suspect, will be valid and lawful.

Second, the police have entered Mr Allison's house in his absence. Though PC Eddison tried to stop him, Mr Allison got into his car and drove off and PC Fisher then relayed a message to the headquarters giving details of the car for it to be intercepted. This procedure is lawful. The issue is whether their entry into the home of Mr Allison is lawful. Clearly there is no search warrant on the police, and as such entry without a search warrant will be examined. Section 17 PACE 1984 allows a constable to enter and search premises without a warrant if he has reasonable grounds to believe that the person sought after is on the premises or that the suspect is hiding incriminating evidence or prohibited articles on his person or in the premises. As it was not known to PCs Eddison and Fisher that the person who drove off in the car was in fact Mr Allison, this belief could be justified by the police. Moreover, the door was unlocked and PC Eddison did ask if anyone was inside and whether they could enter. There was no response forthcoming, at least no negative response. The police could say that they feared that the person inside may have been injured or needed help or assistance. Entry on this basis is also allowed by s17 PACE 1984 without a warrant. Hence, the police could justify lawful entry under the circumstances. Since their entry is lawful, s19 PACE 1984 confers a general power to seize property once the police have lawfully entered into the premises. A police officer may seize anything which he has reasonable grounds to believe is evidence or can be used as such in relation to an offence under investigation, or any other offence for which the suspect is detained. Therefore, the items taken away by the police from Mr Allison's home do not in any way give rise to any improper procedure on the part of the police.

English Legal System

Next, the arrest of Mr Allison. The powers of the arrest are contained in ss24–25 PACE 1984. For serious offences which are arrestable by virtue of the nature of the offence, no warrant of arrest is necessary. However, for non-arrestable offences, the police may arrest without a warrant if the service of a summons is inappropriate (this is so in the case at hand), and if the general conditions of arrest as stipulated by s25(3) PACE 1984 are satisfied, for example, the name of the suspect is unknown or cannot be discovered, or the suspect must be prevented from escaping investigation. Therefore, the police can stop the car in question in order to ascertain the identity of the driver. They seem to have done this, and in fact they have arrested Mr Allison. Under s117 PACE 1984, the police can use such force as is reasonable under the circumstances to effect the arrest. Section 28 PACE 1984 dictates that a caution must be administered by the police before or at the time of the arrest. The suspect must be told why he or she is being arrested, and must then be immediately (or as soon as is practicable) taken to a police station. As there is no contrary information in the question, I shall proceed on the basis that the arrest has been properly executed.

Once arrested, the suspect has several rights at the police station. For example, he or she is entitled to consult the Codes of Practice. Section 56 PACE 1984 provides that the suspect is entitled to have his or her next of kin informed of the arrest. Section 58 PACE 1984 gives the suspect a right to legal representation. Therefore, Mr Allison is by law entitled to consult a solicitor. His request to see one was refused by the Superintendent on the basis that Mr Allison may belong to an organisation and that the solicitor may alert the others (inadvertently, of course). The question is whether the Superintendent's refusal is justified. First, it is submitted that it is not up to the police to determine matters of professional conduct to be exercised by a solicitor. In *R v Samuel* [1988] 2 WLR 920, the court stated that this fundamental right can only in exceptional circumstances be denied. This view was reiterated in *R v Alladice* [1988] Crim LR 608. Hence, by denying Mr Allison the right to consult a solicitor, the Superintendent has acted unreasonably and in contravention of PACE 1984 and the Codes of Practice.

Finally, the issue of the interrogation and the use of the confession evidence. Section 60 PACE 1984 states that all interviews must be tape recorded. This is fine. Mr Allison was detained for six hours prior to his first interview: why six hours? Could he not have been interviewed sooner? This raises the issue of the validity of the detention. Did the police caution Mr Allison prior to his first interview commencing? Suspects are entitled to have a lawyer present during the interview. This was not the case here. The first interview lasted for two hours. The Police and Criminal Evidence Act 1984 states that there must be a break at least every two hours. An hour later, Mr Allison is interviewed again. Was he cautioned by the police before the second interview commenced? It seems unlikely that this was done on the facts, and this raises the presumption of a breach of both PACE 1984 and the Codes of Practice on the part of the police.

Generally, confessions are admissible evidence unless the confession has been obtained by oppression (s76(2)(a) PACE 1984), or the confession is unreliable on the basis of anything said or done in procuring it (s76(2)(b) PACE 1984). In any event, the court may exercise its jurisdiction under s78 PACE 1984 to exclude any evidence which has been unfairly or improperly obtained. On the facts of this question, whilst it may not amount to torture, repeated interrogation in short intervals may be tantamount to degrading treatment. Additionally, it may also fall foul of the rights conferred by the European Convention on Human Rights, as incorporated by the Human Rights Act 1998.

Worst still is the conjecture fabricated by the police in order to elicit a confession. The police officer knew that what he was saying was untrue, and this in fact amounts to oppression, which is not allowed by s76 PACE 1984. Clearly this is irregular and the court should in all fairness exclude this evidence.

In conclusion, therefore, it is submitted that whilst the pre-arrest procedures were valid, lawful and in compliance with PACE 1984, the post-arrest procedures, on the other hand, have been seriously compromised.

QUESTION TWO

The police have been informed by Garnet that: 'a group of foreign people are meeting regularly at the local church hall and planning terrorist attacks ... I know because I've seen them carrying guns inside'. PC Blake and PC Flint are dispatched to observe the church hall. They see two men leave the hall and drive off in a car after having carried out a bag with what appears to be a rifle sticking out of it. The police follow the car to a house. As the two men carry the bag inside the house PC Blake runs over and calls out: 'Stop ... show me what you have in that bag!'. The two men manage to get inside the house and slam the door in his face.

PC Flint asks to be let inside but receives no response; he then calls for backup. When it arrives the police break down the door and search the premises. The bag contains a quantity of items that appear to be light machine guns and rifles as well as old army clothing. PC Flint says to the two men: 'What have you got to say about all of this?'. The two men just look terrified and begin yelling in a language none of the police can understand. PC Flint replies: 'Don't try those tricks on me ... anyway you are arrested, come with us'. As he takes the arm of one of the men the man pushes him and tries to run out of the door. PC Blake manages to trip him and he falls heavily, hitting his head, which begins to bleed profusely.

The men are taken to a local police station where they are questioned. They continue to speak loudly in a language no one can understand. A police constable bandages the injured man's head but no doctor is called. Police Superintendent White decides that no solicitor should be called as: 'that might alert others who are involved'. The men are kept in separate cells overnight. In the morning a solicitor and interpreter are called. Shortly afterwards the Vicar of the local church arrives. He explains that the men can hardly speak English and that they are the leaders of a drama group organising a play about the terrible events they survived in Bosnia, the production of which is sponsored by funds from the Arts Council. The weapons turn out to be actors' props. The men are released shortly afterwards.

English Legal System

Assess the police behaviour and validity of the procedures and advise whether the suspects have any claims against the police.

University of London LLB Examination
(for External Students) English Legal System June 2000 Q8

General Comment

The conventional problem-type question on police powers makes yet another appearance. Students must be fluent with the relevant provisions of the Police and Criminal Evidence Act (PACE) 1984 as well as the Codes of Practice affecting police powers.

Skeleton Solution

Police powers in general – powers of stop, search, entry into premises, questioning and detention – PACE 1984 – remedies available against police.

Suggested Solution

Police powers, having grown in a piecemeal fashion, are governed by both common law and statute. Firstly, in relation to the powers of stop and search, common law states that the police have general powers to stop and search anyone in any place where the public have free access, although this power must be based on reasonable grounds of suspicion. Under statute, the Police and Criminal Evidence Act (PACE) 1984 provides for the same in ss1–7. Here, the police are acting on information which is quite sensitive given its nature (ie, foreigners, local church, terrorist attacks, carrying guns etc). The police have therefore acted in the public interest and on the grounds of having reasonable suspicion that criminal activities are occurring, or that a criminal activity is about to materialise. Hence, the attendance of PC Blake and PC Flint at the church hall is justified.

The next issue is whether the PCs could 'stop' the suspects. The PCs saw two men leave the hall and drive off, carrying a bag which the police believed to be a firearm. The police follow the car to a house, whereupon PC Blake calls out to the men to stop and reveal the contents of the bag, but the two men quickly go indoors and shut the door. Reasonable suspicion would entitle the police officers to stop a suspect for the purposes of effecting an inquiry or an investigation, but according to the Code of Practice 'A' which relates to the use of stop and search powers, reasonable suspicion must be supported by non-personal factors, and that is evidently clear in this case in that the suspects seem to be carrying a rifle, or something that appears to be a rifle.

Although the PCs asked to be let in, they received no response from the suspects, who were clearly indoors. If the PCs were let inside, then their entry would have been lawful. However, in this case, the police were not let in, as a result of which backup was called, and when it arrived the door was broken down and the police entered the premises and effected a search. The powers of entry and search will now be examined.

Arrest, Search and Seizure; Interrogations and Confessions

Although the court in *McLeod v Commissioner of Police of the Metropolis* [1994] 4 All ER 553 commented that the police have a common law right to enter premises in order to prevent or deal with a breach of peace, even though the breach is in a private property, this power is only exercised in exceptional circumstances. The police should have obtained either an arrest warrant, or a search warrant from the local Magistrates' Court which would be valid for one month from the date of issue: s16(3) PACE 1984. There is no problem in establishing reasonable grounds for believing that there is 'incriminating evidence' to be found in the premises. The warrant would have justified both the entry and the search, as well as any subsequent seizures, if made.

Upon entry, the police find items that appear to be light machine guns and rifles as well as old army clothing. When PC Flint asks for an explanation, no response was made, whereupon PC Flint proceeds to arrest. The question does not state whether the police seized the 'incriminating articles', but a reasonable and procedural assumption would allow that inference. What is surprising is the fact that these so-called 'guns and rifles' which were merely actors' props was not discoverable by the police on the inspection at first instance. If the police had a search warrant, then their entry, search, seizure and arrest would have been lawful and justified. In the absence of it, the court may declare these actions as unlawful and may invalidate the arrest. The issue of damages or compensation will be dealt with at the end.

In any case, s28 PACE 1984 states that any person who is being arrested must be informed of the reasons for the arrest in plain and simple English, and they must be made aware that they are being arrested. This does not seem to have been complied with by PCs Blake and Flint. The fact that the police have powers to arrest under s24 PACE 1984 is immaterial to this fact. If, on the other hand, the two suspects had been arrested outside the house, then s32 PACE 1984 allows the police to exercise powers of entry and search immediately after arrest without a warrant, as stated in *R v Badham* [1987] Crim LR 202. The next issue is the use of force by the police to effect an arrest. Section 117 PACE 1984 allows the police to use such force as is reasonable under the circumstances to effect an arrest. What is reasonable force is a question of fact which is dependent upon the facts of each case. PC Blake's method of tripping the suspect, causing him to fall and suffer an injury, may be deemed as unreasonable force on the basis of *Director of Public Prosecutions v Greene* [1994] 3 All ER 513.

Section 30 PACE 1984 states that the arrested person must be taken to a local police station soon after arrest. This appears to have been done in this case. Once at the police station, however, the men are entitled by virtue of s56 PACE 1984, to have their next of kin (or someone) informed of their arrest. Further, under s58 PACE 1984, they are entitled to legal representation without any delay, as illustrated in *R v Samuel* [1988] 2 All ER 135 and *R v Alladice* (1988) 88 Cr App R 380. The men are kept overnight. No doctor was called to attend to the injury suffered by one of the men, although a police constable was said to have tended to the man's head injury. A solicitor and interpreter were called the following morning. The vicar of the local church also arrives and explains that the men were drama artists merely practising for a play, and the weapons

English Legal System

are only actors' props. They were all involved in a legitimate activity funded by the Arts Council. The police then released the men.

It is likely that the men would be successful in claiming compensation in the law of tort against the police for false imprisonment and unlawful arrest. This, of course, does not include breaches of PACE 1984 and the Codes of Practice, although this may enable the men to complain to the Police Complaints Authority, which may result in a disciplinary action against the officers concerned: s67 PACE 1984.

QUESTION THREE

'The Police and Criminal Evidence Act 1984 achieves a satisfactory balance between the interests of the community and the rights and liberties of suspects.'

How far do you agree with this statement? Support your argument by reference to the provisions of PACE and recent case law.

University of London LLB Examination
(for External Students) English Legal System June 1999 Q8

General Comment

This is a broad question about the panoply of powers provided by the Police and Criminal Evidence Act (PACE) 1984 which needs to be structured so as to address the question of how those powers impinge on the rights and liberties of a suspect, and whether in so impinging a satisfactory balance is maintained between their particular rights and interests and the interests of the remainder of the community. The effect of the Criminal Justice and Public Order Act (CJPOA) 1994 should be mentioned, but the question clearly requires that the focus of the answer lies with PACE. Reference to recent case law is essential.

Skeleton Solution

The purpose of PACE 1984 and the Codes of Practice and introduction to CJPOA 1994 – PACE 'stop and search' powers (s1); procedure under s2; new CJPOA powers (s60) – PACE powers of entry, search and seizure on premises (ss15–17 and 19) – interrogation of suspects and obtaining confessions (s56); exclusion of confessions from evidence (ss76 and 78) – balance of public and private interests; new caution under ss34–37 CJPOA; role of Criminal Cases Review Commission.

Suggested Solution

This is a broad question about the panoply of powers provided by the Police and Criminal Evidence Act (PACE) 1984, how those powers impinge (as they inevitably do) on the rights and liberties of a limited sector of the community, namely those who at the relevant time are 'suspects', and whether in so impinging a satisfactory balance is maintained between their particular rights and interests and the interests of the remainder of the community. Firstly, therefore, a brief examination of the scope of PACE is required.

The Act was passed because of recommendations of the Royal Commission on Criminal Procedure (1981) (Cmnd 8092) and deals mainly with police powers that have to be exercised subject to Codes of Practice issued by the Home Secretary, which operate as guides to the way the police should conduct criminal investigations. Further police powers were created by the Criminal Justice and Public Order Act (CJPOA) 1994, and there is subsequent criminal law and administrative legislation that is not directly relevant to the subject under discussion here.

First, therefore, there are police 'stop and search' powers under s1 PACE which apply to individuals and vehicles, where a police constable has reasonable grounds for suspecting that stolen or prohibited articles will be found ('prohibited articles' would include offensive weapons and equipment made or adapted for use in burglary or theft). The Codes of Practice stipulate when the grounds are sufficiently strong to cause suspicion, and s2 PACE goes on to establish the procedure to be followed once the s1 conditions are satisfied.

New powers of stop and search are provided by s60 CJPOA 1994, where a senior police officer (of the rank of superintendent or higher) has reasonable belief that incidents involving serious violence might occur on his patch, ie in any locality in his area. Here, on his written authority, a 24-hour policy can be put in force to stop and search, and if the circumstances are imminent and serious an officer of inspector rank can take the decision. The Criminal Justice Act (CJA) 2003 extends police powers of stop, search, entry and seizure. Section 1 CJA 2003 extends stop and search powers where criminal damage is suspected, and s2 allows persons accompanying the police under a warrant to actively assist in searching premises.

PACE also provides powers of entry, search and seizure on premises, where generally a warrant has to be issued if there are reasonable grounds for believing that a serious arrestable offence has been committed, by virtue of s116. This is where the police are looking for materials that are likely to be of substantial value to criminal investigations and would be relevant evidence. Sections 15 and 16 deal with issue of warrants in this regard. These powers are reinforced by s17, which allows a constable to enter and search premises where he has reasonable grounds for believing that someone he is trying to apprehend is on the premises, or where he is trying to recapture an escapee or is seeking to save life, limb or to prevent serious damage to property.

Section 17 goes further, preserving the old common law power to enter premises to prevent a breach of the peace from being committed, but this is fraught with danger for the police, as was evidenced by *O'Loughlin* v *Chief Constable of Essex* [1998] 1 WLR 374. Here the plaintiff and his wife had caused a fracas and damage to a neighbour's property when returning home from a night out, before barricading themselves into their own home. When the police arrived the couple were shouting and swearing and the wife spat at a police officer. The police entered the premises and the man received a black eye; he was subsequently bound over to keep the peace. However, he also subsequently obtained nearly £8,000 damages against the police for assault, and this was upheld by the Court of Appeal who took the view that, notwithstanding the couple's abusive and irrational behaviour, the police had not been justified in forcing entry.

There is also a power of seizure of property under s19 PACE, where police are lawfully on premises under the powers previously referred to. Under s24 there exist powers of arrest both for the police and for private citizens, where sentence is fixed by law and for offences where the punishment is a minimum five-year sentence. One relevant question here for the ordinary citizen is how she/he is supposed to know this in the heat of the moment, as her or his behaviour may only subsequently be legally justified in the light of the severity of the sentence available to punish the accused. It might be preferable from the community's point of view if the citizen's actions were judged by the reasonableness criterion, because in attempting to uphold the law or assist the police the individual may fall foul of an action for false imprisonment after what turns our to be a wrongful arrest, as in *R v Self* [1992] 1 WLR 476.

Further provisions of the 1984 Act deal with interrogation of suspects and obtaining confessions. Protection to the suspect is provided by s56 which allows the arrested person to have a friend or relative informed of their detention, with delay in doing this only available and justified if the alleged offence is serious and a superintendent authorises it. The balancing of the public's and suspect's interests element here is the risk that there might be tampering with evidence or witnesses if premature disclosure of police action takes place. There is the right to consult a solicitor and to request a copy of the Code of Practice.

Under s76 PACE a suspect's confession may be excluded from evidence if it is obtained by oppression or in circumstances that might render it to be unreliable, and this is reinforced by s78 which allows a trial judge to exclude evidence at his discretion if its admission would be likely to have an such an adverse effect on the proceedings that it would be unfair to admit it, eg if it were obtained in circumstances involving trickery or deception.

A good example of the dilemma which arises in attempting to balance public and private interests here is the new caution that was introduced by virtue of ss34–37 CJPOA 1994, because now a court is permitted to draw inferences from a suspect's silence after having been charged and the caution read out to him. The words 'it may harm your defence if you do not mention when questioned something which you later rely on in court' now appear in the caution, which detracts from the previous absolute right of silence that applied to an accused person. The public's interest in this is avoiding wrongful convictions: there may be many reasons why an accused fails or omits to mention something, which is not in fact indicative of guilt, but which now makes him run the risk of conviction – fear, ignorance, failure to understand the language, illness and so on.

The law, procedure and police practice prior to PACE was demonstrably causative of injustice, as various subsequent appeals have horrifically demonstrated, whether the cause was police corruption or scientific incompetence. This is further exemplified by the need to establish the Criminal Cases Review Commission with its very heavy workload. The more tightly drafted police powers under PACE and the CJPOA 1994, together with the Codes of Practice, should go some way towards redressing the balance. (The new Codes of Practice A–F were issued in July 2004.) The general public have quite legitimate expectations that villains should be apprehended and impeded, but every case of oppression, wrongful arrest or worse still wrongful conviction is a stain on civilised society. It is probably reasonable to conclude that the balance is never entirely satisfactory, and that in some regards the remedial legislation has not fully addressed the risks that exist for people who turn out to have been innocent, but who were in the wrong place at the wrong time.

QUESTION FOUR

Essex police have been called to a burglary at the premises of a small, highly specialised company, named Exhale. The managing director tells them that the only things taken were some files and computer chips containing the latest information on certain lines of product development. He also tells the police that the information would only be of interest to a competitor and that he had recently sacked a relatively senior employee, Mary Francis, when he discovered that she was in negotiations to join a rival firm, Extreme Vision. A search using the police computer reveals that she has previous convictions for fraud and for handling stolen goods.

The police make inquiries and discover Mary has recently joined Extreme Vision as product development manager. Two constables are dispatched to her home. Upon opening the door she is immediately arrested and taken to Essex central police station. Other constables take the opportunity to search the house and discover quantities of photocopied files relating to the products of Exhale.

At the police station, her request to have Mr Booker of Booker and Co, Solicitors informed of her detention is refused when Superintendent Sullivan learns that Mr Booker is also the solicitor for Extreme Vision. Mary is detained for 24 hours and questioned every three hours for periods of up to an hour. She consistently denies any knowledge of the burglary and claims the photocopies related to the fact that she often worked at home on the projects she had been previously involved with. At the end of the questioning the officer questioning her asserts 'that is very strange, since the only copies we have found match the details of those stolen' (a statement the officer knew to be untrue). In response Mary states 'you had better talk to Dick Mitchell, the Managing Director of Extreme Vision about that'.

The police obtain a search warrant to search the premises of Extreme Vision and seize all the files and computer disks in the product development section. Some of the files relate to new products which seem very similar to those developed at Exhale. The next day Dick Mitchell is arrested.

English Legal System

Assess the police procedures.

University of London LLB Examination
(for External Students) English Legal System June 1998 Q8

General Comment

A straightforward problem-type question on police powers of the type frequently found on these examination papers. The important thing is to concentrate on issues directly arising from the facts of the problem and avoid general narrative of the law of police powers. Reference must be made both to the provisions of the Police and Criminal Evidence Act 1984 and the Codes of Practice issued under it (latest issue July 2004).

Skeleton Solution

Powers of arrest (ss8, 15 and 16 PACE); for arrest without a warrant (s17 PACE) – powers of entry, search and seizure; seized business records (s14 PACE) – rules for charge and release on bail (s27 CJPOA) – entitlement to a solicitor (s58 PACE); detention, oppressive interrogation, cautions (s76 PACE).

Suggested Solution

Acting upon the information provided to them as in the initial paragraph above, the first action instituted by the Essex police was to send two constables to Mary's home, where she was immediately arrested apparently without caution, warning or discussion, and removed to the central police station. Immediately thereafter, her house was searched. These two procedures will be assessed first of all.

The exercise of the power of arrest by the constables should be based on the issue of a warrant by a magistrate, on the grounds that a serious arrestable offence has been committed, any material found upon her premises is likely to be of substantial value to the police investigations, and any material found is likely to be needed as relevant evidence in a prosecution. Sections 8, 15 and 16 of the Police and Criminal Evidence Act (PACE) 1984 apply. Some business records can only be seized by permission of a circuit judge under s14 PACE, so this may be an additional complication for the police.

A warrant remains valid for one month, and would then lapse, and a search should take place at a reasonable time, although what is reasonable is fairly subjective. The premises to be searched, however, should be precisely and clearly identified in the warrant: *R v South Western Magistrates' Court, ex parte Cofie* [1997] 1 WLR 885. It appears this procedure was not followed, but to arrest without a warrant s17 PACE would authorise a constable to enter and search premises if he has reasonable grounds for believing Mary was there and had committed an arrestable offence. It would seem that this might possibly provide a justification, although a warrant should preferably have been obtained. However, strict requirements are stipulated by the courts even where warrants are issued. For example, photocopies of a warrant unaccompanied by schedules of what was to be searched for were not acceptable in *R v Chief Constable of*

Lancashire, ex parte Parker [1993] 2 WLR 248. Powers of arrest without warrant should only be used in particular cases – for example, for offences against public order, where the offender might give false details, or involving children – but not in cases such as this one.

If the police were lawfully on the premises they would have a general power of seizure of property if they had reasonable grounds for believing that the materials were obtained in consequence of her having committed an offence and it was necessary to seize the photocopies in order to avoid concealment, loss or alteration. It would appear that they should have obtained a warrant to justify this, and it may well be doubtful whether at that stage they had sufficient grounds for doing so.

As an example of the considerations to be borne in mind, the court considered the need for an arrestable offence to have been committed in *Chapman v DPP* (1989) 89 Cr App R 190 where a police constable Sneller was called to assist another police officer who was being assaulted by some youths. PC Sneller tried to enter some premises to apprehend a youth, but the youth's father resisted as he was in his own home at the time. He was charged with obstructing a constable in the execution of his duty and was acquitted on the basis that the assault on PC Sneller's colleague was not an arrestable offence, so he had no power of arrest himself when he chased the youth into his father's premises. This is not a very satisfactory state of affairs either for police officers, nor for members of the public who might be seeking to assist the police in the execution of their duties.

Following Mary's arrest she should have been charged and released without bail unless one of a number of grounds applied, for example if she were likely to abscond, or would be likely to commit an offence. The police might argue that they had reasonable grounds for believing that her detention was necessary to prevent her from committing a (further) offence, which was a ground of refusal created by the Criminal Justice and Public Order Act (CJPOA) 1994, but on the face of it that seems a weak argument here. If bail is justifiable, it can now be conditional under s27 CJPOA 1994.

Mary is entitled to ask for a solicitor under s58 PACE, and to ask for a copy of the Codes of Practice. It is not up to the police to determine matters of professional conduct to be exercised by the solicitor, so the excuse that they used for not allowing her to see Mr Booker is insufficient, and in any event even if it were justified she should have been allowed to choose an alternative legal adviser. Her detention for 24 hours without charge and with repeated interrogation is oppressive under s76 PACE, which reflects the European Convention on Human Rights definitions. Police actions here would clearly not amount to torture, but they could amount to inhuman or degrading treatment, and any evidence obtained in such circumstances could be excluded by the trial judge were she ever to be prosecuted, if he formed the opinion that its admission could have an adverse effect on a fair trial. Her repeated protestations of innocence, and the reasons she gives for possession of the materials, are plausible and do not justify 24 hours of repeated interrogation without access to legal advice.

No mention is made of any caution being administered, and the police officer who talked about the copies matching the stolen materials when he knew that to be untrue is attempting to obtain a confession by oppression which would also come within the terms of s76 PACE. The belated obtaining of a search warrant after all these irregularities, and the subsequent arrest of Dick Mitchell, only serve to cloud the issues further. The police at that stage might have to start considering the possibility of conspiracy which is outside the scope of the considerations here.

All in all the investigation has been bungled and procedures seriously compromised.

QUESTION FIVE

The police receive an anonymous phone call which states that a large consignment of drugs is about to arrive by lorry into England. An increased watch is ordered on all trucks and lorries coming into the UK. A decision is made to follow a lorry belonging to Osal, a well-known Turkish freight company, which has returned from a trip to Turkey. The lorry is followed by PCs Johnston, Peters and Burrows into London. It does not go to the company warehouse but stops outside a private house. The driver is observed carrying several large bags inside. PC Johnston rings the door bell and asks if the driver, Asif, would mind answering a few questions. Asif repeatedly refuses to co-operate and tells PC Johnston to 'clear out' and tries to close the door. PC Johnston forces himself into the house and grabs Asif stating 'I am arresting you on suspicion of drug smuggling. You do not need to say anything but it will harm your defence if you do not mention when questioned something which you later rely upon in court. Anything you say will be used in evidence.'

PC Burrows and Peters search the cargo of the lorry damaging several items, but find no drugs. They then enter the house and search for the bags which had been taken inside. They find that the bags contain clothing but also a significant quantity of cannabis.

Asif is taken to the local police station. He is held for several hours and questioned repeatedly but denies any wrongdoing. He is denied access to a solicitor. After six hours of questioning he is told 'the cargo is now in our hands and you had better come clean'. Asif then states that he was pressurised into transporting drugs by James, a superior at Osal, who would otherwise have sacked him. The police obtain a warrant to search James's house and in their search find a substantial sum of money.

Assess the legality of the police behaviour and whether the drugs, Asif's statement and money found at James's house will be admissible in future court proceedings.

University of London LLB Examination
(for External Students) English Legal System June 1997 Q8

General Comment

A standard problem-type question on police powers conferred by the Misuse of Drugs Act 1971 and the Police and Criminal Evidence Act 1984 (PACE). Familiarity with the contents of the most recent (July 2004) Codes of Practice issued under the 1984 Act is also required. It is important to distinguish between police illegalities (which may give rise to civil or criminal proceedings against the police), and police improprieties (breaches of the Codes, which do not give rise to such proceedings but which may be relevant to the question of admissibility of evidence). A general narrative of police powers should be avoided; instead address only the precise issues which arise from the facts given.

Skeleton Solution

Police powers to question and interview suspects – the need to caution when interviewing – effect of a failure to caution – nature of 'reasonable suspicion' to form the basis for making an arrest – need to state fact of, and reasons for, an arrest – the need to caution a person under arrest – searches of premises following an arrest: scope of s32 PACE – power of seizure under s19 PACE and of retention under s22 PACE – need to keep written records of arrests and searches – procedure for detaining suspects at police stations – suspects' statutory rights under ss56 and 58 PACE; grounds for denying such rights – admissibility of evidence; discretion of trial judge to exclude improperly obtained evidence under s78 PACE – admissibility of evidence; requirement to exclude confessions obtained by oppression and/or unfair inducements under s76 PACE – admissibility of evidence found as a result of an inadmissible confession: scope of s76 PACE.

Suggested Solution

I am asked to advise on the legality of police behaviour and on the admissibility of certain items of evidence as a result of the facts set out in a problem situation.

Legality of police behaviour

A number of issues arise under this category.

PC Johnston's forcible entry into a private house and his subsequent arrest of Asif

Since police suspicion in this case fell upon possible illegal importation of drugs, the relevant stop and search powers (of persons, vehicles and premises) are conferred by the Misuse of Drugs Act 1971, though in practical terms they are broadly similar to the general police powers contained in the Police and Criminal Evidence Act 1984 (PACE). PC Johnston had no statutory power to simply question Asif, so that any such questioning depends on the consent and co-operation of the person subject to it. If the questioning amounts to an 'interview' about a specific offence (as seems likely in this case) PC Johnston should have cautioned Asif as to his right of silence under Code C, para 10. If, however, the questions were of a general exploratory nature, no such caution need be given: *R v Christou* [1992] 3 WLR 228. In any event, failure to caution, although a procedural impropriety, is not an unlawful act upon the part of a police officer: s67 PACE.

English Legal System

Whether PC Johnston acted lawfully in entering the house and arresting Asif depends upon whether he had reasonable grounds for entering and making an arrest, and whether he used reasonable force in doing so. The facts disclose that the police had been motivated by an anonymous tip off and, as a result of a general watch, became suspicious when Asif's lorry unloaded at a private house rather than a company warehouse. This may arguably make the suspicion 'reasonable' because it provides some objective evidence for the suspicion (it is more than a mere 'hunch' or instinct). Further, a police officer is entitled to form a suspicion on the basis of what he has been told. It is not necessary for the officer to show that the information was accurate: *O'Hara v Chief Constable of the Royal Ulster Constabulary* [1997] 1 All ER 129. Further, the officer is under no obligation to delay an arrest in order to conduct further questioning or enquiries: *Holgate-Mohammed v Duke* [1984] 1 All ER 1054. On the facts given it is suggested that PC Johnston had an honest and reasonable belief that Asif was involved in the commission of a serious arrestable offence and that he used reasonable force to enter the house in order to arrest Asif.

The arrest could still be unlawful on other grounds. Every arresting officer must make plain the fact of an arrest (especially to someone who may have difficulty understanding English), and must also specify the reasons for the arrest: s28 PACE. PC Johnston seems to have complied with these requirements. Upon arrest the suspect must be cautioned as to his right of silence and, again, PC Johnston seems to have complied with this requirement because his minor deviations from the wording of Code C, para 10 did not destroy the true sense of that caution. The precise wording of the caution is as follows:

> 'You do not have to say anything. But it may harm your defence if you do not mention when questioned something which you later rely on in court. Anything you do say may be given in evidence.'

PC's Burrows' and Peters' searches of the lorry and the private house

The two officers are probably protected by the powers granted to them by the Misuse of Drugs Act 1971 since presumably they were acting on the same suspicions as PC Johnston. Further, under s32 PACE searches may be conducted on the premises on which Asif was arrested or in which he was present immediately before his arrest (ie the lorry), in order to discover evidence relating to the offence for which the arrest was made. The discovery of the cannabis is evidence of crime which may be seized by the police under, for example, the general power conferred by s19 PACE (assuming they were lawfully on the premises). The evidence may then be retained for so long as is necessary, eg for use at Asif's trial: s22 PACE. It appears that all three police officers in this case failed to keep written records of the arrest and searches, as required by PACE 1984.

Asif's treatment at the police station

The responsibility for such treatment is that of the custody officer, who should have ensured that Asif was accorded the rights for suspects provided by PACE 1984 and Code C of the 2004

Code of Practice. Two illegalities may have occurred.

a) Asif was entitled to have someone informed of his arrest and of the place where he was being held: s56 PACE. It may be that the custody officer will be able to rely on the statutory excuse provided by s56 for failure to do this, namely that a delay was necessary in the interests of the proper administration of justice, eg to prevent accomplices from being tipped off.

b) Asif was entitled to consult privately with a solicitor: s58 PACE. Again there is a similar statutory excusal for denying such access (ie that delay is necessary in the interests of justice), but it is much more difficult for the police to establish such excuse under s58 since they would need to show that the solicitor chosen by Asif could not be trusted to act properly (ie that he/she might tip off accomplices). Access to legal advice when under arrest at a police station has been described as a 'constitutional fundamental', and a breach of s58 may therefore amount to the tort of breach of statutory duty and, arguably, turn a lawful arrest into a false imprisonment: *R v Samuel* [1988] 2 All ER 135.

Any breaches of the Code of Practice on Detention at the police station will not involve illegalities but may affect the admissibility of evidence (below), as will the illegalities highlighted above.

The admissibility of evidence

The drugs

It has already been advised above that these were lawfully seized and that therefore they may be given in evidence at any trial.

Asif's statement

Since the statement followed a denial of access to a solicitor in probable breach of s58 PACE, this in itself may be a ground for the trial judge, using his discretion, to exclude the statement on the ground that to admit it would prejudice the fairness of the trial proceedings: s78 PACE. Any serious and substantial breaches of Code C may also persuade the trial judge of this point, eg failure to tape record the statement, failure to offer the suspect reasonable breaks during questioning, and failure by the custody officer to review the need for continued detention after the first six hours' detention – all of which may have occurred on the facts given. Further, under s76 PACE, the trial judge *must* exclude any confession obtained by oppression or which might be unreliable because the suspect was offered an improper inducement. Arguably the repetitive nature of the questioning, and the words 'you had better come clean', could be construed as sufficiently intimidatory in character as to amount to oppression, which was defined in *R v Fulling* [1987] 2 All ER 65 as the exercise of authority in a harsh or burdensome manner. In *R v Miller* (1993) 97 Cr App R 99 confessions were excluded after it was revealed that the police had shouted at suspects what they wanted them to say, even though they had denied involvement over 300 times during their interrogation.

The money found at James's house

Since the police had conducted a lawful search under a warrant the money could be seized as evidence of the profits of drug dealing, even though the basis for the issue of the warrant may have been an illegally or improperly obtained confession from Asif. This is because s76(4) PACE specifically provides that an inadmissible confession shall not affect the admissibility in evidence of facts discovered as a result of that confession.

Chapter 13

Prosecution and Bail

13.1 Introduction

13.2 Key points

13.3 Key cases and statutes

13.4 Questions and suggested solutions

13.1 Introduction

In October 1986, the system and responsibilities of prosecution underwent major change with the introduction of the Crown Prosecution Service (CPS). However, the police still play a major role in criminal prosecutions. The Glidewell Report (1998) is important as it introduced fundamental changes to the CPS structure. Changes to the CPS were also effected by the Access to Justice Act 1999 and the Crime and Disorder Act 1998. More recently the Government commissioned a White Paper in 2001, entitled *Criminal Justice: The Way Ahead*, to look into reforms in the area of criminal justice and evidence. The Department for Constitutional Affairs' website provides full details of this. See the following websites for further details:

a) www.cps.gov.uk;

b) www.homeoffice.gov.uk;

c) www.criminal-justice-system.gov.uk;

d) www.dca.gov.uk.

Reforms have also been introduced by the Criminal Justice Act 2003 in relation to charging a suspect and bail rights.

13.2 Key points

Prosecution

The police

The police initiate most prosecutions, principally because they are in the best position to investigate crimes and as they have wide powers of arrest. Once the accused is charged, the CPS will take over the prosecution. The police will however continue to assist the CPS in the collecting and giving of evidence.

The Crown Prosecution Service

a) The CPS was created by s1 of the Prosecution of Offences Act 1985. The Director of Public Prosecutions (DPP) is its head and is required to take over all criminal proceedings initiated by the police. The DPP may also take over any other prosecution initiated by a private individual or other body. The DPP acts under the supervision of the Attorney-General.

b) The principal importance of the CPS is its independence from the police and it is the CPS that takes the responsibility of deciding whether a particular prosecution should continue. The CPS is also in a position to discontinue proceedings in magistrates' courts: s23 of the 1985 Act.

The Glidewell Report (1998) has reorganised the CPS into 42 areas with a Chief Crown Prosecutor for each area. Note also that a statutory CPS Inspectorate was created in 2000.

Government bodies

Most non-police prosecutions are initiated by other Government bodies, for example the Health and Safety Executive, the Inland Revenue and the Serious Fraud Office.

Private individuals

Private individuals are in a position to prosecute other individuals, a right retained by s6 Prosecution of Offences Act 1985. They will generally do so where the police display insufficient interest in bringing prosecution.

The decision to prosecute

Not every criminal offence is prosecuted. The decision to prosecute is at the discretion of the prosecutor. It will largely be based upon the extent and quality of evidence available and the seriousness of the offence. The CPS issued a revised Code for its prosecutors in 2000. See, in this respect, *R v DPP, ex parte Kebilene and Others* [1999] 3 WLR 972 (HL).

There is, generally, no prosecution for technical infringements of the law. Often the police will issue instead a caution. This is principally used in relation to juvenile offenders and works by way of warning, so that although no prosecution takes place, the likelihood of prosecution is greater for subsequent offences.

It is extremely rare for the court to interfere with the exercise of the decision to prosecute, see: *R v Commissioner of Police of the Metropolis, ex parte Blackburn* [1968] 2 WLR 893.

A decision not to prosecute is, however, judicially reviewable: see *R (On the Application of Joseph) v DPP* [2001] Crim LR 489, but the courts are loathe to interfere.

Under s28 Criminal Justice Act 2003 the police should refer cases which they would normally charge to the CPS to determine whether proceedings should be initiated and, if so, on what charge.

Commencing a prosecution

The Code for Prosecutors 2003 prescribes a two-stage test:

a) the sufficiency of evidence to provide a realistic prospect of a conviction;

b) it must be in the public interest to prosecute.

Once these two conditions are satisfied, then there are two methods in which a prosecution may commence: laying an information and charging.

a) Laying an information

This is a statement of the suspected offence – either written or oral – and is generally used for less serious offences. The appearance of the defendant may be secured by either an issue of summons or a warrant for arrest.

i) Where a summons is required the information may be dealt with by the magistrates' clerk. Once a summons is obtained, it is issued to the accused and he is informed about when he is to appear before the magistrates to answer the allegations made against him.

ii) Where a warrant is required, the information must be in writing and on oath and it is the magistrate who must deal with the matter.

b) Charging

This is used for more serious offences, generally by the police. The charge is written down on the charge sheet and read over to the accused. He is then either detained or bailed. The charge sheet is then sent to the magistrates' court.

Bail

Bail is defined simply as the release of a person subject to a duty to surrender to custody at a particular time and place. It can be applied for both at the police station and at court. Note that s4 Criminal Justice Act 2003 states that the police can grant bail in the street rather than having to take the suspect to the police station.

A right to bail

a) Section 4 Bail Act 1976 gives the accused a right to bail. However, this does not mean that the accused may not be refused bail. The section does not apply to all stages of the proceedings. The importance of this right is that it is for the prosecution to show why bail ought to be withheld.

b) Section 4 applies to give a right to bail in cases that do not fall within Sch 1 of the Bail Act 1976. In these cases there is no statutory presumption in favour of bail and the defence would have to plead for bail. Section 14 Criminal Justice Act 2003 requires the courts to give particular weight in bail hearings to the fact that the offence under consideration appeared to have been committed while the defendant was on bail for another offence.

c) Cases in which there is no right to bail:

i) There is an absolute prohibition on the grant of bail to a person previously convicted of either murder, attempted murder, manslaughter, rape or attempted rape and who has now been charged with or convicted of one or more of those offences: Criminal Justice and Public Order Act 1994, s25.

However, an exception was created by s56 of the Crime and Disorder Act 1998 (bail may be granted in exceptional circumstances). The 1998 Act added this exception to satisfy the requirements of art 5 of the ECHR (the right to liberty and security) which was incorporated into the English legal system through the Human Rights Act 1998.

ii) Where the magistrates' court has summarily convicted the accused and commits him for sentence to the Crown Court.

iii) Where the accused has been convicted or sentenced by the magistrates or Crown Court and is appealing against conviction or sentence.

Factors to be taken into account

Paragraph 9 of Sch 1, Part I of the 1976 Act gives the court some guidance on approaching the issue of bail. The following ought to be considered in determining whether bail should be granted:

a) the nature and seriousness of the offence;

b) character, antecedents, associations and community ties ie, job, home, wife, children;

c) past record for answering bail;

d) strength of the prosecution's case.

Grounds for refusing bail – imprisonable offence

Schedule 1 lists the circumstances in which bail may be refused. This applies where the defendant is accused or convicted of at least one imprisonable offence.

The defendant need not be granted bail where:

a) the court is satisfied that there are substantial grounds for believing that if he is released he will:

i) fail to surrender to custody; or

ii) commit an offence; or

iii) interfere with witnesses or obstruct the course of justice *or*

b) the court is satisfied he should be kept in custody for:

   i) his own protection; or

   ii) if a juvenile, for his own welfare; or

   iii) where he is already serving a custodial sentence; or

   iv) he has already been bailed, absconded and been arrested.

In addition, s26 of the Criminal Justice and Public Order Act 1994 provides that a person need not be granted bail if:

a) the imprisonable offence is an indictable only offence or an offence triable either way, and

b) it appears to the court that he was on bail in criminal proceedings in respect of another offence on the date of that offence.

The usual considerations must be regarded as applying to a decision under para 9 (eg the nature and seriousness of the offence, etc) above.

This new restriction on the grant of bail is designed to deal with the growing number of offences committed each year by people on bail.

Under s14 Criminal Justice Act 2003 bail can be refused unless there are exceptional circumstances justifying the absolute right to bail. Conversely, if bail is granted for an imprisonable offence, s18 Criminal Justice Act 2003 allows the prosecutor a right to appeal to the Crown Court against the magistrates' decision.

Grounds for refusing bail – non-imprisonable offence

Schedule 1, Part II allows the court to refuse bail if:

a) on a previous occasion the defendant failed to surrender to custody; or

b) the court is satisfied that the defendant ought to be kept in custody for his own protection/welfare; or

c) the defendant is already serving a custodial sentence; or

d) he has already been bailed, absconded and been arrested.

Conditions on bail

The court may grant unconditional bail under s3 Bail Act 1976, in which case the only obligation is to surrender to custody at the time and place required.

However, the court is permitted to attach whatever conditions it deems fit. The most common conditions are:

a) to ensure the defendant surrenders to custody, the court may require a surety to undertake to pay a sum of money to the court if the defendant fails to surrender; no forfeiture will be order if the defendant absconds after surrendering to the custody of the court, eg after arraignment: *R v Central Criminal Court, ex parte Guney* [1996] 2 All ER 705 (HL);

b) the defendant may be required to report to a particular place at particular intervals;

c) the defendant may be required to live at a particular address;

d) the court may impose a curfew on the defendant.

Appealing against refusal to grant bail

Where bail is refused, a record is made of the decision and the reasons for it. The defendant may if he wishes obtain a copy.

Appeal against a magistrates' decision may be made to the Crown Court pursuant to s18 of the Criminal Justice Act 2003 in relation to all imprisonable offences. Section 22 of the Criminal Justice Act 1967 governs the jurisdiction of the High Court in this respect and provides for the High Court to grant bail or vary any conditions to bail imposed by the magistrates.

Appeal to the Crown Court is also possible. The Crown Court may grant bail, if it is refused by magistrates, in the following cases:

a) where the magistrates remanded the defendant in custody after hearing a full bail application; or

b) where the magistrates have committed the defendant to the Crown Court for trial or sentence; or

c) where the defendant was convicted by the magistrates and refused bail pending appeal to the Crown Court.

Appealing against/reconsidering a grant of bail

By virtue of s1 of the Bail (Amendment) Act 1993, where a magistrates' court grants bail to a person who is charged with or convicted of an offence punishable by a term of imprisonment of five years or more or an offence under s12 (taking a conveyance without authority) or s12A (aggravated vehicle taking) of the Theft Act 1968, the prosecution may appeal to a judge of the Crown Court against the granting of bail. This applies only where the prosecution is conducted by or on behalf of the Director of Public Prosecutions or by a person who falls within such class or description of persons as may be prescribed by the Secretary of State.

Such an appeal may be made only if the prosecution made representations that bail should not be granted and the representations were made before it was granted.

The appeal before the Crown Court is by way of re-hearing. The appellant has no right to be present. Although amendments to the Crown Court Rules make it clear the appellant may be present if either he is unrepresented or a Crown Court judge gives leave. The judge may remand the appellant in custody or grant bail on any terms he thinks fit.

In addition, s30 of the Criminal Justice and Public Order Act 1994 inserts a new s5B into the Bail Act 1976 to give a magistrates' court power, on the application of the prosecution, to reconsider a decision to grant bail made by a magistrates' court (or by a custody officer) before the accused's scheduled appearance in court, if new information comes to light. This new power is restricted to offences triable only on indictment or triable either way, ie where the new evidence indicates that the accused, if allowed to stay on bail, may be a social danger. The new power includes power to vary bail conditions or to impose new conditions to withdraw bail (in which case the accused, if before the court, must be remanded in custody or, if not before the court, must be ordered to surrender forthwith to the court; failure to surrender can be dealt with by arrest without warrant).

Failure to surrender

A person released on bail is guilty of an offence if he fails to surrender to custody: see s6(1) of the Bail Act 1976.

Note, however, all issues in relation to bail is now subject to arts 5 and 6 of the ECHR and the courts are bound to consider the jurisprudence of the European Court of Human Rights in deciding this issue: s3 Human Rights Act 1998.

13.3 Key cases and statutes

- *Cabellero* v *United Kingdom* (2000) 30 EHRR 643 (ECHR)
  Provides an illustration of the UK's violation of art 5 of the European Convention on Human Rights

- R v *Director of Public Prosecutions, ex parte Kebilene and Others* [2000] 2 AC 326
  A decision not to prosecute is judicially reviewable

- R v *Havering Magistrates' Court, ex parte Director of Public Prosecutions* [2001] 1 WLR 805 (QBD)
  Addresses issues in relation to fairness of the trial

- Access to Justice Act 1999 – gave Crown Prosecution Service lawyers advocacy rights in the Crown Court

- Bail Act 1976 and the Bail (Amendment) Act 1993 – govern the granting of bail in various circumstances

- Crime and Disorder Act 1998 – created new offences and gave new powers to the police and the Crown Prosecution Service

English Legal System

- Criminal Justice Act 2003 – creates new powers in respect of the CPS and bail rights
- Criminal Justice and Public Order Act 1994 – extended police powers significantly

13.4 Questions and suggested solutions

QUESTION ONE

Answer *both* parts:

a) Describe in outline the organisation of the Crown Prosecution Service in England and Wales; and

b) 'It has never been the rule in this country – I hope it never will be – that suspected criminal offences must automatically be the subject of prosecution' (Lord Shawcross). Discuss.

University of London LLB Examination
(for External Students) English Legal System June 1987 Q4

General Comment

This is a difficult question in both parts. Both parts of the question are sufficiently general to be capable of being handled in so many ways that it is hard to penetrate the mind of the examiner to see what he may have been seeking for when the question was set. This is not to say that questions have a particular answer that the examiner expects, it is just that one can usually recognise some of the points that are likely to be found in an answer.

Skeleton Solution

a) Historical perspective on the Crown Prosecution Service (CPS) – role of the Director of Public Prosecutions – role of CPS lawyers.

b) Reasons for close scrutiny of cases – public benefit for undertaking prosecution – consideration of available evidence.

Suggested Solution

a) The Crown Prosecution Service (CPS) was set up in October 1986 as a result of the Royal Commission on Criminal Procedure (1981). This seminal report gave rise to the Police and Criminal Evidence Act 1984 and the Prosecution of Offences Act 1985. The intention was to redefine police powers with regard to search, seizure, arrest and interrogation and to put the prosecution of offences into the hands of a completely new body. The two Acts may be seen as complementary in this respect. Until then prosecutions had been undertaken by the police themselves who had fulfilled two functions. First, to decide in what situations to prosecute. This is essentially an executive decision quite divorced from investigative or fact-finding tasks of the police or their functions in detecting or preventing crime. It is not unreasonable to assume that the decision to prosecute should be left to another body.

The second function undertaken by the police before the CPS was initiated was the actual conduct of the prosecution. This relates to the marshalling of the appropriate evidence and the presentation of the case of the court. It is not surprising that in view of the specialised forensic nature of the process that many police authorities had already recruited their own Prosecuting Solicitors' Departments. This formed the basis of the CPS. The prosecuting solicitors could conduct a case in the magistrates' court and would brief barristers when a case was to be dealt with in the Crown Court. The Glidewell Report (1998) has restructured the entire CPS. It has 42 areas with a Chief Crown Prosecutor for each area.

Before the establishment of the CPS the more serious crimes were dealt with by the Director of Public Prosecutions, and police forces were obliged to report these offences to the Director and sometimes could not prosecute without his authority. The Director of Public Prosecutions was the natural head of the new service. It was hoped that the CPS would provide for greater national consistency in the prosecution of offences for, although it remains a regionally based service, it is nationally organised.

It might be churlish to say that it would be easier to write about the *dis*organisation of the CPS. There have been many accounts of lost papers and poor preparation and advocacy. Many agents – barristers and solicitors in private practice – have had to be employed at higher rates than full-time members of the service because of the shortage of staff and this is generally attributed to the relatively poor pay offered to full-time Crown Prosecutors. Staff shortages have been linked to a somewhat hasty timetable of reorganisation and morale is undoubtedly low. Nonetheless, the concept of a CPS remains a good one and, even if the current difficulties are more than teething troubles, it must be made to succeed.

b) A major criterion in deciding whether to prosecute an offender must be the likelihood of success. Failure is both expensive and embarrassing in that the defendant has been put to unnecessary trouble and exposure to risk while the prosecutor may appear to be incompetent or the law and the prosecution a species of harassment. Of course, not every suspected criminal offence can be the subject of prosecution. First, it is necessary to see whether an actual offence has occurred, second, whether a perpetrator can be identified and apprehended. It seems unwise in general to prosecute an offence without a proper consideration of whether there is a criminal offence disclosed in the particulars of indictment.

To prosecute for a suspected criminal offence where none turns out to have been committed seems an equally strange way of proceeding. Coroners' juries are no longer able to name the person they believe guilty of a murder because it tends to force the hands of the police and, in any event, it may be ill-considered allegation.

If fresh evidence were to be discovered subsequently to an unsuccessful prosecution it could not be used, for the defendant, once acquitted, is not subject to double jeopardy, and could plead 'autrefois acquit'. The automatic prosecution of suspected offences might involve too much premature shooting of the police's bolt.

Another major criterion is the consideration of the public benefit to be derived from a prosecution. Although there is not a time limit for the prosecution of indictable offences, summary offences must be prosecuted with six months. An offence committed many years before might not be worth prosecuting at a later date. It might be considered oppressive to do so.

For that matter the prosecuting authorities have a discretion as to whether to prosecute at all. The police cannot attempt to prosecute every actual offence and there must be some reasonable discretion at this stage. Thus the dropping of litter is unlikely to be prosecuted and most police officers would not even warn a person in those circumstances. Even first offences of the possession of small amounts of the less harmful controlled drugs are unlikely to be the subject of prosecution. In these circumstances the police are more likely to issue a caution, either formally or informally. There are regular provisions for the administering of a formal caution by a uniformed police officer and this is often used in the case of juveniles or minor shoplifting cases.

There are many cases where prosecution will not be merited in the circumstances of a case but there are at least two problems that flow from this. One is the assumption which may easily be made that a person brought before the courts has been previously cautioned and that this therefore is effectively a second offence. Secondly, there is a visible danger in allowing anyone other than an open court of law to decide on the appropriate course of action once a person has been accused of having committed an offence. There are occasional allegations that people of influence have been able to avoid prosecution, although this normally refers to minor offences. It is both impossible and undesirable that every suspected person or offence should be subject to formal prosecution. Commonsense must be allowed to enable some discretion to be used in these situations.

QUESTION TWO

Critically assess the advantages of TWO of the following:

a) tape recordings of confessions of accused persons in the police stations;

b) the general right to bail created by the Bail Act 1976;

c) the discount on sentence allowed to an accused person who pleads guilty.

University of London LLB Examination
(for External Students) English Legal System June 1988 Q2

Note: para (b) is the subject of this chapter. Paragraph (a) was dealt with in Chapter 12 and paragraph (c) is covered in Chapter 16. For convenience the entire solution to all three parts of the question is set out below.

General Comment

The key word here is 'critically'; your judgment is asked for on three topical areas of criminal justice. 'Critically assess' means look at the advantages and disadvantages of both the theory and practice of the three areas and perhaps come to a conclusion as to what the Government should now do to remedy any defects. It should not be forgotten that those who do best in exams are generally those who have original ideas on an area.

Skeleton Solution

a) Section 60 of the Police and Criminal Evidence Act 1984 (PACE), introduction of tape recordings – challenges on evidence obtained without recordings – disadvantages of tape recordings.

b) Consideration of s4 Bail Act 1976 – exceptions to the general right to bail – options available to a defendant on refusal of bail – the new rules imposed by the Criminal Justice Act (CJA) 2003.

c) Individualised sentencing – how can guilty pleas be seen as a mitigating factor?

Suggested Solution

a) Section 60 of PACE lays a duty on the Home Secretary to, by statutory instrument, introduce the tape recording of interviews of criminal suspects throughout England and Wales. Since the passing of the Act the new system has been introduced. Before looking at the merits and demerits of tape recording let us examine briefly the advantages and disadvantages of the new and old systems.

The old system involved a police officer, usually together with a fellow officer, when interviewing the suspect in either taking down verbatim in question and answer format what is said. Alternatively, he could keep a note in his 'pocket book' or the fellow officer could keep a note in his pocket book. The trouble was that this pocket book note was often in summary form because the officer wanted to save time by not noting down every word. When the matter came to court there were frequent challenges to statements obtained by either of the above methods because it was said other things were said by the police or the accused which were not recorded in the note book. These challenges wasted a lot of time at the trial. Also the police officers wasted a lot of time writing up interviews, either verbatim or later on where pocket book notes were transferred to sheet paper.

The trouble with the new system is that it is expensive and slow. It is expensive because the equipment is more costly and sometimes several tapes are needed for one interview and because the interviews are slower and therefore wasteful of police manpower. Tape recorded interviews are slower because every word of the interview is recorded start to finish, even requests for a cup of tea. Much irrelevant material is recorded which has no bearing on the case and sometimes the jury have to listen to this at the trial. The advantages are a dramatic reduction in the number of challenges at the trial and at other stages. There can be no doubt about what was said. Eventually therefore, the new system should speed up the trial and make the criminal justice system a little more efficient.

b) Bail is a right not a privilege as the Bail Act 1976 makes plain: s4. However, this 'right' is not in practice a right because there are a wide range of circumstances where bail will not be granted. There is much concern also that magistrates do not grant bail in all the cases that they should do and there are often cases where, against the strict letter of the law, magistrates refuse bail and it is necessary for the accused to go to a higher court before being granted bail (often to the consternation of the judge). Bail may also be granted by the police prior to the accused's first appearance before court. Bail is also governed by the CJA 2003 which empowers police to grant bail on the streets as opposed to at the police station.

Section 4 provides that the accused 'shall be granted bail except as provided in Sch 1'. This right to bail continues from the date of the first appearance up to the date on which he is acquitted or convicted. Therefore the right continues during the trial and the judge must give reasons for overnight (and sometimes over lunch) detention. The exceptions to this general right provided in Sch 1 are that, in the case of an imprisonable offence:

i) The accused would:
- fail to surrender to custody;
- commit an offence while on bail;
- interfere with witnesses or otherwise obstruct the course of justice. Or

ii) The accused needs to be kept in custody for his own protection. Or

iii) Because of lack of time since commencement of proceedings the court is unable to say one way or the other because it does not have the information required to answer (i) or (ii) above.

The Criminal Justice and Public Order Act (CJPOA) 1994, s26 adds a further ground for refusing bail in the case of an imprisonable offence which is indictable only or triable either way, namely, that it appears to the court that the accused was on bail in criminal proceedings in respect of another offence on the date of that offence. This new restriction is designed to deal with the problem of offences committed each year by people on bail, although statistical research indicates this is a comparatively small percentage. See now s14 of the CJA 2003 which justifies the refusal of bail in specific circumstances.

Further, s25 CJPOA 1994 provides an absolute prohibition on the grant of bail to a person previously convicted of either murder, attempted murder, manslaughter, rape or attempted rape and who has now been charged with or convicted of one or more of those offences.

However, this refusal must now be read in the light of the exceptions introduced by the Crime and Disorder Act 1998 which was brought in to satisfy the Convention requirements in art 5.

If the magistrates refuse bail at one appearance the defendant can only make a renewed application to the bench if there has been a 'change of circumstances'. In practice it is very difficult to show this; for example, a grant of legal funding is not considered a change of circumstances. Therefore most defendants who are refused bail either go (most commonly) to the Crown Court or to the High Court to a judge in chambers, to argue that the magistrates at the lower court exercised their discretion in the wrong way. Often they do; a high percentage of appeals against refusal of bail are successful. It has recently been suggested that the change of circumstances restriction on reconsidering applications for bail in the lower court should be removed, as appeal to the higher court is wasteful of time and money and unjust to the accused.

Criticism of the present system centres around the high percentage of cases in which bail is refused rather than over-liberality. Research has shown that in cases where bail is granted pending trial only a very small number of defendants commit offences while on bail, less than one per cent. Also on moral grounds it must be right to try and incarcerate as small a number of people as possible pending trial or conviction. These people are after all innocent until proven otherwise – why should they be treated like criminals?

Therefore it has been said that the law needs to be drafted in a clearer way so that magistrates are in no doubt of the accused's right to bail. Also perhaps magistrates need better training in such matters. Such things as the change of circumstances restriction need to be removed. At a time of prison overcrowding it is now imperative that something is done, both for practical and for moral reasons.

c) Depending on the potential effect and strength of mitigation personal to the defendant on the trial judge, it may lead the sentencer to pass an individualised sentence whose aim is not to punish the defendant but to help rehabilitate him, or, if a tariff sentence is imposed, to a penalty somewhat less severe than that warranted by the offence viewed in isolation.

A common mitigating factor pleaded on behalf of defendants is that the defendant pleaded guilty. A judge must not increase the sentence he passes because the accused pleaded not guilty, even if he believes that the accused has committed perjury; or because the defendant's defence involved grave allegations against the police; or because by pleading not guilty the defendant has forced the prosecution to call witnesses who found giving evidence distressing or harmful, eg child witnesses to sexual offences.

However, it is well established that a guilty plea attracts a lighter sentence than a conviction following a not guilty plea.

Pragmatism is probably the major reason for treating a guilty plea as mitigation. If every defendant pleaded not guilty, the legal system could not cope with the extra work involved. If there was no advantage to pleading guilty, why should any defendant give up the chance of an acquittal, however remote? Therefore, in order to save public time and money, defendants should be encouraged to plead guilty. It is in the public interest to give a discount on sentence even if a guilty plea was not motivated by the defendant's contrition for the past and his determination to reform for the future. There is no precise percentage by which the sentence should be reduced on account of a guilty plea. The Court of Appeal (Criminal Division) cases have suggested that between one-quarter and one-third off the tariff custodial sentence would be proper, though this percentage may be reduced the stronger the case is against the defendant, ie had he pleaded not guilty he would have stood little chance of an acquittal.

Section 48 CJPOA 1994 makes it a formal requirement for a sentencing court to take account of the stage in the proceedings at which the offender indicated his intention to plead guilty and the circumstances in which this indication was given. Section 48 applies to all courts which are sentencing for an offence.

Chapter 14

Classification of Offences and Committal Proceedings

14.1 Introduction

14.2 Key points

14.3 Key cases and statutes

14.4 Question and suggested solution

14.1 Introduction

The classification of offences is vital to determine the mode by which they are to be tried. For this purpose offences are divided into three main categories, namely, offences triable only on indictment, offences triable summarily and offences said to be triable either way. Note that the Courts Act 2003 will support improvements to case preparation and progression by providing for binding pre-trial rulings in magistrates' courts, in line with the current procedure in the Crown Court.

14.2 Key points

Classification of offences

a) Indictable offences are generally the more serious offences such as murder, manslaughter, robbery, rape. These offences are triable only on indictment, ie triable by both judge and jury in the Crown Court.

b) Summary offences are the least grave offences, many of which do not carry a sentence of imprisonment. The offences are triable summarily in the magistrates' court.

c) Triable either way offences are offences of medium gravity. These offences vary in seriousness and include offences such as theft and handling stolen goods. As such they are triable in either the magistrates' or the Crown Court.

Criminal damage involving more than £5,000 is triable either way, but below that figure the offence must be tried summarily: Criminal Justice and Public Order Act 1994, s46(1).

Determining the mode of trial

In 1999 and 2000 the Government tried to remove the defendant's right to elect trial by jury at the Crown Court, but on both occasions the Bill was rejected by the House of Lords. However, s41 and Sch 3 of the Criminal Justice Act 2003 amend the existing procedure to be followed by magistrates' courts in determining whether cases that are triable either way should be tried summarily or on indictment.

The Auld review (2001) (see: www.criminal-courts-review.org.uk) recommended in this respect that offences punishable by up to two years' imprisonment should be tried by a 'hybrid' court consisting of a district judge and two lay magistrates.

Section 49 of the Criminal Procedure and Investigations Act 1996 introduces the plea before venue procedure, which requires the magistrates, before determining the mode of trial in triable either way cases, to ascertain the accused's plea.

Where an offence is summary or indictable, it must be tried accordingly. A choice only presents itself in relation to offences triable either way. Under s29 of the Criminal Justice Act 2003 the procedure is commenced by the service upon the accused by the prosecutor of a written charge and requisition to attend court. This replaces the old method of laying of an information and the issue of a summons. The accused may plead guilty by post if it is a non-imprisonable offence. However, if it is an imprisonable offence, the accused has to attend court in order to enter a plea.

If a guilty plea is entered, then the case is adjourned for pre-sentencing reports. If a not guilty plea is entered, then s41 and Sch 3 of the Criminal Justice Act 2003 states that magistrates would have to send to the Crown Court cases which would normally need to go there. This amends the old procedure of magistrates becoming 'examining magistrates' to determine the mode of trial. The new procedures introduced by the 2003 Act are designed to enable cases to be dealt with in the level of the court which is appropriate to their seriousness, and to ensure that they reach that court as quickly as possible.

The new procedure applies only to either way offences and will not affect the right of the accused to elect committal to the Crown Court on a declared plea of not guilty. It will also not affect the power of magistrates to commit for sentence either following a plea of guilty or following a conviction after a plea of not guilty. It follows that there may still occur a number of cracked trials because, for a variety of reasons, the accused indicates a not guilty plea and elects trial by jury even though his real intention is to plead guilty at the Crown Court. This may be the inevitable result of the Criminal Justice Act 2003 which may invariably give rise to two possibilities, namely:

a) magistrates may be tempted to deal with more cases themselves, thus resulting in more lenient sentences than that encouraged by existing Government policy; and

b) there may be more adjournments in the magistrates' court in order for the defence to obtain further information in deciding what plea to indicate.

Once the magistrate decides on trial on indictment or the defendant chooses this mode, committal proceedings will follow.

Committal proceedings

As a result of the Narey Report in 1997 (*Delays in the Criminal Justice System*), as well as the study conducted by the Royal Commission on Criminal Justice (1993), and after the use of pilot schemes to evaluate the utility and efficacy of committal proceedings, the recent Crime and Disorder Act 1998 abolished the practice of committal proceedings through s51. It came into force in January 2001. Since then there are no more committals for indictable offences.

14.3 Key cases and statutes

- *Atlan* v *United Kingdom* (2001) The Times 3 July
  Admittance and/or exclusion of evidence is court's prerogative

- *Jasper* v *United Kingdom* [2000] Crim LR 584
  Prosecutor can apply to court for non-disclosure

- *R* v *Davies, Rowe and Johnson* [2001] 1 Cr App R 8
  Entitlement to disclosure of evidence is not an absolute right

- Crime and Disorder Act 1998 – abolished committal proceedings

- Criminal Justice Act 1988 – added a fourth category of summary offences triable on indictment

- Criminal Justice Act 2003 – introduces changes to summary and triable either way trial procedures

- Criminal Law Act 1977 – divided offences into three categories of summary, indictable and triable either way

- Criminal Procedure and Investigations Act 1996 – introduced new procedural rules for summary and triable either way offences, for example, the plea before venue procedure

14.4 Question and suggested solution

See Question 3 in Chapter 16.

Chapter 15

Summary Trial

15.1 Introduction

15.2 Key points

15.3 Question and suggested solution

15.1 Introduction

Summary trial generally takes place before three lay magistrates or a single district judge. The procedure of summary trials is governed by the Magistrates' Courts Act 1980. The only limitation on the criminal jurisdiction of the magistrates' court is subject to geographical limitations. For an evaluation of the magistracy see Chapter 5.

15.2 Key points

Attendance and representation

In some cases the defendant is not required to be present at summary trial: s12 Magistrates' Court Act 1980 (as substituted by Criminal Justice and Public Order Act 1994). A defendant is permitted to plead guilty by post where the maximum penalty for the offence is no more than three months.

Information and plea

The first stage in a summary trial is the clerk 'putting the information' to the defendant and asking for a plea. Should the defendant plead guilty, sentencing is the next stage. Where the plea is not guilty, the trial will follow. For pre-trial disclosure requirements see Chapter 16.

Summary trial procedure

The Courts Act 2003 introduces new procedures relating to pre-trial rulings in the magistrates' courts.

At any time prior to, or during, a criminal trial, it is common for a defendant to change his plea from 'not guilty' to 'guilty' to one or more counts.

a) The prosecution will begin the proceedings with a short speech that gives some background information on the prosecution's evidence and will include a brief description of the facts of the case.

b) The prosecution must then bring evidence to show beyond reasonable doubt that the defendant is guilty. Usually, witness evidence is called. It is particularly advantageous to have oral evidence, as it allows the magistrate to evaluate a witness's credibility and gives the defence an opportunity to cross-examine.

c) Written statements of evidence may, however, be used in certain circumstances:

   i) Section 9 of the Criminal Justice Act 1967 allows the admissibility of written evidence in cases where the evidence is undisputed and certain formalities are complied with.

   ii) Section 105 of the Magistrates' Courts Act 1980 permits written evidence taken from a witness who is ill and unlikely to recover or is dead. This is permissible so long as notice is sent to the other side.

   iii) Section 42 Children and Young Persons Act 1933 permits certain types of evidence from children to be in written statements.

d) There are three stages in witness evidence: firstly the examination in chief; secondly, cross-examination by the defence, during which time the defence has an opportunity to ask questions and attempt to discredit the witness; and finally re-examination, which allows the prosecution to deal with any unfavourable answers given in cross-examination.

e) At the end of the prosecution case, the defence may make a submission of no case to answer, and if the magistrates agree with this, they may discharge the defendant.

f) The defence need not adduce any evidence as it is for the prosecution to prove the case.

g) The magistrates will then make their decision, taking advice from their clerk as necessary. The procedure to be followed before sentence is similar to that followed in the Crown Court: see Chapter 16, section 16.2.

15.3 Question and suggested solution

See Question 3 in Chapter 16.

Chapter 16

Trial on Indictment and Plea Bargaining

16.1 Introduction

16.2 Key points

16.3 Key cases and statutes

16.4 Questions and suggested solutions

16.1 Introduction

Indictable offences are tried in the Crown Court by both judge and jury. This mode of trial is also used for triable either way offences, either where the defendant elects it or the magistrate decides it is the suitable mode. The review conducted by Auld LJ sought to introduce changes. For further information: see www.criminal-courts-review.org.uk. Also note the effects of the Criminal Justice Act 2003.

16.2 Key points

Preparing the case for trial: plea and directions hearings, preparatory hearings and disclosure

a) The purpose of a plea and direction hearing (PDH) is to allow the judge to make a number of rulings so that the case can proceed quickly and efficiently to trial: *Practice Direction* [1995] 4 All ER 379. The judges' powers include the power to make binding rulings on the admissibility of evidence or questions of law or both: s40 of the Criminal Procedure and Investigations Act (CPIA) 1996.

b) In complex or potentially lengthy cases a preparatory hearing may be held so as to allow a more detailed investigation of the issues than is possible at a PDH: s29 of the 1996 Act. A preparatory hearing may be ordered at a PDH.

c) The arraignment of the accused (ie his plea) is taken at the PDH or preparatory hearing (unless already taken at the PDH).

d) One of the most important issues to consider at a PDH or a preparatory hearing is whether the new requirements on pre-trial disclosure of evidence by each side have been or are being complied with. These requirements were introduced by ss3–11 of the 1996 Act and also apply to summary trials where the accused intends to plead not guilty. There are three stages to the new procedure:

i) Primary prosecution disclosure – the disclosure by the prosecution of all unused material which might undermine the prosecution case;

ii) Defence disclosure – disclosure of the general nature of the defence (a requirement to disclosure details of alibi evidence already exists under s11 of Criminal Justice Act 1967); defence disclosure under the 1996 Act is mandatory in Crown Court cases but voluntary in the magistrates' court;

iii) Secondary prosecution disclosure – disclosure by the prosecution of any additional unused material which might reasonably assist the defence in the light of the defence disclosure. Note that under the Criminal Justice Act 2003 the prosecution must now disclose all such evidence. The accused will also be required to give more details in their pre-trial defence statement.

See, in this respect, the new Attorney-General's Guidelines on Disclosure (2000): see www.lslo.gov.uk.

Articles 5 and 6 of the ECHR also have implications on the applicability of the CPIA 1996.

Arraignment: pleas and plea bargaining

a) Ambiguous pleas – where a plea is ambiguous, the judge will explain to the defendant the necessity for a clear plea and a second arraignment should follow. Should the plea remain ambiguous, a plea of not guilty will be entered for the defendant.

b) Voluntary pleas – an appeal court may quash a conviction and order a retrial should it be proved that the plea was not made voluntarily. A plea is involuntary if the defendant is placed under pressure by the defendant's counsel or the judge (see the dangers of plea bargaining, below).

c) Inability to plead – where the defendant does not give a plea, a jury is empanelled to decide if the defendant is either:

   i) 'mute by malice', in which case his acts are deliberate and a plea of not guilty will be entered on his behalf and the trial will continue (see s6(1)(c) Criminal Law Act 1967); or

   ii) 'mute by visitation of God', in which case the proceedings will be adjourned to find a method of communication. Where there is doubt, a jury is empanelled to decide whether the accused is fit to be tried.

d) Guilty – sentence will follow such a plea, though there is a procedure for sentencing: see below.

e) Not guilty – the case will proceed to trial.

f) Guilty to a lesser offence – such a plea mus tbe acceptable to prosecution and judge, otherwise plea must be changed: s6(1)(b) Criminal Law Act 1967.

g) Autrefois acquit and autrefois convict – ie that the accused has previously been acquitted or convicted of the charge in question.

h) Change of plea – the defendant may change his plea at any stage of the trial before sentence is passed. Any change is subject to the judge's consent.

i) Plea bargaining – It is a well established practice for judges to give a more lenient sentence where an accused has pleaded guilty, on the ground that the accused has saved the court time and the public expense and has avoided unnecessary character attacks on prosecution witnesses at the trial. The earlier the plea of guilty, the greater the discount, up to perhaps one-third off the custodial sentence. This system of 'implicit bargaining' was examined by the Royal Commission (1993), which recommended that it should be 'more clearly articulated'. Accordingly, s48 of the Criminal Justice and Public Order Act 1994 requires a sentencing court to take account of the stage in the proceedings at which the offender indicated his intention to plead guilty and the circumstances in which this indication was given. The power applies to all courts which are sentencing for an offence. The effect is a formal recognition by a statute of what was previously an informal custom or practice. This has received statutory recognition in the form of Powers of Criminal Courts (Sentencing) Act 2000 which makes it mandatory for a judge to reduce sentences according to the timing and circumstances of the guilty plea.

An alternative way of achieving a more lenient sentence is through a system of explicit plea bargaining between defence and the prosecution, which may result in a 'plea arrangement' whereby the defendant pleads guilty to a lesser offence in exchange of the more serious charges being dropped. The prosecution may be prepared to indulge in this practice either to save costs of a trial ('costs bargaining') or because of uncertainty of winning on the original set of charges ('odds bargaining'). There are careful guidelines as to how the system should operate in order to avoid the defendant being pressurised and to prevent the judge from appearing biased: see guidelines of Lord Parker in *R v Turner* [1970] 2 QB 321 at 326, confirmed by *Practice Direction* [1976] Crim LR 561. This guidance puts emphasis on the need for any charge bargaining to take place in the presence of the judge (preferably in open court). Both prosecution and defence counsel are prohibited from 'sentence canvassing', ie approaching the judge so as to obtain his view on the likely sentence in the event of a specified plea arrangement. The courts have regularly given warnings of the dangers of plea bargaining, and convictions have been set aside in cases where improper pressure was placed on the accused to plead guilty or where the judge responded to improper canvassing: *R v Pitman* [1991] 1 All ER 468 (CA), especially per Lord Lane CJ, at pp470–471; *R v Preston* [1993] 4 All ER 638 at 655 per Lord Mustill; and *R v Thompson* (1995) The Times 6 February (CA). However, in *R v Dossetter* [1999] 2 Cr App R(S) 248 the Court of Appeal reminded advocates that plea bargaining 'forms no part of English criminal jurisprudence'.

By contrast, in America charge bargaining is a regular administrative practice conducted directly by the prosecution with the defence, in which the trial judge often acts as a mere 'rubber stamp' for any deal struck.

Trial procedure

a) Empanelling a jury – a jury panel of between 20–25 people is summoned, out of which 12 will be retained as jurors and sworn in.

b) The prosecution's case – the prosecution will in its opening speech explain the process of the trial to the jury and also inform them of their role. The prosecution will then give the background of its case against the defendant. After this the prosecution will call its witnesses and the defence will have opportunity to cross-examine them. The defence has a right to an opening speech if calling evidence as to facts (ie witnesses).

c) Submission of no case to answer – this submission is made in the absence of a jury and it is for the judge to decide. Should he decide there is no case to answer, the jury is called back and will be directed to acquit; if not the trial will continue.

d) The defence will then put its case, and call its witnesses.

e) Closing speeches will be made by both the prosecution and defence.

f) Summing up – the judge will summarise the case to the jury. There are several issues he must bring to their attention:

   i) the respective roles of judge and jury;

   ii) the burden and standard of proof;

   iii) explanations of the law;

   iv) evidential rules;

   v) reminder of all material evidence;

   vi) direction as to the appointment of a foreman;

   vii) the need for a unanimous decision.

g) The verdict – after the summing up, the jury will retire to the jury room for their deliberations. The three possible verdicts they could return are guilty, not guilty or guilty of a lesser offence.

Majority verdicts are only allowable under the judge's direction where the jury have deliberated for at least two hours and 10 minutes.

h) The Royal Commission (1993) suggested various measures aimed at speeding up the whole process. For example, that opening speeches should be limited to a maximum of 15 minutes each, with concentration on general issues, not the evidence to be called; closing speeches should be limited to a maximum of 30 minutes each; time-wasting tactics by counsel should be stopped by the judge and penalised through reduction in fees on the judge's direction; judges should have power to exclude relevant evidence which is merely confusing, repetitions, etc; and that the judge need not sum up for and against the prosecution case in every case. Note that the Criminal Justice Act 2003 allows witnesses to give evidence using TV links from remote locations if this would be more efficient or effective.

Procedure before sentencing

The Criminal Justice Act 2003 makes major reforms to sentencing practice and sets in statute the purposes and principles of sentencing.

a) Where the defendant pleads guilty to an offence or is found guilty before sentence is passed it is the duty of the prosecution to recount the facts to the judge.

b) The defendant's antecedents must be made known to the judge. Usually a police officer dealing with the case is responsible for this and will give his evidence on oath. The procedure will generally include details of the following:

  i) age;

  ii) education;

  iii) employment;

  iv) domestic and marital status;

  v) income;

  vi) date of his last release from prison;

  vii) previous convictions.

  The defence may cross-examine or challenge the truth of allegations.

c) Reports on the defendant are an important part of this procedure. The major types of reports are:

  i) Pre-sentence reports, prepared by probation officers. These reports will deal with the defendant's social background and will make recommendations as to how he ought to be dealt with.

  ii) Community service reports must be prepared if the court wishes to make a community service order. They are required to consider the defendant's suitability for such a sentence.

  iii) Medical and psychiatric reports must be considered, where a judge wishes to detain a defendant in a mental hospital.

  iv) Reports of juveniles will be required to be prepared by social workers involved.

d) The defence may also make an attempt to persuade the judge to pass a more lenient sentence by entering a plea in mitigation. The defence will ensure that the following issues are considered:

i) any factor that makes the offence look less serious;

ii) any explanation for the commission of the offence;

iii) any developments in the defendant's future to indicate that he is unlikely to offend again.

16.3 Key cases and statutes

- *R v Pitman* [1991] 1 All ER 468 (CA); *R v Preston* [1993] 4 All ER 638; *R v Thompson* (1995) The Times 6 February (CA)
  Plea bargaining forms no part of English criminal jurisprudence

- *R v Turner* [1970] 2 QB 321
  Provides guidelines on plea bargaining

- *R v Ward (Judith)* [1993] 1 WLR 619
  Prosecution's duty of disclosure is higher than the defence's

- Crime and Disorder Act 1998 – abolishes the 'old' committal proceedings and introduces 'new' 'sending for trial' procedure

- Criminal Justice Act 1967, s11 – relates to the defence of alibi

- Criminal Justice Act 2003 – introduces new procedural rules governing criminal litigation

- Criminal Procedure and Investigations Act 1996 – introduced new procedural rules, such as plea before venue, plea and directions hearings, preparatory hearings and rules on disclosure

- European Convention of Human Rights, arts 5 and 6 – relates to fair trial and right to liberty and security

- Powers of Criminal Courts (Sentencing) Act 2000 – judges can now give sentence discounts based on guilty pleas

16.4 Questions and suggested solutions

QUESTION ONE

'Even the guilty are entitled to due process of law: a system of plea bargaining may undermine this principle, as it allows the state to secure convictions based on unproven allegations.'

Discuss.

University of London LLB Examination
(for External Students) English Legal System June 2001 Q5

General Comment

This would be a difficult question to attempt if the student is not thoroughly acquainted with the philosophy and practice of 'plea bargaining'. It requires an examination of whether true justice is being served, and whether 'due process' prevails.

Skeleton Solution

The nature of the criminal justice system – the practice of 'plea bargaining' – its rationale – a comparison of 'crime control' versus 'due process' – conclusion on the utility of plea bargaining.

Suggested Solution

One of the cornerstones of the English criminal justice system is its rigid compliance to the doctrine of the Rule of Law, which states that no one can or should be punished unless they are proven to be guilty of having committed a breach of the law. It is perhaps this rule that led to the presumption, in criminal trials, of innocent until proven guilty. Hence the ideal contained in the question at hand, ie that even the guilty are entitled to the due the process of the law. The issue to be addressed is the practicality of plea bargaining, and whether this practice lends support to the fact that it facilitates convictions which are unfounded, or created by way of a consensus or agreement between the prosecution and the defence on the basis of unproved allegations.

The benefit of case law or legislation would disclose that it is undeniable that at any time prior to or during a criminal trial, it is common for a defendant to change his plea from not guilty to guilty in respect of one or more counts. This may be attributable to a number of factors and, more importantly, it wastes court time and public resources. In fact, this was identified as being the main reason for plea bargaining by the Royal Commission of Justice.

Judges are more sympathetic towards defendants who clearly admit guilt and who are filled with remorse. One reason for this may be that by admitting their guilt, the accused has saved court time and costs (apart from the fact that the judge has to write lengthy grounds of judgment!). The case proceeds to sentencing, and once the appropriate pre-sentencing reports are received by the court, sentence is passed. Of course, if the sentence is excessive or disproportionate to the charge or charges, the accused may appeal against sentencing. Therefore, where is the unfairness of the practice or convention of plea-bargaining? Evidently, the guilty plea avoids any form of 'combat in court' between the prosecution and the defence, and this arguably cuts the costs of employing QCs.

To ensure that it was fair, this system of 'implicit bargaining' was examined by the Royal Commission in 1992, and the Commission recommended that it should be 'more clearly articulated'. This may be attributable to the fact that the practice was purely informal and lacked regulation. Accordingly, s48 Criminal Justice and Public Order Act 1994 requires a sentencing court to take account of the stage in the proceedings at which the defendant indicated his intention to plead guilty, and the circumstances in which this indication was given. The effect is a formal recognition by Parliament (through a statute) of what was previously an informal custom or practice. Recently, further statutory recognition compounded the practice of plea bargaining. The Powers of Criminal Courts (Sentencing) Act 2000 now makes it mandatory for a judge to reduce sentences according to the timing and circumstances of the guilty plea. Whether this acts as an inducement to plead guilty is questionable, but why would any accused what to plead guilty if he or she is innocent? Also, the fact that barristers should provide the best possible legal representation in the interests of justice, and certainly in the interest of the accused, would challenge any notion of irregularity.

Perhaps an acceptable way or method of plea bargaining would draw more nods of approval. There are careful guidelines as to how the system should operate in order to avoid the defendant being pressurised, and to prevent the judge from appearing biased. For instance, Lord Parker provided some guidelines in *R v Turner* [1970] 2 WLR 1093 and this was subsequently confirmed by a *Practice Direction* [1976] Crim LR 561. This guidance puts emphasis on the need for any plea bargaining to take place in the presence of the judge (preferably in open court). Both the prosecution and defence counsel are prohibited from 'sentence canvassing', which means approaching the judge so as to solicit his view on the likely sentence in the event of a specified plea arrangement.

Whilst the practice does undoubtedly exist, it is surprising that the Court of Appeal saw fit to remind practitioners that plea bargaining 'forms no part of English criminal jurisprudence' in the case of *R v Dossetter (Anthony William)* [1999] 2 Cr App R(S) 468. This is nothing new, because the courts have in the past regularly given warnings of the dangers of plea bargaining. A contrasting argument to that would be the fact that our appeal system is solid, and cases such as *R v Pitman* [1991] 1 All ER 468 and *R v Preston* [1993] 4 All ER 638 illustrate the fact that convictions have been quashed by the Court of Appeal where there is evidence of improper pressure on the accused to plead guilty, or in instances where the judge has positively responded to improper canvassing.

With the advent of the Human Rights Act 1998, the position of an accused is now strengthened in that improper pressure or an unfair plea bargain will vitiate the defendant's right to a fair trial, as he or she is entitled to under art 6 European Convention on Human Rights. Therefore, it cannot be seen as something that prejudices the accused's right to be tried fairly and justly.

In conclusion, it is submitted that there are sufficient safeguards to ensure that the practice of plea bargaining is not over-encouraged, and, if followed or practised, the right of the defendant or accused to the due process of law is never compromised. This Rule of Law shall, and always will, prevail over any other notion of administrative convenience.

QUESTION TWO

'It is inevitable that bargaining will take place in criminal cases. There is no reason why the practice should lead to injustice. Rather, it smoothes the processing of cases and avoids wasting public funds.'

Discuss.

University of London LLB Examination
(for External Students) English Legal System June 2000 Q6

General Comment

This question requires an evaluation of the concept or practise of plea bargaining and the arguments in support or against it.

Skeleton Solution

The rationale for plea bargaining – the types of plea bargaining – arguments for and against – Powers of Criminal Courts (Sentencing) Act 2000.

Suggested Solution

Whenever an accused appears before the court, he or she is asked to enter a plea during the process of arraignment. The plea is either 'guilty' or 'not guilty'. Criminal statistics reveal that the vast majority of offenders plead guilty. If a guilty plea is entered, the accused may be convicted and the process of sentencing commences. If, however, a 'not guilty' plea is entered, then the case must be tried and this could either be at the magistrates' court itself or at the Crown Court, depending on the nature and seriousness of the offence.

It is undeniable that at any time prior to or during a criminal trial, it is common for a defendant to change his plea from 'not guilty' to 'guilty' in respect of one or more counts (charges). This wastes court time and public resources and, as Darbyshire (Eddey & Darbyshire, *English Legal System* (7th edn, 2001)) observes, this has also been one of the concerns of the Royal Commission of Justice. Perhaps this explains the philosophy behind the practice of plea bargaining.

It is a well established principle of practice for judges to give a more lenient sentence where an accused has pleaded guilty, on the ground that the accused has saved court time and costs (public expenses). The fact that unnecessary character attacks on prosecution witnesses at the trial has been avoided is also of help, and is thus taken into consideration. The earlier the plea of guilty, the greater the 'sentence discount', up to perhaps one-third off a custodial sentence. This system of 'implicit bargaining' was examined by the Royal Commission in 1993 and it recommended that it should be 'more clearly articulated'. Accordingly, s48 Criminal Justice and Public Order Act 1994 requires a sentencing court to take account of the stage in the proceedings at which the defendant indicated his intention to plead guilty, and the circumstances in which this indication was given. The power applies to all courts which are sentencing for an offence. The effect of this is a formal recognition by statute of what was previously an informal custom or practice. This statutory recognition comes in the form of the Powers of Criminal Courts (Sentencing) Act 2000, which makes it mandatory for a judge to reduce sentences according to the timing and circumstances of the guilty plea. As to whether this encourages a form of 'forced' guilty plea or acts as an inducement for such pleas is arguable, but the fact that it paves the way for the quicker disposal of cases cannot be overlooked. Saving public expenses is another advantage.

Perhaps an alternative way of achieving a more lenient sentence is through a system of explicit plea bargaining, as is the practice between the defence and the prosecution. This may culminate in a 'plea arrangement' whereby the accused will plead guilty to a lesser offence in exchange for the more serious charges being dropped. The prosecution may be prepared to indulge in this practice either to save costs of a trial ('costs bargaining') or because of the uncertainty of winning on the original set of charges; this may be attributable to a lack of sufficient evidence, or the unavailability of prosecution witnesses or other issues. This is also known as 'odds bargaining'.

To preserve the notion of justice and fairness, careful guidelines have been drawn up on how the system should operate in order to prevent the defendant from being pressurised, and to prevent the judge from appearing biased. These guidelines were first given by Lord Parker in *R* v *Turner* [1970] 2 WLR 1093, and subsequently affirmed by the then Lord Chancellor in a *Practice Direction* [1976] Crim LR 561. This guidance places emphasis on the need for any charge bargaining to take place in the presence of the judge and preferably in open court. Both prosecution and defence counsel are prohibited from 'sentence canvassing', ie approaching the judge so as to obtain his view on the likely sentence in the event of a specified plea arrangement.

The courts have regularly given warnings of the dangers of plea bargaining, and convictions have been set aside in cases where improper pressure was placed on the accused to plead guilty or where the judge had responded to improper canvassing. This point is illustrated in *R* v *Pitman* [1991] 1 All ER 468, *R* v *Preston* [1993] 4 All ER 638 and *R* v *Thompson* (1995) The Times 6 February. It, therefore, is unsurprising that the Court of Appeal in the recent case of *R* v *Dossetter (Anthony William)* [1999] 1 Cr App R(S) 248 commented that plea bargaining, whilst practised, forms no part of English criminal jurisprudence.

It is further arguable that plea bargaining may now be challenged as violating the defendant's right to a free trial under art 6 European Convention on Human Rights. It cannot be viewed, for obvious reasons, as a regular administrative practise conducted directly by the prosecution with the defence, in which the trial judge often acts as a mere 'rubber stamp' or any deal struck between the parties.

This must, however, be balanced with the fact that at all times the accused has the benefit of legal advice of counsel, and therefore is protected from any allegation of being affected by unfair practices. It would also be unethical, as well as a breach of the

English Legal System

code of professional ethics, if the accused is not given the representation he deserves, and counsels engage in the act of plea bargaining purely for the sake of convenience. Ultimately, the fact that it saves the court time and resources, more importantly public expense, must be the main reason why the practice is allowed or followed. After all, if it helps oil the wheels of the criminal justice system, then why not?

QUESTION THREE

Your client Pierre (37), a hotel porter, has been arrested and charged with the theft of a ring worth £5,000 from a hotel guest. He tells you he is not guilty. Advise him:

a) in which court he will be tried and how this will be determined;

b) whether he will be entitled to legal aid to prepare and conduct his defence; and

c) on the merits of an application for bail. Pierre worked in England for 10 years; he lives at the hotel and is unmarried with no relatives in this country. He had no police record. He fears he will now lose his job.

University of London LLB Examination
(for External Students) English Legal System June 1987 Q6

Note: paragraph (a) is covered in this chapter and also Chapter 14. Paragraph (b) is covered in Chapter 9 and paragraph (c) was dealt with in Chapter 13. For convenience the entire solution to all three parts of the question is set out below.

General Comment

This is not a difficult question for those who have worked hard to understand the basics of procedure in the criminal trial. It is made harder to answer in that it also requires the candidate to have revised legal aid and the matter of bail. These are, however, all quite easy to deal with if the candidate has done the work because this question needs only the minimum of thinking or planning, although it is vital to be fast because of the amount of material to handle and thus it is important to be clear and precise.

Skeleton Solution

a) Classification of the offence – determination of mode of trial – Pierre's election and advice on the effect of his choice – committal proceedings for trial on indictment.

b) Application to Crown Court – the means and merits test and how it is applied.

c) Possible reasons for the police to object to bail – likelihood of refusal.

Suggested Solution

a) Theft is an offence triable either way, ie the offence may be dealt with either by the magistrates or by the Crown Court. The procedure is that Pierre will be brought before the magistrates at the earliest possible opportunity and then the prosecution and the defence will make representations as to the appropriate mode of trial. In view of the sum of money concerned and the circumstances of the theft (which involve a breach of trust) it is likely that the magistrates would decline to try the case themselves. In any event, as Pierre may well prefer trial by jury, this is not a problem. Even if the magistrates are willing to try Pierre summarily he must be asked if he consents to this mode of trial. This process is now governed by the Criminal Justice Act 2003 as well as the Courts Act 2003.

The magistrates would not proceed to immediate trial in any event as Pierre is going to plead not guilty and this would involve an adjournment in order for the prosecution to prepare its case. However, we must now turn to what will happen if the magistrates decide on, or Pierre insists on, a trial by jury at the Crown Court.

Committal proceedings for all indictable offences were abolished by ss51 and 52 of the Crime and Disorder Act 1998, but as theft is a triable either way offence the new style (short form) committal will be applicable. Under the new style committal – s6(2) of the Magistrates' Courts Act 1980 – no oral evidence will be heard. Only written statements, depositions and other documents will be submitted by the prosecution. No witness for either the prosecution or the defence will be required to give evidence. Pierre must be present throughout this process. The examining magistrate will then decide if there is sufficient evidence for the case to be committed to the Crown Court. If there is insufficient evidence, then the case will be heard summarily at the magistrates' court. Pierre would have no say or choice in the outcome of the case at this stage.

If Pierre wishes to give evidence of an alibi at his Crown Court trial he must give notice to the Crown Court of this intention within seven days from the committal of the proceedings to the Crown Court for trial, otherwise he will not be permitted to call alibi evidence without special leave of the trial judge: Criminal Justice Act 1967, s11 as amended by s5(7) of the Criminal Procedure and Investigations Act 1996.

The 1996 Act also requires each side to disclose relevant material to the other, though the defence will only need to supply a statement of the general nature of the defence. The burden is heavier on the Prosecution which must make disclosure of all unused material which might assist the defence.

b) As far as legal funding is concerned, the old system of criminal legal funding has been, since April 2001, replaced by the Criminal Defence Service (CDS). The CDS is administered by the Legal Services Commission (LSC). State-funded criminal defence will however continue to be given on a demand-led basis. The old criminal legal aid was means tested. The new scheme under the CDS abolishes this. Decisions to grant representation in individual cases are made by the magistrates' courts. Representations are always granted when it is in the interests of justice, particularly where, if the accused is found guilty, it will lead to imprisonment.

Further, to be refused legal funding or bail without a sound reason or ground would also violate the accused's rights under the European Convention on Human Rights. Article 6 would be breached in that the accused could claim that he or she was not given a fair trial.

Therefore, taking into account Pierre's circumstances, in all probability he would be granted legal funding under the new scheme of the CDS.

c) There is an entitlement to bail but the police may object although there is no special reason to think that they are likely to do so here. The reasons most relevant here for objecting to bail may be summarised as follows:

   i) The defendant is likely to abscond. This obviously relates to the seriousness of the charge and the roots that the defendant has in the community. Certainly, Pierre has something of a problem here but there are always possible conditions that can be attached to bail, such as the need to surrender a passport, or a requirement that the accused should reside in a certain place. Equally, the defendant may be required to report to the police station daily and Pierre could always make an offer to be bound by some condition or offer a surety, although it may not be necessary.

   ii) The defendant is likely to re-offend whilst on bail. There is no suggestion of this and it would seem highly unlikely. It would be important to see what the reaction of the hotel would be in these circumstances as Pierre might well be suspended from work and this would have a negative effect on the chances of obtaining bail. A helpful reference from his employers would go a long way here.

   iii) The defendant is likely to interfere with witnesses or obstruct the course of justice. This seems unlikely in the present case.

It therefore seems likely that Pierre would obtain bail. It must however be borne in mind that the refusal of bail does not contravene the rights of the accused under the European Convention on Human Rights.

QUESTION FOUR

Plea bargaining is prohibited because it is said to place unfair pressure upon the accused and to militate against a fair trial. Could a similar criticism be made about the practice of awarding sentence concessions to those who plead guilty?

University of London LLB Examination
(for External Students) English Legal System June 1992 Q3

General Comment

This question requires a great deal of careful thought. Although the information that must be dealt with is not particularly complex, to tackle the question effectively necessitates careful planning and consideration of structure.

Skeleton Solution

Clarify the actual status of sentence concessions, etc, in this jurisdiction – results in unfair pressure? – results in unfair trial? – conclusion, including attitudes of the profession and future status.

Suggested Solution

Plea bargaining and sentence concessions are among the most controversial areas of the criminal legal system and, with the recent proposals from the Bar Council's working party, they are again topical. This practice first received a statutory nod of approval in the form of s48 of the Criminal Justice and Public Order Act 1994 and more recently 'sentencing discounts' were recognised by the Powers of Criminal Courts (Sentencing) Act 2000.

The exact status of sentence concessions for guilty pleas in the English legal system is not without confusion. In practice, the technical guidelines and the realities are often different. So far as any form of plea bargaining exists, it takes two forms. Firstly, that of offering a guilty plea to the sentence charged. Secondly, pleading guilty to a lesser offence on the indictment in return for no evidence being offered for a more serious offence – 'the plea arrangement'. One needs to examine the use of these before considerations of fairness and pressure can be looked at. The case of *R* v *Turner* [1970] 2 QB 321 offers a valuable illustration.

The offering of a guilty plea is a well-known practice. While no promises are, or can be, given by the judge, it is established practice that a plea of guilty will count as a mitigating factor as it allows the defendant to show his contrition and remorse. Unofficially, it has been suggested that it may serve to reduce the sentence by a quarter or one-third. The plea arrangement is also widely used and is, in reality, a form of plea bargaining. However, the frequency with which these situations arise has in no way served to eradicate the problems that seem to come with them.

The use of the guilty plea is relied upon by the adversarial system. Without criminal cases being 'settled' in this way, the courts simply could not cope with the volume of work. Over 70 per cent of crown court cases are dealt with by a guilty plea. This clearly is an advantage in that it may allow more 'important' cases to be heard fully and sooner. Similarly, it relieves some of the pressures of lack of funding and saves witnesses the ordeal of giving evidence. If one could be sure it was only used by the guilty, the use of the plea could be advantageous. For the defendant it guarantees a sentence of less severity than a conviction of guilty. For the prosecution it alleviates the problems of a heavy case load and the time and expense of conducting the trial, as well as being a guaranteed 'win'. However, Baldwin and McConville (among others) believe they have clearly identified a problem of the innocent pleading guilty. This may start in the police station with an innocent detainee making a confession in order to obtain bail. However, even the slightest suggestion by the police that a plea of guilty would lead to a mitigation of sentence would make any resulting confession inadmissible under s76 of the Police and Criminal Evidence Act 1984. But it has already been suggested that it is common knowledge and may not require an overt suggestion from the police for the detainee to feel under pressure to plead guilty in order to go home, believing he can prove his innocence at a later date. Criticism has also been made of undue pressure from counsel and a lack of fight on the part of legal representatives. An abnormally high rate of guilty pleas on the North Eastern circuit was explained by one judge as being due to northern common sense!

The plea arrangement is also not without criticism. There are allegations of overcharging, where the prosecution will overload the indictment with more offences than they could realistically prove in order to obtain a guilty plea to the offence they are most concerned with. Similarly, it may mean the prosecution obtains a successful outcome for a case that may have proved very weak at trial. It obviously could act as pressure on the innocent defendant who may feel the 'system' is against him and decide not to risk being convicted of a more serious offence.

Clearly, the potential for undue pressure is there. This would undoubtedly mitigate against a fair trial as the defendant who pleads guilty never has the opportunity to put his case and force the prosecution to fulfil its legal and evidential burdens. But it should also be noted that there are attempts to alleviate the problem. Unlike some other jurisdictions, the English prosecution cannot exert any influence or make any suggestions on the length or type of sentence. It can only 'bargain' about the charges that will be offered. The role of judge and counsel in this area is confused, but attempts have been made to clarify this by case law and rules of professional conduct. With regard to plea arrangements, the judge cannot interfere and so it is up to the prosecution counsel what charges should be pursued and which should be left on file. But the judge does not have to agree with the plea arrangement, the most notorious example of this being in the trial of the 'Yorkshire Ripper' where the judge refused to accept a plea of guilty to manslaughter on the grounds of diminished responsibility, regarding it as in the public interest that a full trial for murder should take place (and the defendant was subsequently convicted). The case of *R v Turner* [1970] 2 QB 321 and the subsequent *Practice Direction* [1976] Crim LR 561 sought to make the role of counsel and judge in plea 'bargaining' crystal clear. While it is perfectly permissible for the counsel to advise his client that a plea of guilty may lead to a lighter sentence, it should always be emphasised to the defendant that he must only plead guilty if he is! The accused must have and feel that he has complete freedom of choice. There should be complete freedom of access between *both* counsel and the judge, but no indication of length of sentence must ever be given, nor implied to the client in conference. The judge must never be seen without both sides being present and the practice has become that approaches to the judge in chambers should only be made if absolutely necessary and may be turned down. Counsel is under a duty to relay to his client what exactly happened in the judge's chambers so no false assumptions can be made or inferences drawn. While these might appear to be ample safeguards, subsequent case law has shown that abuses of the system remain. Private communications between counsel and judge were condemned in *R* v *Pitman* [1991] 1 All ER 468, and *R* v *Thompson* (1995) The Times 6 February.

The evidence would seem to suggest that the risk of undue pressure is great, although not perhaps so great as in some other jurisdictions where the prosecution plays a more active and direct role in the sentencing decision. The future status of the practice is uncertain. Recent case law suggests the rules of conduct are unclear or ignored. This situation looks unlikely to change if the proposals of the Bar's working party are to be followed in which the working party suggested that plea bargaining is an option to be recommended to obtain the efficient disposal of business in the crown court, and that guidance on sentence lengths would help the guilty defendant come to a decision sooner and stop wasting court time. More recently, the Royal Commission on Criminal Justice (1993) recommended that the whole system should be clarified and kept under review. It is also recommended that the size of discount for a guilty plea should be proportionate to how soon in the proceedings it is given and that the judge should be able to indicate the maximum sentence he is inclined to give in the case.

Section 48 of the Criminal Justice and Public Order Act 1994 makes it a formal requirement for a sentencing court to take account of the stage in the proceedings at which the offender indicated his intention to plead guilty, and the circumstances in which this indication was given. The power is available to all courts which are sentencing for an offence: see Powers of Criminal Courts (Sentencing) Act 2000.

Revision Aids

Designed for the undergraduate, the 101 Questions & Answers series and the Suggested Solutions series are for all those who have a positive commitment to passing their law examinations. Each series covers a different examinable topic and comprises a selection of answers to examination questions and, in the case of the 101 Questions and Answers, interrogams. The majority of questions represent examination 'bankers' and are supported by full-length essay solutions. These titles will undoubtedly assist you with your research and further your understanding of the subject in question.

101 Questions & Answers Series

Only £7.95 Published December 2003

Constitutional Law
ISBN: 1 85836 522 8

Criminal Law
ISBN: 1 85836 432 9

Land Law
ISBN: 1 85836 515 5

Law of Contract
ISBN: 1 85836 517 1

Law of Tort
ISBN: 1 85836 516 3

Suggested Solutions to Past Examination Questions 2001–2002 Series

Only £6.95 Published December 2003

Company Law
ISBN: 1 85836 519 8

Employment Law
ISBN: 1 85836 520 1

European Union Law
ISBN: 1 85836 524 4

Evidence
ISBN: 1 85836 521 X

Family Law
ISBN: 1 85836 525 2

For further information or to place an order, please contact:

Mail Order
Old Bailey Press at Holborn College
Woolwich Road
Charlton
London
SE7 8LN

Telephone: 020 8317 6039
Fax: 020 8317 6004
Website: www.oldbaileypress.co.uk
E-Mail: mailorder@oldbaileypress.co.uk

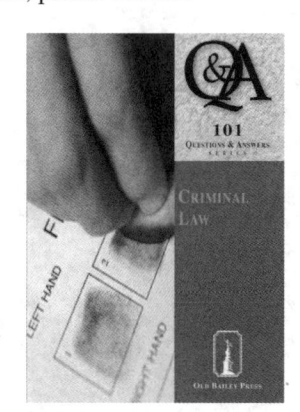

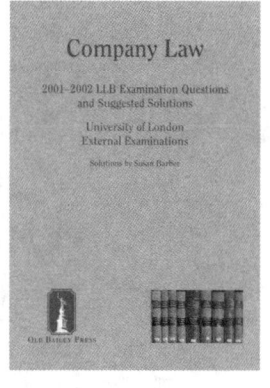

Unannotated Cracknell's Statutes for Use in Examinations

New Editions of Cracknell's Statutes

Only £11.95 Due 2004

Cracknell's Statutes provide a comprehensive series of essential statutory provisions for each subject. Amendments are consolidated, avoiding the need to cross-refer to amending legislation. Unannotated, they are suitable for use in examinations, and provide the precise wording of vital Acts of Parliament for the diligent student.

Commercial Law	**Family Law**
ISBN: 1 85836 562 7	ISBN: 1 85836 566 X
Company Law	**Medical Law**
ISBN: 1 85836 563 5	ISBN: 1 85836 567 8
Conflict of Laws	**Public International Law**
ISBN: 1 85836 564 3	ISBN: 1 85836 568 6
Evidence	**Revenue Law**
ISBN: 1 85836 565 1	ISBN: 1 85836 569 4

Succession
ISBN: 1 85836 570 8

For further information or to place an order, please contact:

Mail Order
Old Bailey Press at Holborn College
Woolwich Road
Charlton
London
SE7 8LN

Telephone: 020 8317 6039
Fax: 020 8317 6004
Website: www.oldbaileypress.co.uk
E-Mail: mailorder@oldbaileypress.co.uk

Old Bailey Press

The Old Bailey Press Integrated Student Law Library is tailor-made to help you at every stage of your studies, from the preliminaries of each subject through to the final examination. The series of Textbooks, Revision WorkBooks, 150 Leading Cases and Cracknell's Statutes are interrelated to provide you with a comprehensive set of study materials.

You can buy Old Bailey Press books from your University Bookshop, your local Bookshop, directly using this form, or you can order a free catalogue of our titles from the address shown overleaf.

The following subjects each have a Textbook, 150 Leading Cases, Revision WorkBook and Cracknell's Statutes unless otherwise stated.

Administrative Law
Commercial Law
Company Law
Conflict of Laws
Constitutional Law
Conveyancing (Textbook and 150 Leading Cases)
Criminal Law
Criminology (Textbook and Sourcebook)
Employment Law (Textbook and Cracknell's Statutes)
English and European Legal Systems
Equity and Trusts
Evidence
Family Law
Jurisprudence: The Philosophy of Law (Textbook, Sourcebook and
    Revision WorkBook)
Land: The Law of Real Property
Law of International Trade
Law of the European Union
Legal Skills and System
    (Textbook)
Obligations: Contract Law
Obligations: The Law of Tort
Public International Law
Revenue Law (Textbook,
    Revision WorkBook and
    Cracknell's Statutes)
Succession (Textbook, Revision
    WorkBook and Cracknell's
    Statutes)

Mail order prices:	
Textbook	£15.95
150 Leading Cases	£12.95
Revision WorkBook	£10.95
Cracknell's Statutes	£11.95
Suggested Solutions 1999–2000	£6.95
Suggested Solutions 2000–2001	£6.95
Suggested Solutions 2001–2002	£6.95
101 Questions and Answers	£7.95
Law Update 2004	£10.95

Please note details and prices are subject to alteration.

To complete your order, please fill in the form below:

Module	Books required	Quantity	Price	Cost
		Postage		
		TOTAL		

For the UK and Europe, add £4.95 for the first book ordered, then add £1.00 for each subsequent book ordered for postage and packing.
For the rest of the world, add 50% for airmail.

ORDERING

By telephone to Mail Order at 020 8317 6039, with your credit card to hand.

By fax to 020 8317 6004 (giving your credit card details).

Website: www.oldbaileypress.co.uk
E-Mail: mailorder@oldbaileypress.co.uk

By post to: Mail Order, Old Bailey Press at Holborn College, Woolwich Road, Charlton, London, SE7 8LN.

When ordering by post, please enclose full payment by cheque or banker's draft, or complete the credit card details below. You may also order a free catalogue of our complete range of titles from this address.

We aim to despatch your books within 3 working days of receiving your order. All parts of the form must be completed.

Name
Address

E-Mail
Postcode   Telephone

Total value of order, including postage: £
I enclose a cheque/banker's draft for the above sum, or

charge my   ☐ Access/Mastercard   ☐ Visa   ☐ American Express

Cardholder: ....
Card number
☐☐☐☐ ☐☐☐☐ ☐☐☐☐ ☐☐☐☐

Expiry date   ☐☐☐☐

Signature: ....Date: ....